The Stage
Manager's Toolkit

D0218060

The Stage Manager's Toolkit

Templates and Communication Techniques to Guide Your Theatre Production from First Meeting to Final Performance

Laurie Kincman

Focal Press
Taylor & Francis Group

NEW YORK AND LONDON

First published 2013
by Focal Press
70 Blanchard Rd Suite 402
Burlington, MA 01803

Simultaneously published in the UK
by Focal Press
2 Park Square, Milton Park, Abingdon, Oxon OX14 4RN

Focal Press is an imprint of the Taylor & Francis Group, an informa business

© 2013 Taylor & Francis

The right of Laurie Kincman to be identified as the author of this work has been asserted by her in accordance with sections 77 and 78 of the Copyright, Designs and Patents Act 1988.

All rights reserved. No part of this book may be reprinted or reproduced or utilised in any form or by any electronic, mechanical, or other means, now known or hereafter invented, including photocopying and recording, or in any information storage or retrieval system, without permission in writing from the publishers.

Notices
Knowledge and best practice in this field are constantly changing. As new research and experience broaden our understanding, changes in research methods, professional practices, or medical treatment may become necessary.

Practitioners and researchers must always rely on their own experience and knowledge in evaluating and using any information, methods, compounds, or experiments described herein. In using such information or methods, they should be mindful of their own safety and the safety of others, including parties for whom they have a professional responsibility.

Product or corporate names may be trademarks or registered trademarks, and are used only for identification and explanation without intent to infringe.

Library of Congress Cataloging-in-Publication Data
Kincman, Laurie.
  The stage manager's toolkit: templates and communication techniques to guide your theatre production from first meeting to final performance/Laurie Kincman.
     pages cm
  Includes bibliographical references.
1. Stage management. I. Title.
  PN2085.K57 2013
  792.068—dc23

2012039238

ISBN: 978-0-415-66319-9 (pbk)
ISBN: 978-0-203-55250-6 (ebk)

Typeset in Times New Roman
Project Managed and Typeset by: diacriTech

Printed in China by China Translation & Printing Services Ltd.

Table of Contents

Foreword

All stage managers believe they are good communicators. Yet, every stage manager can recount at least one instance when failed personal communication had an impact upon his or her work. Communication is the cornerstone of a collaborative production, and the stage manager is the keystone holding the various parts of communication together.

As a professional stage manager, you must adapt and learn quickly not only how to communicate with cast, crew, and production team but also how to decipher the pertinent information from a myriad of communication styles these people present to you. This is a skill that many will argue is innate, and excellent stage managers simply hone their ability to discern information. But even those who have great communication skills are constantly striving to improve their ability to relay and exchange information.

As a university educator, it became my job to help young stage managers find these skills within themselves. There are a plethora of books about stage managing and forms that professional stage managers and educators can turn to for foundational support. Some of these books are considered seminal to the education of stage managers today. Yet none of them tackles in depth the materials you are about to read.

The Stage Manager's Toolkit explores not only the information stage managers must discern and communicate but also the psychology behind its presentation. By considering not only what you are telling people but also the various audiences you tell, Laurie Kincman has filled a void in the education of managers in live performance.

This book, while aimed at stage managers, gives thought to presenting identical information to various people or departments in different manners that make the information clear to those people's specific needs. Something as "simple" as a weekly schedule holds vast amounts of information, so much so that it may need to be distributed in multiple versions, ensuring information important to one department is not lost in other information, which, while important to some, is cacophony to others.

The positive and negative sides of technology are discussed as we become more and more an instant-information society. The desire to communicate quickly must be tempered by taking the time to consider what information you are sharing and how it will be received in the form you are choosing to communicate. *The Stage Manager's Toolkit* discusses not only the types of communication but also the psychology of humans and how they respond to information. It also looks at the practical side of these choices. For example, while the brain responds well to color, theatre budgets and the cost of color printing do not always allow for such expense. These types of pro and con considerations give this text a practical approach in every way.

Perhaps the greatest aspect of what is contained in this book is that the author does not advocate a one-size-fits-all approach. While the information to be shared in a production lifespan is generally similar from show to show, the manner in which it must be presented can vary from production to production and company to company. By sharing not only techniques but also the necessary questions to ensure the use of the technique is appropriate to the moment, Laurie Kincman has given us a truly useful and practical text that applies to the art of management across all live-performance disciplines.

David Grindle
Executive Director
USITT

Acknowlegments

The spirit of theatrical collaboration is alive and well in this book. I would first like to thank the theater artists who shared their work and thoughts with me: stage managers Keith Michael, Holly Burnell, Kristen Harris, and Nicole Smith; designers Mandy Hart and Sean Michael Smallman; production managers Al Franklin and Susan Threadgill; and musical director Gary Walth. I am also grateful to my "on-scene photographers," David Hartig and Chris Anaya-Gorman.

The support I received from the University of Wisconsin–La Crosse has made this book possible. I extend thanks to Ruthann Benson, dean of the College of Liberal Studies; Julia Johnson, associate dean and director of the School of Arts and Communication; and Joe Anderson and Beth Cherne, current and past chairs of the Department of Theatre Arts.

This book would never have come together without the expertise of the team at Focal Press. I am grateful to Denise Martel for her thoughtful comments on draft chapters of this book, Meagan White for her coordination of the cover design and Emma Elder for her assistance in negotiating the proof process. Most importantly, I offer a very special thanks to Stacey Walker for believing in the value of this material from the outset and for shepherding it to the finished product in your hands.

This book is designed for student and early-career stage managers and is an outgrowth of my love of teaching. That love has come from a number of wonderful young stage managers I have had the pleasure to mentor in my career. I celebrate your ongoing successes (and continue to put pins in the map). I also owe a debt of gratitude to those who have inspired me to be both a better stage manager and a better teacher– my parents; teachers Maggie Kline and Michael Van Dyke; colleagues Mary Leonard, Michael McNamara, and Jerry Dickey; and stage managers Julie Haber, Mary Yankee Peters, and Peter Van Dyke.

To love what you do and feel that it matters—how could anything be more fun?
—Katharine Graham

Introduction: The Stage Manager as Communicator

One of the most important roles in any theatrical production is that of the stage manager. A clearinghouse for information, the stage manager is responsible for organizing rehearsals and running performances. The requirements for the job include confidence, strong organizational and management skills, understanding and compassion, a sense of humor, and the motivation to initiate tasks and follow them through to completion. The stage manager works as a team with the director, production manager, designers, technicians, and actors, facilitating a process in which creativity can flourish.

In less official terms, the stage manager might be thought of as the "air-traffic controller" of a theatrical production, coordinating the flow of information into and out of the theatre and guiding the participants to a finished product that reflects the artistic considerations of all.

Professionally, many theatrical stage managers belong to Actors' Equity Association, the union of actors and stage managers first formed in 1913. Men and women can find themselves working under one of several contracts on Broadway, in regional theatres, or in a variety of other companies around the United States. The appendix of this book provides an overview of the union and a sampling of the theatres whose employees it represents. A look at just a portion of the AEA definition of a stage manager makes clear the wide variety of skills and experiences necessary to execute the job.

A Stage Manager:

- *Shall be responsible for the calling of all rehearsals, whether before or after opening.*

- *Shall assemble and maintain the Prompt Book, which is defined as the accurate playing text and stage business, together with such cue sheets, plots, daily records, etc., as are necessary for the actual technical and artistic operation of the production.*

- *Shall work with the Director and the heads of all other departments, during rehearsal and after opening, schedule rehearsal, and outside calls, in accordance with Equity regulations.*

- *Assume active responsibility for the form and discipline of rehearsal and performance, and be the executive instrument on the technical running of each performance.*

- *Maintain the artistic intentions of the Director and the Producer after opening, to the best of his/her ability, including calling correctional rehearsals of the company when necessary and preparation of the Understudies, Replacements, Extras, and Supers.*

- *Keep such records as are necessary to advise the Producer on matters of attendance, time, health benefits, or other matters relating to the rights of Equity members.*

- *Maintain discipline as provided in the Equity Constitution, By-Laws, and Rules where required, appealable in every case to Equity.*

Actors' Equity Association[1]

In order to meet this set of requirements, perhaps the most important characteristic of a successful stage manager is his or her communication skills. In his book *Essentials of Stage Management*, author Peter Maccoy defines the creation of a theatrical production as a "dynamic and evolutionary process" and identifies the stage manager as the conduit through which information flows. The rehearsal room serves as a laboratory of sorts, and the results of the director's experimentations need to be shared in a precise and timely manner with the other creative artists working on the project, so that the vision for the show develops collectively and respects both aesthetic considerations and practical safety and logistical issues.[2]

The combination of the AEA definition and Maccoy's explanation highlight several ways in which a stage manager communicates: in person, during meetings and rehearsals; in writing, through reports, lists, and other documents; and electronically, through emails and postings to show websites. Depending on the nature of the information and its intended audience, a stage manager will use one or more of these methods to share details on a daily basis. It is, therefore, very important to understand how to use a variety of communication techniques.

COMMUNICATION VERSUS SELF-EXPRESSION

It is easy to think that any time we are imparting information to another person we are communicating. In actuality, the term *communication* reflects a very specific relationship between you and the people with whom you are talking or writing.

In her book *It's the Way You Say It*, Carol A. Fleming offers a terrific clarification of what communication is and is not. And although not written specifically about the stage manager or theatre artists at all, it reinforces the point of view through which the SM must interact with every director, actor, designer, and technician.

> *What is self-expression? It means that you say what you want to say in the manner that comes to you naturally. It will be your take on the matter, in the words you normally use, perhaps with the narrative flow of your experience. It's a solo performance in front*

of people with 100 percent of your attention on finding and speaking your thoughts, as opposed to communication where the listener is foremost in your mind as you speak. You speak their language, you speak to their concerns, and you get to the point insofar as it concerns them.[3]

A successful stage manager does not just deliver facts or ask questions; he or she *communicates*. Our concern is for the show as a whole. We invest time to learn the right terms, pay attention to how individual elements affect the big picture, and present information through paperwork and conversations that unite individual collaborators in a way that respects them as both artists and people.

FORMAT OF THIS BOOK

This book sets out to provide the stage manager with a road map to discovering and sharing show information with that perspective in mind. It is organized on the chronology of a typical theatrical production: pre-production work, rehearsals, the tech period, performances, and post-production duties. In each of these major sections, the book will outline the objectives for the stage manager and the communication techniques that can ensure success. We will take a look at what is to be done and how to approach the task—whether that is how to record character entrances and exits and prepare for your first meeting with the director, or how to organize the backstage tasks of your crew and prepare for understudy rehearsals.

Explanation of the process is paired with samples from several theatre productions, allowing the reader to see both what to do and why it works. Basic verbal communication strategies are discussed, paired with suggestions and checklists for meetings. And as a major element of the stage manager's communication is paperwork, the book explores that in detail as well. Throughout the chapters you will find samples of many of the key documents to be created. The book includes variations for plays and musicals, shortcuts for shows on an abbreviated timetable, and strategies for maintaining consistency and legibility. The book highlights differences the stage manager may encounter when working on professional and academic productions. Key components of the Actors' Equity Association rules are presented—largely in generalities. The appendix offers an overview of some of the most common union employment categories, but readers will find the document library of the AEA website to be the best source for examining the specific details of each of the many individual agreements.

The paperwork showcased in this book and the related software references primarily address the Microsoft Office suite for PC—largely due to the author's preference and available equipment. That is not, however, the only way to approach these documents. The Macintosh platform has word processing and spreadsheet programs that function virtually identically, and many additional software suites can be found both for free and for purchase. This book is also not intended to be a software tutorial. Tips are provided on occasion, but a quick trip to the Internet or the bookstore will provide readers with a host of how-to manuals for their preferred software, which will provide details on the intricacies of working with a specific program.

The final component of the book provides the reader with templates for his or her own production use. Located online through the page for this book on the Focal Press website (www.focalpress.com), this will allow you to put the ideas presented in this book to work for you. Whether professional or academic, every theatre has specific needs. And even within a single company, shows can vary widely. A well-laid-out starting point allows the stage manager to insert theatre logos, make personal font choices, add and delete color, and meet other administrative requirements.

You can also adapt the template so that the principles can apply to both the four-character one-act and the multiset ensemble musical with relative ease. As stage managers, we all look for ways to make time spent doing paperwork more efficient. This book endeavors to provide you with just that.

CHAPTER 1

Avenues of Communication

Early in my teaching career, I asked a group of students to identify the images that to them best represented a stage manager. Responses included a headset, an unending pile of paper, a roll of spike tape, and a stopwatch. All of these objects symbolize information with which the stage manager interacts and items through which he or she communicates.

But this list also demonstrates a second truth: communication is not limited to a single method. The stage manager receives information through a variety of channels and employs multiple techniques to share those details. One of our most important jobs is to combine many facts into a single point of information—what the scenic design drawings tell you about the stairs to your set's second floor, what the director asks an actor to do during scene three, and what the costume shop shares about the length of the skirt that actor is wearing at the time. Just as you rely on more than once source to formulate the big picture of that moment, you will use a combination of written and verbal communication strategies to ensure the cast and production team members not only understand all the facts but also how those facts impact one another. A rehearsal note is valuable but so is facilitating a conversation that allows designers to discuss and coordinate their efforts. As more people become involved, especially if compromise will be needed, the stage manager should consider whether the chart or the chat best serves the production as a whole.

In other instances, successful communication occurs by reframing the information for different audiences—what the production team needs to know versus the actors or the publicity office. The stage manager's goal is to provide actionable information, which means it must be accessible. Facts should be consistent and accurate, but, as we will see in many instances throughout this book, the style of delivery and level of detail vary based both on the recipient and the method of exchange.

TACTFUL, TIMELY, AND SPECIFIC

The author offers these three words as the key elements of successful communication, whether it is in person or in writing. They demonstrate respect for both the production and its personnel, and will enable the stage manager to facilitate creativity and collaboration in a highly successful manner.

FACE-TO-FACE COMMUNICATION

The stage manager does a lot of talking. This includes everything from the job interview to the production meeting. Being able to choose your words carefully, convey details concisely, and maintain a spirit of collaboration is important. Our role in the process is a neutral one—we are not on the "side" of any one part of the team. As such, there are many things to consider.

Many books have been written about communication theory and techniques for successful interaction in the workplace. On the day I first began this chapter, I typed the words *face to face communication* into the search engine on Amazon.com and received a list of over five hundred books available for purchase on the subject. Typing the same phrase into Google generated over five million links. If you are a stage manager who wants to devote time to in-depth study of the topic, multitudes of options exist. But here are a few basic points to get you started:

Word choice, pronunciation, and grammar. Clarity and comprehension will get you far. You may not have all the information you need about a particular subject, but knowing how to ask questions and speak thoughtfully with others will generate much better answers.

Tempo and tone. If it takes five minutes to explain a problem, you are unlikely to get a good solution. You have probably lost your conversation partners along the way. Similarly, if every sentence you utter ends with an upward inflection, it will sound like a question even if you are presenting confirmed facts, thereby undermining perceptions about your knowledge or authority.

Body language. Standing with your arms crossed over your chest implies you are not open to help or information. Hands placed on your hips may convey hostility. An inability to make eye contact will suggest a lack of confidence or trust. Your demeanor will say as much as your words, if not more. Successful stage managers learn to be aware of their nonverbal cues and to read them in others.

By keeping the above three principles in mind, face-to-face communication can work in your favor: (1) The exchange is immediate. You can get a response right away. (2) Information comes through more than one channel. You can monitor how the information is received by reading body language while you are talking, and adjust your speed or tactic if necessary. (3) The process is flexible. You can clarify yourself to correct a misunderstanding instantly and can ask additional questions right away if an answer is unclear. (4) The scope of the exchange

Nonverbal behavior	Interpretation
Standing with hands on hips	Readiness, aggression
Sitting with legs crossed, foot kicking slightly	Boredom
Sitting with legs apart	Open, relaxed
Sitting with hands clasped behind head, legs crossed	Confidence, superiority
Hands clasped behind back	Anger, frustration, apprehension
Arms crossed on chest	Defensiveness
Hand to check	Evaluation, thinking
Rubbing hands	Anticipation
Touching, slightly rubbing the nose	Rejection, doubt, lying
Stroking chin	Trying to make a decision
Rubbing the eye	Doubt, disbelief
Head resting in hand, eyes downcast	Boredom
Pinching bridge of nose, eyes closed	Negative evaluation
Tapping fingers	Impatience
Steepling fingers	Authoritative
Tilted head	Interest
Looking down, face turned away	Disbelief

Figure 1.1 Common nonverbal behavior and what it means.[1]

is specific. You can choose how public to make a comment, opting for a group discussion or a one-on-one conversation. (5) The tone of the exchange is personal. You can speak either formally or informally, based on the information and the people to whom you are speaking—and can make adjustments if the situation changes.

But face-to-face communication also comes with challenges. (1) The immediacy of the conversation brings constraints. You don't have time to consider every word before you say it, and repeatedly going back to correct yourself can hamper your credibility. (2) The conversation is in real time. You can't take it back. If this turns out to be the wrong moment to pose a question or make a comment, it may be impossible to ask someone to forget that you spoke. (3) The multichannel nature of the exchange works both ways. Just as you can read the body language of your colleagues, they can read yours. (4) People are subject to emotional influence, intentional or not. You can be drawn into the state of your conversation partners and inadvertently alter what you are saying or how you are saying it if you get caught up in their anger or excitement. (5) Even if you are not influenced, working in the "emotion zone" can be tricky. In the moment, it can be tough to recognize the difference between someone who is venting—yelling toward you—and someone actually yelling at you.

These constraints by no means undercut the value of a meeting or an in-person conversation. Rather, the stage manager must simply be aware of these factors when interacting with others.

WRITTEN COMMUNICATION

Just as some information is best shared in person, other details are more appropriately communicated in writing. It can be quicker to post the change to next week's rehearsal schedule on the callboard than to call each actor in your cast. It will be more efficient to share an update with the entire production team in an email rather than to wait a week to announce it during the next meeting, and certainly more practical if the production team is spread across the country—or even just across the city. It is more effective to share large amounts of detailed information in a chart or list rather than to explain each fact over the period of an hour. And if the idea of thinking about inflection and body language is daunting, it may seem safer to share news in writing. Surely it is easier to convey a director's dislike of a new prop or the unavailability of an actor for a costume fitting when there is no chance of an immediate in-person negative response.

Written communication provides a level of personal control over the information. You can rewrite a rehearsal note several times before actually printing or emailing a report to make sure it is "just right." You can use font and color to draw attention to updates on a document, whether posted or sent electronically. Throughout this book you will discover the how and why for creating individual forms and reports. Once created, it is the method of distribution that becomes important. Each avenue that is available for sharing written communication comes with a set of considerations a successful stage manager should keep in mind.

EMAIL

It is almost impossible today to imagine a world without email. Whether for personal or professional communication, email provides us the opportunity to share information at any time—whether or not the recipient is available at that moment. It also makes communicating across distance easier. A stage manager can pose a question to an out-of-town designer, share a schedule update with the director after he or she has left for the day, or deliver a note simultaneously to the entire cast. The introduction of email was a major step forward in the process to streamline the flow of information.

Email also provides a targeted avenue for communication. Details can be specifically sent to individual personnel, lessening the chance important information will be missed because your coworker's route out of the building at the end of the day did not include a trip past the callboard or your office. Email is timelier than distributing hard copies of reports, even for local personnel. If your costume designer is considering whether or not to go shopping on his or her way to the theatre, receiving a rehearsal report at home and knowing the first fitting will take place at 1:00 p.m. rather than 10:00 a.m. will make a difference.

But despite the conveniences of email, in many ways it can be as public as a callboard. The stage manager cannot send out a report or an individual message and put a "do not forward" blocker on it. This means that any message sent electronically can be subsequently sent to anyone else—even those for whom it was not intended. For these reasons it is best to anticipate that anything put into writing will become public information and to approach email with a set of guidelines similar to those in place for face-to-face conversations.

Word choice and grammar again—and now spelling too. Clarity and comprehension are back, and are even more important now than they were during our face-to-face encounters. Taking the time to write in complete sentences, with correctly spelled words, greatly improves the odds that your message will be understood. Most word-processing programs have proof-reading tools built into them to check spelling and grammar. Take the time to use them! Not every theatrical term may be catalogued in Microsoft Word's library, but in general those red and green squiggly lines that appear under your typing are an indicator that something did not translate quite right from your head to the page. But don't rely solely on software—it won't catch content errors. Is that fitting at 1:00 or 1:30? Make sure to check your own work for accuracy with names, dates, or times.

Formality and professionalism. Written communication is generally considered to be a more formal method of communication than talking in person. This is again due to the distance factor and the reader's lack of access to the context in which something was written. The stage manager does not need to write notes in paragraphs, but should take the time to be thorough and professional. "Text-speak" has no place in an email.

Context becomes fluid. Email may facilitate the immediate delivery of information, but it doesn't transport the stage manager along with the message to explain it. He or she loses control of a message as soon as the Send button is clicked. Not only should written communication be grammatically correct and professionally composed, it also should be neutral and objective. You may think your sarcastic sense of humor is worthy of a Mark Twain Prize, but not everyone does. The stage manager has no way to predict if the recipient of a report has just stubbed a toe on the corner of a desk, received bad news from a family member, or forgotten to pick up extra diapers and had to go back out in the rain. If your information is read as unclear or inappropriate, you may inadvertently alienate a key member of your team.

THE CALLBOARD

The theatre callboard is the most traditional and most public means of disseminating informa-tion. It is particularly useful for sharing details with a large group, especially if its members will not all be in the same place at the same time. It is also a recognizable location that can house permanent materials that may not be constantly needed.

Just as there are things that belong on a callboard, there are also things that do not. For privacy reasons, it is generally a poor choice to post a contact sheet that contains home phone numbers and addresses. In an academic theatre department, this may even be a violation of federal student-privacy laws.

Some theatres have preferences about posting rehearsal reports or meeting minutes. Typically this has less to do with personal privacy and more to do with the location of the callboard and

Figure 1.2   A callboard outside a rehearsal room at the Milwaukee Repertory Theatre. Photo by David Hartig.

the opportunity for outsiders to read and misunderstand the notes. A theatre may also have more than one callboard, and the content of postings is related to location—rehearsal reports on the board outside the shops, daily schedules outside the rehearsal rooms, and so on. The theatre company or academic department in which you are working may have official guidelines or more informal traditions that can help you determine what should be posted.

Originally the callboard was solely a physical entity—a large corkboard mounted in the theatre or rehearsal hall. Actors and production team members can check it whenever they need to. It is an ideal location for the rehearsal schedule, announcements, and archival copies of some lists and breakdowns. When working on an Equity production, the union provides the theatre with specific information to be made publicly available to the cast. It is typically not time-sensitive, and sometimes not even specific to an individual show—perfect for posting. If the callboard is close enough to the rehearsal hall, it is also an efficient location for the sign-in sheet. The actors can report to a central location to note they have arrived for the day, and the SM team can look in a single place to determine if everyone is present.

In today's technological age, the callboard is not restricted to physical form. Many theatres have adopted electronic callboards—a website devoted to a single production or season of shows—on which similar information is posted and archived.

The electronic callboard provides several advantages over its hard-copy predecessor. An infinite number of documents can be uploaded and linked. When all that is required on the page is the name of the document, it is easier and cleaner to post many more items than could successfully be pinned to a board. The callboard for a production at the Milwaukee Repertory Theatre shown in Figure 1.2 makes good use of its available space, combining show-specific notices and folders for Equity paperwork, and even finds a home for area menus for out-of-town actors unfamiliar with lunch or dinner options. But the space is nearly full, and could not easily accommodate many more items. An electronic callboard can hold more information and can be subdivided so that actors and production team members visit separate spots to find the details most pertinent to them.

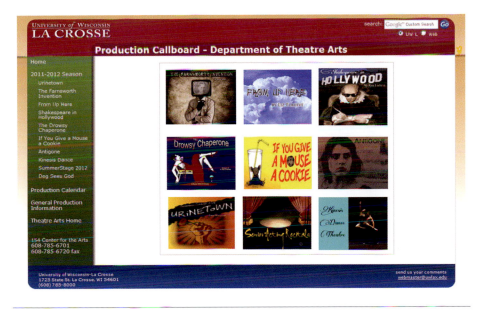

Figure 1.3   The home page of the UW-L Theatre Callboard.

The image in Figure 1.3 shows the home page of the electronic callboard for the University of Wisconsin–La Crosse Department of Theatre Arts. The home page includes both written and graphic identifiers of each production in the season, either of which can be clicked to deliver personnel to the correct show pages. The overall template for the site is a university-mandated and nonnegotiable design standard—the red, green, and blue borders are required, as is placement of the navigation bar (written list of page links) on the left side of the screen. But within this template, the specific information for the theatre department is organized in a way that is both unique to this web page and specific enough that users can understand it.

As seen in Figures 1.4 through 1.6, clicking on the *Urinetown* icon will take actors and team members to a subset of pages devoted to this show. And following the next set of links will deliver users to the information specific to their needs. It is easy to see that this callboard contains more documents than the "old school" version and contains both items that may be needed on a daily basis and archival copies of paperwork that has previously been distributed. Actors or designers can obtain duplicates for themselves at any time, should a piece of information be misplaced.

In instances where both the actors and designers require the same information, web programming allows the stage manager to type in one place but reference that information in multiple locations. The first two entries under the "Documents" heading on the production team page are the weekly schedule and the current costume fittings. But although these appear to be links to paperwork like the other items listed in this section, they are in fact bookmarks to the spot on the actor page where that information is typed out. This allows designers to quickly access the details if they need to, and allows the stage manager to update them only once.

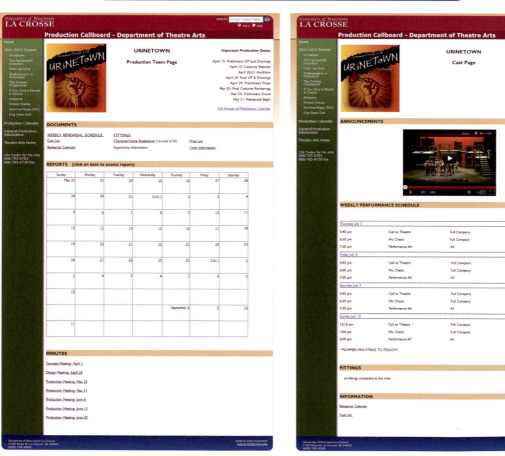

Figures 1.4–1.6 The *Urinetown* home page, along with the subpages for the cast and production team.

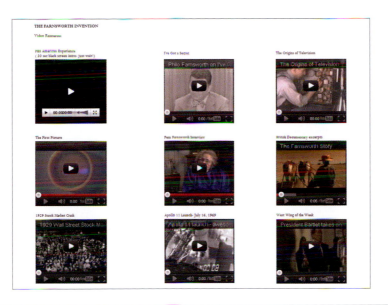

Figure 1.7 The video resource page for *The Farnsworth Invention*.

The electronic callboard also makes possible the posting of information that is not specifically paperwork. For a production of *The Farnsworth Invention* in the same season, the stage manager was asked to help collect a series of video resources for the show. An additional page was added to this section of the website on which nine separate video files could be cataloged and made available (Figure 1.7). No other show in the season required this type of information, but the electronic callboard allows for customization by show as required. It would also be impossible to post anything as useful on a traditional callboard. A typed page with web addresses of the various video sources would be the most feasible option, but hardly as useful. Here the video can be directly embedded and immediately available. And there is even room for a little fun—because the play is written by Aaron Sorkin, a "*West Wing* of the Week" slot existed in the bottom corner. This might be useful as indirect research for actors on how to deliver lines in Sorkin's writing style, but it also provided some humor to the many fans of the television series who were working on the production. No one was required to view it, but the stage manager was able to maintain this bit of enjoyment for interested viewers throughout the rehearsal period.

BLENDING METHODS

In the end, determining the best avenue for sharing information comes down to the stage manager's judgment. Consider the three communication basic principles again: *be tactful, be timely, and be specific*. Is there too much room for misinterpretation about a note to put it in writing? That may lead you to an in-person conversation. Is there not enough time to deliver a piece of information personally to several people? This could argue for email distribution. Is this general information requiring little or no action? Perhaps it is a candidate for the callboard.

There are times when you will resort to more than one method. Early blocking rehearsals are notorious for generating a large number of prop notes. A morning visit to the shop provides the opportunity for in-person clarification of the list from the night before. A multi-area question can be posed at a production meeting, with notes from the discussion and subsequent decision reflected in the meeting's minutes. The next day's rehearsal call is typically announced at the end of the day, but then also posted on a callboard or telephone hotline. As these examples show, some duplication can be helpful—especially if it is mixing the active and passive distribution of information. But use caution not to put every piece of information in every possible location. This can lead to distribution overload and cause members of your cast or production team to start ignoring callboards and emails by thinking, "I've been told everything already."

In the next chapter we will consider some general principles for written communication of any kind—looking at how format affects the understanding of information, no matter which avenue you choose for delivery.

CHAPTER 2

Principles of Document Design

You may have arrived at this chapter thinking to yourself, "Why should I care about something like this? My job is to present substance—not worry about style." And while document design does not appear in the bulleted list of a stage manager's duties, style has a very significant impact on that substance for which we are responsible. If the recipient of a schedule or chart cannot understand the information you have provided, it is as if you haven't provided it at all. By understanding some basic concepts about font, layout, and continuity, the stage manager can ensure that the time spent preparing and sharing paperwork is not wasted effort.

Anyone who has written a paper for a high school or college course can likely remember formatting instructions accompanying the assignment prompt. The wording resembled the following: "Times New Roman, 12 point font, double-spaced, references presented in a Works Cited page at the end of the paper. Names should be typed in the upper-left corner of the page, and page numbers centered within the bottom margin."

The instructor included these requirements not to hamper your creativity but to provide some commonality among the submissions and to keep the focus on the content of the paper. Savvy students receiving less-detailed guidelines, perhaps only a minimum or maximum page length, learn how to game the system: adjusting margins to be a quarter of an inch larger or smaller than the standard one inch, or writing in a font of 11.5 or 12.5 size—all intended to make a paper appear longer or shorter without adjusting the amount of written material. (Truth be told, instructors can see this trick at work, so it does not actually work to a student's advantage as much as he or she might hope.)

This is, in fact, a form of document design! The overall visual style may not be the student's choosing, but he or she is using typography and layout, however subtly, to affect the organization of information on the page.

This is the same principle at play for the stage manager when creating lists, charts, and reports. Document design in our case is intended to maximize the accessibility of the content by providing structure to the way in which the information is presented. By guiding the reader's eye, the stage manager helps him or her to understand details, identify changes, and prepare for actions.

IDENTIFYING YOUR AUDIENCE

The stage manager's first pair of considerations in designing a document is the audience to which it will be distributed and the avenue of communication you will use. These factors can help you to determine the relative importance of the other design choices you will face. A list posted on the callboard may require a larger font size in order to be legible from a distance. A chart of duties distributed to the crew can afford a smaller font, since each technician will have a copy, but will need additional organization to identify what is done, when it is done, and specifically by whom. Formatting a web page is different from formatting a page to be printed. The screen size will vary in proportion to the size of the monitor, so margins and tabs are more relative—and less useful for placing items in a specific location. Details sent simply in the body of an email will not need formatting at all, but will instead rely on our clear written communication tips from the previous chapter, along with an appropriate subject line so that the recipient can immediately identify what information the message contains.

INFORMATIVE OR INTERACTIVE?

The next consideration for the stage manager is how the recipient will use the document. An **informative** document filled with detail probably requires more assistance to guide the reader's eye, and therefore more of the formatting techniques. Calendars and shift plots are examples of informative documents. A prop list is an **interactive** document—one in which multiple users enter information. Interactive documents still need some organizational principles, but the stage manager wants to make sure the formatting is simple enough to prevent the prop master from adding details differently from the ASM simply because the prop master did not understand where they belonged on the page.

PAGE LAYOUT

With these clarifications in mind, layout becomes the first design decision. How much information needs to be presented? Is it narrative or a series of categories? How many individual entries are required? Particularly if it will take more than one page to present all the details, the stage manager should give thought to how one page will relate to the next, and how that will improve or hamper the accessibility of the information—known as **pagination**.

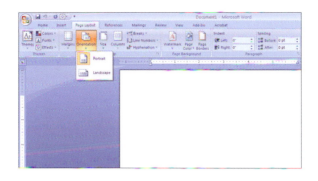

Figure 2.1 The page layout selection tab in Microsoft Word, showing portrait and landscape options.

The first component of layout is page orientation. This selection, available in every word-processing and spreadsheet program, provides a choice between using either the height or the width of the page as the primary determinant of how much information will fit (see Figure 2.1).

Even something as simple as a cast list can require thought, as seen in Figures 2.2 and 2.3. A large cast with actors playing fewer individual roles can successfully be presented in a traditional portrait orientation. But when documenting a show where a smaller ensemble plays a multitude of roles, it may be clearer to change to landscape orientation so that all roles for a single actor can fit on a single line without compromising font size or available margin space.

If you are faced with a large number of actors playing a large number of roles each, the stage manager may have to choose between a smaller font size to fit everything on a single page and splitting the cast information across two pages. In this instance, the primary concern would be to keep all roles for a single actor together to minimize potential confusion. Continuing the cast list on page two will be less confusing if it begins with Actor 20 than if it starts with the leftover roles for Actor 19 that did not fit on page one. Use the page break function (available in nearly all word-processing and spreadsheet programs) to control how information is grouped together.

The quantity of information will be determined by the nature of the document itself. A cast list is complete with only character and actor names. In contrast, a schedule needs to communicate day, time, pages to be rehearsed, actors called, and, if variable, location. As the number of categories increases, so does the need for providing visual distinction. The relationship of actor names to roles can be achieved by placing the two lists in columns opposite one another. The reader can negotiate the space between lists with no assistance. The schedule, which has five kinds of details to be included, will require more groupings.

As the information becomes more complex, the stage manager can choose between two tools to help the page remain accessible—lines or white space. **White space** refers to blank room on the page, and it is useful because it gives the reader's eye a chance to rest and to distinguish one set of details from another. The sample weekly schedule from *Twelfth Night* found in Figure 2.4 demonstrates how white space can assist the actors in distinguishing one day's work from another, as well as locating the individual components of each day—when they are called and what will be accomplished.

Twelfth Night

Cast List

ORSINO, *Duke of Illyria*	Justin Cooke
SEBASTIAN, *brother of Viola*	Matthew Matuseski
ANTONIO, *a sea captain, friend to Sebastian*	Kevin Fanshaw
SEA CAPTAIN, A PRIEST	Jacob Voss
VALENTINE, SAILOR 3, OFFICER 1	Austin P. Hernandez
CURIO, SAILOR 1, OFFICER 2	Luke Prescott
SIR TOBY BELCH, *Olivia's kinsman*	Jacob Gustine
SIR ANDREW AGUECHEEK	Tim McCarren
MALVOLIO, *Steward to Olivia*	Andrew Kelly
FABIAN, *servant to Olivia*	Donnie Mezera
FESTE, *Olivia's jester*	Alden Hedges
OLIVIA, *a countess*	Allyssa Dunn
VIOLA, *sister to Sebastian*	Claire Ganshert
MARIA, *Olivia's gentlewoman-in-waiting*	Amy Nelson
LORD 1, SAILOR 2, OFFICER 3	Brian Coffin
LORD 2, OFFICER 4	Don Hart
ATTENDANT to OLIVIA 1	Emily Ware
ATTENDANT to OLIVIA 2	Lindsay Van Norman
MUSICIAN 1	Suzanne Clum
MUSICIAN 2	Shelby Krarup

THE FARNSWORTH INVENTION
CAST LIST

Kevin Fanshaw	Philo T. Farnsworth
Austin Hernandez	David Sarnoff
Lindsay Van Norman	Pem Farnsworth
Amy Nelson	Lizette
Jake Voss	Officer, Pem's Father, Cliff Gardner, Trader, Broker,
Cody Wesner	Man 1, Atkins, Gifford, Douglas Fairbanks, Solomon
Seth Steidl	Young Philo, Police Officer, Photographer, Howard, Schenck,
Lewis Youngren	Student, Crowd, Wilkins, Analyst, Ridley, Man, Usher, Bartender
Nick Brandt	Officer, Everson, Zworkin,
David Holmes	Young Sarnoff, Executive/James, Doctor 2
Sean Mason	Man 2, Crowd, Stan Willis, Advisor
Bryce Wilson	Man 3, Gorrell, Maitre D/Waiter, Sales Rep, Louis, Judge
Quinn Masterson	Justin Tolman, RCA Chair, Jim Harbord, Doctor, Fed Chair
Ryan Vodnik	Sarnoff's Father, Simms, Lippincott, Houston Control, Banker
Natalie Goodman	Student, Sexy Woman, Betty
Brian Coffin	Student, Crowd, Harlan Honn, Radio Announcer, Lennox,
Andrew Kelly	Russian Officer, William Crocker, Banker, Crowd
Colleen Schulz	Sarnoff's Mother, Woman in Crowd, Pem's Mother, Agnes Farnsworth, Mina Edison
Douglas Nogrady	Wachtel, Banker, Lawyer
Kaylyn Forkey	Student, Sexy Woman, Mary Pickford, Speakeasy Woman, Lippincott's Secretary, Stenographer

Figures 2.2 and 2.3 Two options for presenting casting information.

When white space is not enough, the stage manager can choose to format information in a chart. This can be done by using a word-processing table or a spreadsheet. Rows and columns, with lines and clear headings, help the reader to find each entry and understand the individual components of that entry. Consider the sample page from a series of line changes for the same play seen in Figure 2.5. By by presenting the information in this manner, the reader can navigate a similar set of details for each individual entry and keep them separate. It is also worth noting, though, that there is a bit of white space at work even here. The bottom line in each row has been adjusted to provide additional space between entries. This is helpful because several boxes contain large blocks of text, and, even with the lines, the page could become overwhelming. You might also note the use of color in the line change document—more about that later!

THE SPREADSHEET AS ELECTRONIC GRAPH PAPER

Microsoft Excel and other similar spreadsheet programs are designed to be powerful analytical tools, capable of complex processing of numbers and other collections of data. The use to the stage manager, however, is much more basic. Because the basic setup of a spreadsheet page is a collection of cells, it is essentially always in table format. By adjusting the height of rows or widths of columns, you can convert the sheet into a piece of electronic graph paper, allowing you to create forms with relative ease. Text can be typed into individual cells, and the program's formatting capabilities allow the same insertion of colors, shading, and lines as a word-processing program does. As you progress through this book and visit the online templates, you will be able to see how this can work to your advantage.

A few final layout considerations include **justification, identification,** and **repetition.** Text can be justified—in other words, aligned—with either the left or right edge of a page, or it can be centered. Paperwork should always be identified at the top (in the header) with the name of the show and the title of the document and at the bottom (in the footer) with the creation or revision date and page number. To ensure that multiple pages are kept together, this identification should be repeated on every page. When creating something that will inevitably be modified during the rehearsal process—such as an overall rehearsal schedule—it is advisable to include the note "subject to change" within that header or footer to alert readers to the possibility of more-current information, and to help a production combat late-appearing conflicts that come with the explanation, "That wasn't on the calendar I got at the beginning."

It is always best to number the pages in a document so they can be kept in sequential order. But just noting "page 2" may not be enough. Identifying a sheet as "page 2 of 5" not only keeps the paperwork in order but also allows the readers to confirm they have all of it!

Twelfth Night

Weekly Rehearsal Schedule
November 8-12

Monday November 8

6:30-7:30 pm	Finish I-5	Olivia, Viola
7:30-8:00 pm	II-2 ring speech	Viola
8:00-9:30 pm	II-1 and III-3	Antonio, Sebastian

Tuesday November 9

6:30-7:30 pm	Work I-2	Viola, Sea Captain (no sailors needed tonight)
Also 6:30-7:30 pm	Music Rehearsal	Alden, Shelby, Suzanne
7:30-8:30 pm	Work I-3	Toby, Andrew, Maria
8:30-9:30 pm	Put Tim into IV-1	Sebastian, Toby, Andrew, Fabian, Olivia, Feste

Wednesday November 10

6:30-7:30 pm	Block III-2	Toby, Andrew, Fabian, Maria
7:30-9:30 pm	Block III-4	Toby, Andrew, Malvolio, Fabian, Olivia, Maria, Lindsay, Emily, Antonio, Viola, Officers 1-4

Thursday November 11

6:30-8:00 pm	Work I-1, I-4, II-4	Orsino, Valentine, Curio, Lord 1 & 2, Viola, Feste, Suzanne, Shelby
8:00-8:30 pm	Review II-3	Toby, Andrew, Malvolio, Feste, Maria
8:30-9:30 pm	Work IV-2	Toby, Malvolio, Maria, Feste

Friday November 12

6:30-9:30 pm	Stumble Through Show	Full Company

Twelfth Night

Line Changes

Updated 11/18/10

Act	Scene	Page	Line(s)	Character	Action	Words	Notes
II	5	43	117-118	Fabian	CUT	Sowter will cry upon't for al this, though it be as rank as a fox	Malvolio's lines continue from "Softly, M.O.A.I" to his next speech beginning "M- Malvolio…"
II	5	43	121	Toby	CUT	The cur is excellent at faults	Line now ends with :… work it out?"
III	1	45	2	Viola	CHANGE	TABOR to MUSIC	
III	1	46	9-10	Viola	CUT	or, the church stands by thy tabor, if thy tabor stand by the church	Line now ends with "… dwell near him"
III	1	46	11-13	Feste	CUT	To see this age! A sentence is but a chev'ril glove to a good wit. How quickly the wrong side may be turned outward!	Line now ends after "You have said, sir."
III	2	52	29	Andrew	CUT	I had as lief be a Brownist as a politician	Line now ends after…"for policy I hate."
III	2	53	42-43	Toby	CUT	although the sheet were big enough for the Bed of Ware in England,	Line now skips from "… lie in thy sheet of paper" to "set 'em down."
III	2	53	48	Toby	CUT	at the cubiculo	Line now reads "We'll call thee. Go."

Figures 2.4 and 2.5 A weekly rehearsal schedule, using white space to separate pieces of information, and a page from a line-changes document using rows and columns.

FONTS

As seen in our term-paper example, the font and its size will affect how much information can fit on a single page. But font choices are not based on quantity. The selection of typeface is a major contributor to overall legibility, both as a document to be printed and copied and as one to be shared by email.

Entire books have been written about fonts. For purposes of this tutorial, what is important is to have a general understanding of the basic categories and their use to the stage manager in creating paperwork. In her book *The Non-Designer's Design Book*, author Robin Williams presents six major categories.[1]

1. Oldstyle. These fonts are based on hand lettering. When looking at this category, you can imagine a pen making each stroke. Oldstyle fonts have what is known as a serif—a small end stroke on most letters.

2. Modern. These fonts evolved from oldstyle, and still have a serif, but one that is horizontal rather than diagonal.

3. Sans serif. As the name implies, this category has no end stroke. It appears a bit more modern, and is often used in presentations and web text.

4. Slab serif. A cousin of the sans serif fonts, this group is characterized by thick letters and can appear to always be in bold.

5. Script. These fonts resemble calligraphy or cursive writing, and often denote a sense of elegance. It is common to find script fonts on something like a wedding invitation.

6. Decorative. These are the "fun fonts." Their commonality is their uniqueness. These are fonts we often associate with logos.

Graphic designers will spend a great deal of time making font choices. As stage managers, we should be concerned with two basic things—(1) does the font have too much "personality" and interfere with overall legibility, and (2) is the font common enough to exist on both your computer and those of the people who will be receiving your paperwork.

In general, fonts that fall into the first three categories above are the best options for the majority of your writing. They will be neutral and available. Beyond that, personal choice can come into play. When creating signs or announcements that need a larger size, you may find that sans serif fonts are easier to read. Some fonts are thinner than others by design, requiring slightly less room to fit text into the cells of a table.

The final three categories (slab serif, script, and decorative) are best reserved for titles. Injecting some personality into your paperwork is not a bad thing—you just want to do so judiciously and without compromising the main details. If you remember the sample paperwork from *Twelfth Night*, you can recall that the name of the show appears in a different font from the rest of the page, one that falls into the script category. The stage manager chose the font in an effort to reflect the tone of the show and its design. Figures 2.7 through 2.9 demonstrate what happens when the same information is presented for different shows, changing only the title font. *Biloxi Blues* makes use of a font reminiscent of the lettering on military crates, and

Oldstyle	Goudy Old Style Palatino Times New Roman Perpetua
Modern	**Bodoni MT** Minion Pro PERPETUA TITLING
Sans serif	Gil Sans MT Arial Calibri Verdana
Slab serif	**Cooper Black** **Myriad Pro Black** **Impact**
Script	Calligraph421 MT *Vladimir Script* Bradley Hand ITC
Decorative	Earwig Factory Chiller **STENCIL** GALLERY

Figure 2.6   Popular variations of the six major font categories.

Figures 2.7–2.9 How to make use of distinctive fonts in your paperwork.

How the Grinch Stole Christmas employs one that pays tribute to the type in Dr. Seuss's books. All three are thematically appropriate. And yet, using that title font for all the written information would be a mistake in all three instances. The script font is light and could become illegible when it gets small or is photocopied; the slab font will be overwhelming if everything is in bold; the decorative font is larger and rounder than other choices and will require wider columns and more pages to communicate the same information.

FONT STYLE

Within a single font or family of fonts, variations exist. Size—the number of points—can be changed to distinguish between heading and body content. The **bold** variation is useful to make a title stand out or to denote changes on a revision. Important notes may be written in ALL CAPS to provide another version of emphasis. Italics are used for titles, but can also reflect a commentary (*that means a detail about the information separate from the information itself; a built-in explanation of sorts*). <u>Underlining</u> text can be used for titles in some instances, but can also be used for emphasis. The ~~strikethrough~~ option is useful to denote something is no longer needed, especially when simply deleting it may cause confusion—the cutting of a prop on a prop list, for example, or a line in a script.

UNDERSTANDING TRENDS OUTSIDE THE WORKPLACE

Although this book clearly advocates against the use of slang writing techniques for professional communications, the stage manager does want to be aware of them. One specific example is the use of writing in all capital letters. While it certainly emphasizes the words on the page, in today's chat and blogging communities this indicates yelling. Even if that is not your intent, writing a message or note in all caps is likely to come across as hostile based on our common understanding of that convention. Remembering the cautions about the fluidity of context, you can see why it is better for the substance of a message to come through without an inadvertent tone.

COLOR AND SHADING

When lines or white space aren't enough, the stage manager can employ color or shading to help provide emphasis or guide the eye. The update to a call time or addition of an actor to a rehearsal day may stand out more when placed in another color than if it is underlined or even in bold. The individual sections of a long chart will be more identifiable if headings are visually distinct.

But while these are both useful tools, there are some important things to keep in mind. Color is only useful if it is always present. Before investing time and effort into creating paperwork with a rainbow of hues, return to the decisions you made about distribution avenues. Placing an update in color and then sending the page through a black-and-white photocopier obviously negates its use.

Using color on a sign to be posted, or on a document for which you can reasonably print all necessary copies, is fine. It is equally useful on a website or a piece of paperwork that will be distributed electronically.

Shading is a good alternative to color when you need too many copies to print each one yourself. It can provide the same emphasis and visual break on a page. Just be certain that you find the correct level for your copier. Shading that is too light may disappear, and shading that is so dark it provides little contrast between the background and the text it is emphasizing is also wasted effort.

Let us take a look at a few successful examples of color and shading, shown in figures 2.10 and 2.11. The first is the return of the page of line changes (Figure 2.10). Instead of focusing on the table itself, now note the use of blue text. Cumulative information, collected and amended throughout the rehearsal process, is more usefully presented as a single comprehensive list of changes rather than a series of separate documents. A designer may wait until the end of

Twelfth Night
Line Changes
Updated 11/18/10

Act	Scene	Page	Line(s)	Character	Action	Words	Notes
II	5	43	117–118	Fabian	CUT	Sowter will cry upon't for al this, though it be as rank as a fox	Malvolio's lines continue from "Softly, M.O.A.I" to his next speech beginning "M- Malvolio…"
II	5	43	121	Toby	CUT	The cur is excellent at faults	Line now ends with :… work it out?"
III	1	45	2	Viola	CHANGE	TABOR to MUSIC	
III	1	46	9–10	Viola	CUT	or, the church stands by thy tabor, if thy tabor stand by the church	Line now ends with " … dwell near him"
III	1	46	11–13	Feste	CUT	To see this age! A sentence is but a chev'ril glove to a good wit. How quickly the wrong side may be turned outward!	Line now ends after "You have said, sir. "
III	2	52	29	Andrew	CUT	I had as lief be a Brownist as a politician	Line now ends after…" for policy I hate. "
III	2	53	42-43	Toby	CUT	although the sheet were big enough for the Bed of Ware in England,	Line now skips from " … lie in thy sheet of paper" to "set 'em down."
III	2	53	43	Toby	CUT	at the cubiculo	Line now reads "We'll call thee. Go."

Figure 2.10 Successful color and shading at work.

REVISED REHEARSAL SCHEDULE

September 28-30

Wednesday September 28

6:30-7:30 pm	Work Stock Market sequence: pp. 61-68	Philo, Sarnoff, Brandt, Coffin, Goodman, Holmes, Kelly, Mason, Masterson, Nogrady, Steidl, Vodnik, Voss, Wesner, Wilson, Youngren
7:30-8:30 pm	**Work all Lab Scenes: pp. 34-44, 69-73, 78-79**	**ADD Pem, Schulz, Novak** **RELEASE: Masterson, Nogrady**
8:30-9:30 pm	Work All Pem/Philo and Lizette/Sarnoff Scenes & Sarnoff Monologue: pp. 27-30, 32-34, 39-40, 81-84-100	RELEASE all but Philo, Sarnoff, Pem, Schulz, Voss ADD: Nelson

Thursday September 29

6:30-9:30 pm	Work Act One	Full Company

Friday September 30

6:30-9:30 pm	Work Act Two	Full Company

Figure 2.11 Successful color and shading at work.

the rehearsal process—as he or she is preparing for tech and needs to give the stage manager specific locations for cues—to input the changes. A designer can reference a single piece of paperwork that covers the entire script at once rather than opening five or six separate documents and returning to individual scenes multiple times to make edits. But the actors will likely double-check their scripts each week when the changes are published. By noting the revision date and the new entries in blue, they are able to focus on what has changed rather than what simply exists in print. This use of color makes the document work for multiple audiences at the same time with very little additional work on the part of the stage manager.

Figure 2.11 is a rehearsal schedule that has been changed midweek. Because many of the work sessions contain multiple pages and characters, the days themselves are separated and shaded for clarity. Also due to the density of information, the addition of a new call in the middle of Wednesday night is much easier to find when placed in red. The schedule revision was posted on both the traditional and electronic callboard, and a copy was printed for the stage manager's prompt book. Color is practical in this instance, since only two hard copies are needed.

ACCESSIBILITY

Not all documents need advanced formatting to be accessible. The pair of lists presented in Figures 2.12 and 2.13 makes good use of available space without many bells and whistles. Despite their reduction for purpose of inclusion in this book, both documents actually exist at full-page size. The top item is a general performance schedule posted above the actor sign-in sheet during performances. The information is presented in portrait view, because it allows both versions of the call times to be listed on a single page, and in a font size large enough to read from some distance. A simple line separates the two entries. The cast needs only to read the information, not interact with it, so there is no need for additional lines, shading, or other formatting options. Below it is a very simple table—the sign-in sheet itself. This time the same portrait view is appropriate because it allows for the listing of all 20 names on a single page and all workdays during this week of technical rehearsals and performances. This is an interactive document. Each actor will initial upon arrival each day in the given week. And while it is still very simple, the layout needs a bit more help to be functional.

The stage manager could simply post a list of actor names each day and ask actors to initial next to their name. But because the column of names takes up only a small amount of the available room on the page, it would be a waste of paper to produce seven documents instead of one. Similarly, by day five it could become difficult to take attendance without the grid lines. As presented, the stage manager simply looks for empty boxes when checking arrivals at call time. Without the grid, the stage manager might have to count the number of initials next to actors' names to determine who has arrived on day five as opposed to day four—not a complicated task, but also not an efficient use of time.

CONTINUITY

Our final consideration for the visual appearance of paperwork is continuity. It is first defined as commonality among all documents created for an individual show or theatre—in essence, sticking to your choices once you have made them.

If you select a title font for paperwork, use it on everything. If you have decided that your show logo is an aesthetically pleasing addition to your header and is not subject to photocopier

EVENING SCHEDULE

5:30 pm	Dressing Rooms Available
5:45 pm	Cast & Crew Call
6:30 pm	Mic Check- Mr. Coffin
7:00 pm	House Opens
7:30 pm	Curtain

MATINEE SCHEDULE

12:00 pm	Dressing Rooms Available
12:15 pm	Cast & Crew Call
1:00 pm	Mic Check- Mr. Coffin
1:30 pm	House Opens
2:00 pm	Curtain

THE FARNSWORTH INVENTION
CAST

PLEASE SIGN IN!

	Mon 10/10	Tues 10/11	Wed 10/12	Thur 10/13	Fri 10/14	Sat 10/15	Sun 10/16
Nick Brandt							
Brian Coffin							
Kevin Fanshaw							
Natalie Goodman							
Austin Hernandez							
David Holmes							
Andrew Kelly							
Sean Mason							
Quinn Masterson							
Amy Nelson							
Douglas Nogrady							
Jandrea Novak							
Colleen Schulz							
Seth Steidl							
Lindsay Van Norman							
Ryan Vodnik							
Jake Voss							
Cody Wesner							
Bryce Wilson							
Lewis Youngren							

Figures 2.12 and 2.13 A performance schedule and sign-in sheet to be posted on a theatre callboard.

decay, keep it as well. This will help the items belonging to your show to be instantly recogniz-able as such. Theatre companies or departments producing several shows in a season may have a general format for lists or reports. This level of document design may not be up to you. If your company has determined that effort is better spent finding the details in a document rather than understanding a new style of presenting those details for each show, you should accept the form given to you. But if your prop list is one of five identical documents on someone's desk, then that may not be in your best interest either. Simple identifying factors such as that title font or logo can help keep these similar documents separate.

It is also advisable to keep the same body font for all paperwork and present revision dates and page numbers in the same location and in the same style for everything.

The second definition for continuity—and one which is perhaps more important than the first one—is that the paperwork looks the same no matter who opens it and prints it. After spending time and effort to choose a legible font, adjust margins to make everything fit, and employ shading or color to guide the eye, it would be a shame for that work to be lost.

Every computer that is connected to a printer will recognize that printer's settings as the best default format for a document. Laser and inkjet printers have different capacities for printing close to the edges of a page; a Mac computer and a PC will have slightly different sets of fonts in their factory options.

In order to combat these differences, the stage manager has two lines of defense. First, when originally generating the paperwork, **choose common fonts that are universal rather than ones that are special to you**. If you had to purchase it, probably not everyone has it. It would be possible to email that font to all the members of your cast or production team and ask them to install it as well, but it is unlikely everyone will do that.

But while that could solve your font problem, it won't help page-layout changes. In that case, your best option is to **turn the document into a PDF**. First created by Adobe Software Systems in 1995, the Acrobat Portable Document Format (PDF) finds its usefulness in its ability to "preserve source file information — text, drawings, multimedia, video, 3D, maps, full-color graphics, photos, and even business logic — regardless of the application used to create them and even when compiled from multiple formats."[2]

Essentially, the PDF is a snapshot of the document as originally created, with content and format that will be unchanged when opened on any computer or mobile device. Acrobat Reader is a free program, downloadable onto any computer, to allow the user to open any PDF docu-ment. Translating a document into a PDF can be done with a full version of the Adobe Acrobat program, with several freeware versions, or within many office software suites. For example, as of the 2007 version, Microsoft Office provides conversion to PDF as a standard task in Word, Excel, PowerPoint, and other programs simply by selecting the "Acrobat" tab and clicking a "create PDF" button, as seen in Figure 2.14.

The PDF can be printed, emailed, or uploaded to the web. This makes it an ideal format for preserving your document-design efforts. It also provides a minimal level of protection for the file itself. Although not difficult to acquire, a user will need to own the full version of the Adobe

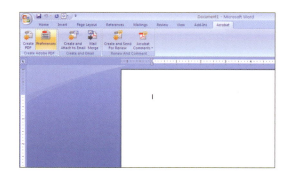

Figure 2.14 The PDF creator built into Microsoft Word.

Acrobat software in order to modify a PDF document. If you are distributing something that should not be changed by others, the PDF provides a level of discouragement.

WHAT'S IN A NAME?

An easy-to-overlook component of creating paperwork is the actual title of the document. You might only be stage managing a single production, but most theatres produce multiple shows in a season, some of which will overlap. Just like the PDF ensures your formatting work remains consistent, effectively naming a document ensures it can be found.

Emailing the prop list for your show simply named "prop list" is asking for it to get lost in the prop master's computer. Always include the name of the show. If a document is sent out multiple times, you should also reference the edition attached—either by including the version number or the date. This is particularly key for items like the rehearsal report, which you will send out every day. Each report should be uniquely identifiable by title. The paperwork entitled "*Twelfth Night* RR 907" or "*Urinetown* Prop List Version 2" will not easily be mistaken for something else.

READY TO BEGIN

With these principles in mind, this book now turns its focus to the stage manager's path through a production. In each section we will consider the tasks to be completed and discuss the substance and the style of the communication that will help guide your show to a successful and collaborative conclusion.

CHAPTER 3

Pre-Production

The stage manager's work on a production begins with a self-orientation to the script, the physical production, and the team with whom he or she will be working. In order to most successfully facilitate discoveries during rehearsal, it is important that the stage manager collect as much information as possible in advance. This work will allow you both to provide answers and to know what additional questions need to be asked.

PRE-PRODUCTION TASKS

- Read and analyze the script

- Collect information on the production

- Prepare initial lists and breakdowns

- Create a prompt book

- Meet with the director

- Participate in auditions

- Prepare the rehearsal room

In an academic theatre department, the stage manager may receive an assignment at the end of one year for a show that will happen the following year. Despite the upcoming vacation, you will inevitably be around your future team members and may be asked to perform some preliminary duties for the show right away. This might be a simple task, such as script distribution, or it might be some of the detailed prep work contained in this chapter. Although much of your work will take place nearer to the start of rehearsals, be sure that you understand what is expected of you and when you should perform these tasks. Not every academic theatre department has a faculty member specifically devoted to stage management training. If it is unclear where to go, start with the person who assigned you to the production. He or she should at least be able to get you started and point you toward other resources as needed.

A professional stage manager is traditionally hired much closer to the project's start date. An Equity stage manager will have a contractually defined prep week (the week before rehearsals begin) for analyzing the script and preparing initial paperwork. But if you are a member of a resident team for a theatre, you may be hired for a slate of shows in a season and may similarly be asked questions or given information before it is "time." It will be up to your discretion and availability if you choose to get involved prior to your official start date.

No matter when your assignment is determined, this first set of information-collecting tasks is among your most important.

NEW, BUT NOT A NOVICE

If you are a young stage manager, it is particularly important that you balance how much you ask versus how much you learn. There are certain questions only a director can answer: how he or she likes to organize rehearsals, preferences about visitors or breaks, deadlines for memorizing lines, and so forth. But the director may not be the best person to ask *everything*. Present yourself as someone capable of finding answers, not just asking questions. If you cannot locate the restrooms in the building, for example, or are unaware about procedures for locking up the rehearsal space, look for other information sources. This might be a fellow stage manager, your advisor in an academic setting, or the production manager. Your theatre or department might also have a handbook in which such details are already documented.

GIVEN CIRCUMSTANCES

If you have worked at this theatre or with these team members before, you will have some basic information about logistics and the working styles of the participants. If not, you will need to begin your investigation of the project with those basics before diving into the script itself. The production manager is typically the best place to start. He or she coordinates the artistic and production details for all of the shows in a theatre's season and will have many answers for you. In an academic setting, you should again start with your faculty advisor.

PERSONNEL

1. Who is the director? Have you worked with this person before? Has the theatre?

2. Who are the designers? Have you worked with any of these people before? Have they worked together? For this theatre? With this director?

If you are new to this company or department, it will be helpful to be aware of existing relationships. If your director is familiar with the theatre's procedures, you will be able to focus on communicating reminders of deadlines rather than explaining why they exist. If he or she has worked in the theatre before, blocking in a rehearsal room can be developed with a better understanding of available backstage space. Designers who are resident to the theatre or are frequent guests will also have expectations about what is possible, what exists in stock, or other considerations.

But in addition to preexisting knowledge about the logistics, prior working relationships will affect how the players communicate with one another and, therefore, how you can best facilitate this dialogue. Team members with many successful shows together may have developed shortcuts in their pattern of information exchange—nicknames for people or units, and discussions filled with references to past shows. If you are the newcomer, it will be important to do some homework so that you can better understand this vernacular. This might mean looking at photos or paperwork of these past productions, getting background from a third party, or at times asking specifically for clarification. You won't want to assume you know what someone means and then transmit this information to someone else, only to find you've misunderstood a reference. Conversely, team members may feel they worked together so well in the past that they know what one another is thinking and do not need to convey details or ask as many questions. The stage manager needs to remain the conduit for consistent, clear information, despite this familiarity to help avoid problems later on.

These prior relationships, however, may not necessarily have been positive ones. Negative past experiences, if allowed to fester, can easily taint this new production. Without engaging in gossip, see what you can learn. A designer who missed many of the deadlines set by the theatre in the past may have been given earlier due dates for drawings or paperwork this time around to build in a buffer. And while this might seem unimportant to you, if meeting those deadlines requires seeing a run-through of the show prior to a certain date, for example, it will be helpful to know this at the beginning so the rehearsal schedule can accommodate this need. If your director was unhappy with the execution of a design element in the past, he or she may make comments during rehearsal and ask that these dictates be included in a rehearsal report in a very specific way. As the stage manager, you will need to focus on separating information from the tone in which you received it.

LOCATION

3. Where will the show perform? Where will it rehearse? If these are two different locations, will there be rehearsals on the set prior to tech?

If you are unfamiliar with your rehearsal space or the theatre itself, go see them! If the rehearsal space is smaller than the theatre, you may have to make some compromises when marking the groundplan of the set in tape on the rehearsal room floor. You will want to ask the director about this before you begin, so that you don't find yourself retaping the set at the end of the first rehearsal. It will also be important to know if the SM team can leave tables and furniture set up overnight, if there is a sound system in place for rehearsal cues, if there is a green-room space for actors, and other such details.

Once you have some basics under your belt, turn your focus to the show itself. This will have two parts—dates and details related to the production, and information contained in the script.

> **Groundplan:** A bird's-eye view of the set and theatre architecture, drawn in scale by the scenic designer
>
> **Taping the set:** Replicating the groundplan on the floor of your rehearsal room by measuring the scale drawing and using tape to indicate where walls, platforms, and other scenic units are located.

THE CALENDAR

The production's calendar is an important source of information. In some instances you may be handed a calendar and tasked with seeing that deadlines are met. In other instances you may be collecting information from multiple sources and creating a calendar yourself.

Our earlier definition of the stage manager as seen in the task list created by Actors' Equity Association identifies three separate parts of the job related to this one item: calling rehearsals, facilitating outside activities, and maintaining records. From the perspective of the actors, the stage manager needs to create a document that clearly and succinctly identifies the overall rehearsal and performance dates, when individual members of the cast will be needed during the rehearsal process, how outside activities such as costume fittings and publicity events fit into the mix, and where important milestones such as running the show or line-memorization deadlines will fall.

These details are all essential to the actors, then, yet bear minimal overlap with the needs of the other users who will depend on the calendar. Designers and other members of the production team will be concerned with overall rehearsal and performance dates, but only occasionally with information about actor milestones. A specific charting of the acting work is of little use to them. This second group does have their own distinct needs as well, which include design deadlines, the load-in dates, and any unavailable time in the theatre due to outside events or maintenance issues—which are of no specific concern to the actors.

And actors and production team members are not the only interested parties. The crew members who will join the production to execute the technical elements care nothing about the events that precede their employment, nor do they care what happens in the building when they are not there. The business office is typically more concerned with overall hours and weeks worked in order to process payroll than with the content of that work time. A director will be interested in seeing that all the actor specifics they generated have been correctly outlined. He or she will want to know when to expect work from the designers and will likely need an additional set of publicity deadlines, which may require the director's time and attention but not affect any of these other players.

Our simple calendar has now become an extremely complex item, and the stage manager faces the challenge of collecting and presenting this information in the most useful way to all of these groups.

So where do you start?

The theatre is likely to have an overall production calendar that shows how multiple productions fit together into a single season. Unless you hold a supervisory position in your stage management department, you may play no role in creating this calendar. But you will most certainly want a copy.

THE PRODUCTION CALENDAR VERSUS THE ACTOR CALENDAR

Take a look at the page from a season calendar presented in Figure 3.1. It contains production information for two overlapping shows in two different theatres. As the stage manager for *Twelfth Night*, you are most concerned with the details for that show. But if you share personnel with the production of *Galoshes* running at the beginning of the month, you can identify this as a time when those designers and technicians will have a decidedly split focus—and your show is probably not the priority. You do not need to do anything with this information now, but will want to remember it as that time approaches. (Note: *Galoshes* refers to a children's production of *Galoshes of Fortune* performed in the theatre's other performance space.)

The calendar outlines for you many important production details in your direct purview—deadlines for adding props and sound cues, crew meetings, and prescheduled runs of the show. If everyone on your production team has this general calendar, you may not need to develop one for them. But make note of these details, so that you can help your team meet these deadlines.

Even if you could get access to the original file and delete the items not specific to your show, this would not be a good version of the calendar to distribute to your cast. It does not contain specifics about rehearsal. And simply replacing the *Galoshes* details with your rehearsal schedule will not create a usable document. You would end up with a calendar so overloaded with information that it would be difficult to navigate. It may be possible to make your font size small enough to fit everything, but at what cost? If the calendar is too difficult to read, many won't invest time to do so. Instead, take the relevant details from this production calendar and create a version better suited for the actors.

Now evaluate the actor calendar in Figure 3.2. You will notice several differences right from the start. First, this calendar has been set up to include the entire rehearsal and performance period on a single page, from mid-October to mid-December. Second, each rehearsal has a

Toland Theatre
FREDERICK THEATRE
Department of Theatre Arts
UW-L

UW-L THEATRE
PRODUCTION CALENDAR 2010-2011

NOVEMBER

Sunday	Monday	Tuesday	Wednesday	Thursday	Friday	Saturday
	1 12:05 Dept Mtg Galoshes Sound Load In Galoshes Hang	**2**	**3** 12:05 Twelfth Night Prod Mtg Galoshes Focus	**4** Galoshes Focus	**5** 12:05 Galoshes Paper Tech 6pm Senior Show Galoshes Focus	**6** Galoshes Cueing
7 Galoshes SM Load In Galoshes Cueing *Daylight Savings Clocks 1 hour back*	**8** *Frederick Theatre- Limited or No Class Availability*	**9**	**10**	**11**	**12**	**13** 11:00, 1:00 Galoshes Strike
	8 12:05 Dept Mtg Galoshes Tech	**9** Galoshes Dress	**10** 9:00, 11:00, 1:00 Galoshes 12:05 Twelfth Night Prod Mtg Twelfth Night Prelim Light Plot	**11** 9:00, 11:00, 1:00 Galoshes *Veterans Day*	**12** 9:00, 11:00, 1:00 Galoshes Photocall	
14	**15** 12:05 Dept Mtg Twelfth Night Hang 5:00 Twelfth Night Crew Meeting Twelfth Night Run for LX	**16** Twelfth Night Hang	**17** 12:05 Twelfth Night Prod Mtg Twelfth Night Final Light Plot Prop & Sound Add Deadline	**18** Twelfth Night Early Reservations	**19** 6pm Senior Show	**20**
21	**22** 12:05 Dept Mtg Twelfth Night Focus	**23** Twelfth Night Focus	**24** Twelfth Night Paper Tech Twelfth Night Focus	**25**	**26** Thanksgiving Break	**27** Twelfth Night Cueing
28 Twelfth Night SM Load In Twelfth Night Cueing Thanksgiving	**29** 12:05 Dept Mtg Twelfth Night Box Office Opens Twelfth Night Tech	**30** Twelfth Night Tech				

Figure 3.1 A month from the production calendar for UW-L Theatre's 2010–2011 season.

Twelfth Night

PRELIMINARY REHEARSAL CALENDAR

Sunday	Monday	Tuesday	Wednesday	Thursday	Friday	Saturday
October 24	25 Rehearsal 6:30-9:30 pm	26 Rehearsal 6:30-9:30 pm	27 Workshop 6:30-8:30 pm (cast required to attend- open to all majors/minors)	28 Rehearsal 6:30-9:30 pm	29 **6:00 pm Allyssa Senior Show** Rehearsal 7-10 pm	30
31	November 1 Rehearsal 6:30-9:30 pm	2 Rehearsal 6:30-9:30 pm	3 Rehearsal 6:30-9:30 pm	4 Rehearsal 6:30-9:30 pm	5 Rehearsal 6:30-9:30 pm	6
7 *Daylight Savings Clocks 1 hour back!*	8 Rehearsal 6:30-9:30 pm	9 Rehearsal 6:30-9:30 pm	10 Rehearsal 6:30-9:30 pm	11 Rehearsal 6:30-9:30 pm	12 Rehearsal 6:30-9:30 pm	13
14	15 Rehearsal 6:30-9:30 pm Run through for Lights	16 Rehearsal 6:30-9:30 pm OFF BOOK PART ONE	17 Rehearsal 6:30-9:30 pm	18 Rehearsal 6:30-9:30 pm OFF BOOK PART TWO	19 **6:00 pm Tim & Donnie Senior Shows** Rehearsal 7:30-10 pm	20
21	15 Rehearsal 6:30-9:30 pm	15 Rehearsal 6:30-9:30 pm	24	25	26	27
			Thanksgiving Break			
28	29 **6-10 pm TECH REHEARSAL**	30 **6-10 pm TECH REHEARSAL**	December 1 **6-10 pm TECH REHEARSAL**	2 **10:00 am MATINEE Photo Call**	3 **7:30 pm Performance**	4 **Afternoon Put-in Rehearsal** **7:30 pm Performance (Understudies)**
5 **2:00 pm Matinee**	6	7	8	9 **7:30 pm Performance**	10 **7:30 pm Performance**	11 **7:30 pm Performance**
12 **2:00 pm Matinee Strike**						

As of 10/22/10

Specific Rehearsal Times are Subject to Change
Afternoon Calls for Costume Fittings, etc to be arranged

Figure 3.2 The rehearsal calendar for *Twelfth Night*.

specific time. Items such as the senior shows, seemingly unimportant on the production calendar, do in fact impact rehearsal times. You will be scheduling around them. So they are worth including. The run for lights on November 15 is an important landmark for the actors, so it is transferred, as are notations of holidays and daylight saving time. But you also want to include details not appropriate for the general production calendar—such as the off-book deadlines on November 16 and 18—which you learned from the director.

This is an ideal amount of information to provide actors at the beginning of the process, starting at auditions. Obviously, it does not have enough specifics to guide the work for individual nights of rehearsal. It is not attempting to do so. Once rehearsals begin, the stage manager will create subsequent weekly or daily rehearsal calls to communicate those specifics. Even if you have them at this point, they are not necessary inclusions.

FORMATTING THE CALENDAR

It may seem obvious, but the most important formatting consideration for a calendar is that it looks like a calendar! This means clearly identified months, weeks, and days. Whether you are creating a single page for each month or a multi-month calendar for your entire production process, both calendars make this information available and clear. To help denote that our sample actor calendar contains multiple months, simple shading has been used.

A typical Equity workweek is six days, traditionally Tuesday through Sunday, with Monday as the day off. It may be tempting to move the Monday column to the far left, so that each row of the calendar is a single work week for your show. But what happens when an actor takes your calendar and compares it to a work calendar or even a personal calendar? Ultimately this will probably create more confusion than you intend. Visually the two will not line up, and the difference between an activity happening on a Tuesday versus a Wednesday could be quite problematic if misread.

Another visual aid is at play in the actor calendar, particularly during the performance weeks. Activities occur during two major blocks of time—during the day and at night. Evening performances are lined up lower in the cells than daytime calls. This helps the student matinee on December 2 and the put-in rehearsal on December 4 to stand out. Even though the calendar was initially published without a set time for this rehearsal, keeping it in line with the matinee makes it clear this will be a daytime call and not one immediately preceding the evening show.

The stage manager will find that this calendar is one of the most frequently needed items. You will print or copy it often. And because of this, color is often a poor formatting choice. At the University of Wisconsin–La Crosse, the production calendar is primarily distributed by email and is uploaded to two different theatre websites. Only one hard copy is printed and posted. The calendar contains information for seven different productions, as well as department events and holidays. The volume of information, and the fact that it is not routinely sent through a copier, makes the use of color appropriate to help differentiate the categories. Were this document primarily duplicated and distributed in hard copy, the color distinctions would be less effective. The department would either make different choices to separate individual categories of information or reluctantly accept that the printed version will always be less accessible than the electronic copy. In contrast, the actor calendar—almost exclusively shared in printed form—utilizes the bolding of information for emphasis. This is appropriate based on its distribution method.

SOME THOUGHTS ABOUT CALENDAR PROGRAMS

In today's age of technology, a wide variety of computer programs exist for creating and maintaining calendars. We can synchronize them across multiple computers or even with our phones, set up a series of reminders, and input recurring events by typing them once and clicking a series of boxes. But while these are all useful tools, it does not mean that calendar software is best for theatre productions.

The stage manager's primary concern is not how the calendar functions within a computer, but how well it works in its printed-out form. If the computer program does not let you control the order in which events are listed on a day or doesn't like text-only details without a specific time, you might find that you are changing what you want to include in order to make it conform to what the calendar program thinks you need. Or what if the program limits how many events can be seen on a single day? When the stage manager is looking at a calendar on a computer and sees "plus 4 more" while in month view, it is easy enough to click that link and have the calendar transform itself to a week or day view to access those additional details. But in print, that link is useless and the additional information is lost.

I have personally tried and evaluated many different calendar programs over the course of my career, and despite many promises of ease, I find that control over both format and content is best found not in a calendar program at all. I create my calendars in either Microsoft Word or Microsoft Excel, making use of templates I set up that can be tweaked and customized to fit the needs of any production.

ANALYZING THE PRODUCTION

After mining the calendar for details relevant to your show, the stage manager's next set of tasks during this pre-production time is related to the script itself. Before you can begin to understand what will make this particular production of the show unique, it is important to understand the basics presented on the page.

The stage manager should begin each project by simply reading the script. As difficult as it can be to turn off the part of the brain accustomed to seeking out details, start by absorbing the story and getting an overall sense of the show. With these general observations in hand, return to the script and now look for the specifics provided in the dialogue and stage directions, taking careful notes as you go.

It is essential for the stage manager to understand what the script dictates in order to accurately assess information about your production of it. It is helpful to have a consistent method for taking notes and a common format for recording your discoveries, but this is a tool not necessarily intended for distribution.

The chart in Figure 3.3 provides one method for capturing this information. In this setup, the stage manager can enter each fact as a separate row, noting it in the column or columns most appropriate. It is important to remember that you are simply cataloging your discoveries, not making decisions about them. Consider the following invented dialogue:

Mary: Gosh it's cold in here.

John: You can borrow that sweater if you want.

Mary: Thanks! I feel much better now.

PRODUCTION ANALYSIS

Act/Scene/Page	Cast/Costumes	Scenery	Props	Lights	Sound	Effects/Other

Figure 3.3 A form for recording notes about a production while analyzing the script.

From this dialogue we can infer that there is a sweater belonging to John somewhere on the stage and that Mary puts it on. The stage manager records this information. But all you know is that there is a sweater—not its color, fabrication, or style. Noting that John has a blue cardigan on your chart would be filling in details not provided by the script.

In other instances, it may not be clear to whom a certain detail belongs. When working on a production of Chekhov's *The Seagull*, the stage manager will discover a stage direction in Act Two that details Treplev's entrance "carrying a gun and a dead seagull." The gun itself can be entered on the chart as a prop in the show. A subsequent stage direction in Act Four tells the stage manager that the "sound of a shot offstage" is heard. This effect should also be noted. But does this sound come from the gun you noted in Act Two, a starter pistol fired in the wings, or a recorded sound effect played through a location-specific speaker? Because the stage manager may not know which method will be used, it is best to record the gunshot as both a possible sound effect and a possible functional weapon for now, because two separate production areas would be responsible for executing this effect, depending on the production.

This completed analysis serves as an excellent reference tool for the stage manager's early meetings with the production team. In an academic setting the stage manager may be in attendance for design discussions, while in a professional setting he or she may join the process much later on. Regardless of the scenario, the stage manager can refer to these notes during meetings. If the gun is discussed, for example, with no mention of how the shot will be handled, the stage manager has created a reminder to ask if a decision has been made about the cue. And while this may be an obvious question to ask on a production of this particular play, the stage manager should not expect to memorize every detail of every element in the show. Using the notes helps ensure that details are not forgotten—or not forgotten to be shared with you.

Once your analysis is supplemented with answers either from formal meetings or informal conversations with the director or designers, you will be ready to create paperwork for your full production team based on this chart. It is unlikely that you will be asked to make a preliminary light cue list based on the information the script contains, but the stage manager is very involved in the creation and maintenance of the prop list, and, in some theatres, may create the initial version of the sound cue sheet. The stage manager's specific responsibility for such paperwork will differ from theatre to theatre, so be sure that you are clear on what is expected of you.

THE CHARACTER/SCENE BREAKDOWN

Your next important task will be the character/scene breakdown. This document is a page-by-page detailing of who is onstage. The stage manager collects this information by thoroughly examining the script, and then meeting with the director to get further clarification about ensemble characters who may not have many specific page references.

Twelfth Night
Character/Scene Breakdown

		I-1 Orsino's Palace first day, early morning			I-2 Illyrian Coast simultaneous with I-1			I-3 Inside Olivia's House simultaneous with I-1 and I-2					I-4 Orsino's Palace early morning 3 days after Orsino & Cesario meet		
		3	4	5	5	6	7	8	9	10	11	12	12	13	14
Justin Cooke	Orsino	+X	X	X-									+X	X	X-
Matthew Matuseski	Sebastian														
Kevin Fanshaw	Antonio														
Jacob Gustine	Sir Toby Belch							+X	X	X	X	X-			
Tim McCarren	Sir Andrew Aguecheek								+X	X	X	X-			
Andrew Kelly	Malvolio														
Donnie Mezera	Fabian														
Alden Hedges	Feste														
Allyssa Dunn	Olivia														
Claire Ganshert	Viola			+X		X	X-						+X	X	X-
Amy Nelson	Maria							+X	X	X	X	X-			
Jacob Voss	Sea Captain, Priest				+SC	SC	SC-								
Austin Hernandez	Valentine Sailor 3, Officer 1		+V	V-		+S	S-						+V	V	V-
Luke Prescott	Curio, Sailor 1, Officer 2	+C	C	C-		+S	S-						+C	C	C-
Brian Coffin	Lord 1, Sailor 2, Officer 3	+L	L-		+S	S	S-						+L	L	L-
Don Hart	Lord 2, Officer 4	+L	L	L-									+L	L	L-
Emily Ware	Olivia Attendant 1														
Lindsay Van Norman	Olivia Attendant 2														
Suzanne Clum	Musician 1	+X	X-												
Shelby Krarup	Musician 2	+X	X-												

X Onstage, +X Enter, X- Exit, +X- Enter/ Exit, (X) Onstage "hiding"
Other initials indicate ensemble character

Figure 3.4 The character/scene breakdown for *Twelfth Night*. (Note that the footer has been cropped out for image clarity in this book, not omitted from the document.)

KEY USERS

- Director and stage management team
- Cast
- Costume designer
- Sound designer/engineer on a musical

What it contains

- The actors in the show and the roles they play
- The scenes in the play broken down by page
- Scene nicknames or descriptions developed by the director or SM
- Songs and references to score pages (for a musical)

Why do it?

- To develop a more specific rehearsal schedule
- To identify who may have fast costume changes
- To identify who might be available to help with scene changes
- To discover any incidental characters not yet cast

CONTENT CONSIDERATIONS

Much like the full production calendar, the character/scene breakdown is a detail document. It is intended to present a comprehensive look at when the actors will appear on stage. Your key challenge as a stage manager is to make the breakdown easy to navigate, since you will intentionally include a great deal of information.

The breakdown is best organized as a chart. The use of defined rows and columns will enable you to be consistent in how you enter the specifics. This is not a case where you are striving for someone to quickly glance at the paperwork and learn what they need to know—here you are trying to consolidate many facts in a single location.

Listing Your Cast

If you are stage managing a play or musical in which each actor plays only a single role for the entire production, you could limit your name listing to a single column of only the character names. If, however, some or all of your actors play multiple roles, you will need to list both actor names and character names. One of the goals of this document is to help identify when costume changes will occur, and if characters are not consolidated by actor, you will miss out on this.

Take a look at the two-column name listing in the *Twelfth Night* breakdown in Figure 3.4. It is organized with principal actors at the top and ensemble members below. Although only half the cast plays multiple roles, the breakdown is set up based on the most complex casting, not the least.

Scenes versus Pages

It would, of course, save you both time and paper to include only columns for the individual scenes rather than a page-by-page listing. But as was true for listing only character names, this would require you to omit some information.

Observe the detail provided in the *Twelfth Night* breakdown for the five male ensemble cast members excerpted in Figure 3.5. All five appear in Scene One, Scene Two, or both. A breakdown organized by scene would provide the bare minimum of information. The stage manager might guess that fast costume changes might be required but would not know exactly when.

The page-by-page listing shows us that Austin and Luke are on stage at the end of Scene One, entering late into Scene Two after a potential costume change. In contrast, Brian exits early from the first scene and appears at the top of Scene Two. We can now tell that costume changes, if planned, will be staggered but are essentially simultaneous—as well as very fast (a single page each). The stage management team can see it will need to time this part of the show early in the rehearsal process and work with the costume shop to prepare the actors and backstage areas.

In this production, the actors helped to transform the stage by moving scenic pieces on and off the stage. The breakdown also facilitates identifying the most logical actor to help strike scenery (Don) or bring on new pieces (Jacob). Although both actors play multiple roles, neither will be involved in a costume change during this shift. And while it is not your job to dictate these decisions to the production team, you need to be prepared to answer questions about available actors when the director or scenic designer asks.

The stage manager virtually never has input into the crew hired for a show, but is sometimes asked about the production's needs while that crew is assembled by the technical director or production manager. If we continue to follow the rows across the page, we can see that three

		I-1 Orsino's Palace first day, early morning			I-2 Illyrian Coast simultaneous with I-1			I-3 Inside Olivia's House simultaneous with I-1 and I-2					I-4 Orsino's Palace early morning 3 days after Orsino & Cesario meet		
		3	4	5	5	6	7	8	9	10	11	12	12	13	14
Jacob Voss	Sea Captain, Priest				+SC	SC	SC-								
Austin Hernandez	Valentine Sailor 3, Officer 1		+V	V-		+S	S-						+V	V	V-
Luke Prescott	Curio, Sailor 1, Officer 2	+C	C	C-		+S	S-						+C	C	C-
Brian Coffin	Lord 1, Sailor 2, Officer 3	+L	L-		+S	S	S-						+L	L	L-
Don Hart	Lord 2, Officer 4	+L	L	L-									+L	L	L-

Figure 3.5 A close-up of the male ensemble actors.

of the ensemble men will need to change back before reappearing on stage in Scene Four. But unlike the first change, they now have an entire scene five pages long to do so. The costume crew will need to efficiently reset the costumes after the fast change, but may not need to provide assistance this time—freeing them for other duties that may be required and impacting the potential number of technicians.

Page Numbers

If you look carefully at the row including the script page numbers, you will notice that numbers repeat. It is rare to find a script where the scene break never falls in the middle of a page. By repeating the page numbers that have scene splits on them, you are prepping yourself for easier formatting. More about that later.

Identifying Scenes and Locations

The case has been made for listing out all page numbers. However, this does not mean that individual scenes should not also be detailed. We still need to know where we are in the play! Insert a row to contain scene names and numbers immediately above the page listing.

In this production, time was of great importance to the director; this sample breakdown goes a step further. A significant portion of the first design meeting was devoted to discussions about when the individual scenes occur. Although these notes were included in the meeting minutes, the stage manager repeated this information into the breakdown so that the designers could look in a single place and know when and where we are, along with who is on stage.

Key

Organizing the breakdown by page means that the stage manager can detail not only who is in a scene but also when they enter and exit, if they appear on stage but do not speak, if they sing from the wings, and other specific details. The character/scene breakdown can be thought of as a map of the script and, as such, needs a key (Figure 3.6). This ensures that everyone reading the document can understand it.

A simple *X* will suffice for making entries for principal characters playing a single role— we need to know only if the character is present. Our multi-role ensemble members need a bit more detail. The simplest way to achieve this is to replace the *X* with a role-specific letter abbreviation (one that should coordinate with your blocking key).

Why note something like hiding? To ensure that no one is omitted from a rehearsal call. When flipping quickly through the script, it might be possible to forget that someone is onstage

X Onstage, +X Enter, X- Exit, +X- Enter/ Exit, (X) Onstage "hiding"
Other initials indicate ensemble character

Figure 3.6 The breakdown key.

if the character has not spoken for several pages. That character may, however, still have an important function in the scene. By noting the actor is present but silent, the stage manager is prepared to ask the director if the actor should be called for a particular rehearsal. The focus of that day—blocking versus text work, for example—may prompt different answers from the director.

As you gain experience, you will develop a method to transition with you from show to show, but be ready to address each production's new requirements, and be willing to add or adapt your previous documentation.

FORMATTING THE BREAKDOWN

As mentioned earlier, this breakdown is best formatted as a chart. Depending on the stage manager's software savvy, it can be done in either a spreadsheet or word-processing table. Both provide the separation into rows and columns necessary to navigate the details.

This chart is laid out in landscape format, providing the stage manager sufficient room for the scene details, the two-column cast listing, and a reasonable number of script pages to be laid out horizontally. There is also room for the key, page numbers, and version information while still maintaining enough white space so the document is not overwhelming.

Look at the difference were the document to be set up in portrait format as seen in Figure 3.7. By the time the chart heading information is repeated, the page has become crowded and more difficult to read. It might be possible to squeeze a few more individual pages of the script onto this page of the chart, but the stage manager does so at the expense of accessibility.

To make enough room for the necessary number of rows, their height has been decreased, crowding the text. In order to maintain minimal margins on right and left, Scene Five no longer fits on a single page. This would mean either repeating the scene heading information on the next page or paginating the document such that all of Scene Five falls on page two, leaving a large empty space at the bottom of page one.

In the case of a show with a small cast, the repetition necessary to have multiple-row sets on a single page may not be problematic. But for shows with cast sizes similar to or larger than our sample, there is little benefit to the choice. Remember what we saw with our calendar—if the information is not accessible, it is like you haven't provided it at all.

Guiding the Eye

Whenever you are creating a document intentionally filled with detail, it is essential to help the reader navigate it. An unshaded chart is devoid of focus, and people receiving this breakdown will have to work to find the information they are looking for. Simply by introducing shading, you help focus the reader's eye.

Twelfth Night
Character/Scene Breakdown

		I-1 Orsino's Palace first day, early morning			I-2 Illyrian Coast simultaneous with I-1			I-3 Inside Olivia's House simultaneous with I-1 and I-2				
		3	4	5	5	6	7	8	9	10	11	12
Justin Cooke	Orsino	+X	X	X-								
Matthew Matuseski	Sebastian											
Kevin Fanshaw	Antonio											
Jacob Gustine	Sir Toby Belch							+X	X	X	X	X
Tim McCarren	Sir Andrew Aguecheek								+X	X	X	X-
Andrew Kelly	Malvolio											
Donnie Mezera	Fabian											
Alden Hedges	Feste											
Allyssa Dunn	Olivia											
Claire Ganshert	Viola				+X	X	X					
Amy Nelson	Maria							+X	X	X	X	X-
Jacob Voss	Sea Captain, Priest				+SC	SC	SC-					
Austin Hernandez	Valentine Sailor 3, Officer 1		+V	V-		+S	S-					
Luke Prescott	Curio, Sailor 1, Officer 2	+C	C	C-		+S	S-					
Brian Coffin	Lord 1, Sailor 2, Officer 3	+L	L-		+S	S	S-					
Don Hart	Lord 2, Officer 4	+L	L	L-								
Emily Ware	Olivia Attendant 1											
Lindsay Van Norman	Olivia Attendant 2											
Suzanne Clum	Musician 1	+X	X-									
Shelby Krarup	Musician 2	+X	X-									

		I-4 Orsino's Palace early morning 3 days after Orsino & Cesario meet			I-5 Inside Olivia's House one hour after I-4 (scene continues on next page)							
		12	13	14	14	15	16	17	18	19	20	21
Justin Cooke	Orsino	+X	X	X-								
Matthew Matuseski	Sebastian											
Kevin Fanshaw	Antonio											
Jacob Gustine	Sir Toby Belch								+X-			
Tim McCarren	Sir Andrew Aguecheek											
Andrew Kelly	Malvolio					+X	X	X-	+X	X-		
Donnie Mezera	Fabian											
Alden Hedges	Feste				+X	X-	X	X-	X-			
Allyssa Dunn	Olivia					+X	X	X	X	X	X	X
Claire Ganshert	Viola	+X	X	X-						+X	X	X
Amy Nelson	Maria				+X	X-		+X-		+X	X	X-
Jacob Voss	Sea Captain, Priest											
Austin Hernandez	Valentine Sailor 3, Officer 1	+V	V	V-								
Luke Prescott	Curio, Sailor 1, Officer 2	+C	C	C-								
Brian Coffin	Lord 1, Sailor 2, Officer 3	+L	L	L-								
Don Hart	Lord 2, Officer 4	+L	L	L-								
Emily Ware	Olivia Attendant 1					+X	X	X	X	X	X	X-
Lindsay Van Norman	Olivia Attendant 2					+X	X	X	X	X	X	X-
Suzanne Clum	Musician 1											
Shelby Krarup	Musician 2											

X Onstage, +X Enter, X- Exit, +X- Enter/ Exit, (X) Onstage "hiding"
Other initials indicate ensemble character

Figure 3.7 The breakdown set up in portrait view.

This breakdown uses vertical shading to help distinguish individual scenes. The reader can easily find the relevant scene and then locate the actor in question. You can now see why we repeated the page numbers. Because the duplicates fall into different shading zones, it is not distracting. But we have avoided having to do one more formatting step by splitting those cells and trying to line up the outside margins.

Consider the alternative offered by the chart in Figure 3.8. In this case, the shading separates individual actors. And while it may be simpler to follow the rows across the page, it is more difficult to find where scenes begin and end. And overall, the "striped" version is busier. We haven't helped the reader's eye—we have added a layer of distraction.

The scene distinction is further reinforced by merging cells at the top of the page. Notice that the cells above pages three through five are merged into one. This instantly identifies them as a single scene, and, as a bonus, gives you a bit of extra room for your text.

Twelfth Night
Character/Scene Breakdown

		I-1 Orsino's Palace first day, early morning			I-2 Illyrian Coast simultaneous with I-1			I-3 Inside Olivia's House simultaneous with I-1 and I-2				I-4 Orsino's Palace early morning 3 days after Orsino & Cesario meet		
		3	4	5	5	6	7	8	9	10	11	12	12	13	14
Justin Cooke	Orsino	+X	X	X-									+X	X	X-
Matthew Matuseski	Sebastian														
Kevin Fanshaw	Antonio														
Jacob Gustine	Sir Toby Belch							+X	X	X	X	X-			
Tim McCarren	Sir Andrew Aguecheek								+X	X	X	X-			
Andrew Kelly	Malvolio														
Donnie Mezera	Fabian														
Alden Hedges	Feste														
Allyssa Dunn	Olivia														
Claire Ganshert	Viola				+X	X	X-						+X	X	X-
Amy Nelson	Maria							+X	X	X	X	X-			
Jacob Voss	Sea Captain, Priest				+SC	SC	SC-								
Austin Hernandez	Valentine Sailor 3, Officer 1		+V	V-		+S	S-						+V	V	V-
Luke Prescott	Curio, Sailor 1, Officer 2	+C	C	C-		+S	S-						+C	C	C-
Brian Coffin	Lord 1, Sailor 2, Officer 3	+L	L-		+S	S	S-						+L	L	L-
Don Hart	Lord 2, Officer 4	+L	L	L-									+L	L	L-
Emily Ware	Olivia Attendant 1														
Lindsay Van Norman	Olivia Attendant 2														
Suzanne Clum	Musician 1	+X	X-												
Shelby Krarup	Musician 2	+X	X-												

X Onstage, +X Enter, X- Exit, +X- Enter/ Exit, (X) Onstage "hiding"
Other initials indicate ensemble character

Figure 3.8 The breakdown with horizontal shading.

Shading versus Color

Ultimately the same visual help could be achieved by the subtle introduction of colored columns. As long as the color is not too dark to interfere with the text itself, it can be successful. Choosing between shading and color is determined by distribution format. For example, this breakdown will be distributed to all of the cast members, as well as the SM team, the director, and the costume shop—at this theatre just shy of 30 individuals.

Do you have a color Xerox machine? Does your theatre or department allow unlimited copies? If both answers are yes, then color might be a reasonable option. But if either answer is no, consider how you will produce all the copies. If you print one in color and then copy it in black-and-white, you've defeated the purpose of using color in the first place. And if the color is too light to copy, then you will end up with an unshaded document.

Does the theatre have a color printer? How much ink will you waste trying to print thirty copies of a seven-page chart? And what happens when changes are made and you need to distribute an updated version?

It is easy, as a new stage manager, to think that color is the answer—that it makes your paperwork look pretty and, therefore, more professional. But stylish does not always mean practical. Remember that one of the stage manager's goals is to work efficiently to communicate the information you have. Wasting time and money is not efficient.

That being said, you will notice the introduction of a color logo on the *Urinetown* breakdown in Figure 3.9. For this production, most of the information was distributed electronically to the design team. This meant no major drain on color ink cartridges.

The logo was also tested on the copier and looked just fine in grayscale. The breakdown could be distributed in hard copy to the actors. The color was also used more as an accent rather than as an essential navigational tool. It helped to provide continuity among all the pieces of production paperwork (see Chapter 2), but the loss of color in the logo, when printed in black-and-white, did not hamper the accessibility of the document.

What does this mean? Know both the rules and when it is okay to break them!

EXTRA CONSIDERATIONS FOR THE MUSICAL

When stage managing a musical, the stage manager will have two "scripts" to consider—the libretto and the score. No matter what form the script in your prompt book takes, it is essential that you are able to communicate with everyone. You will need to know both scenes and songs, and page numbers in both of these books.

> The **prompt book** is the stage manager's binder, which contains copies of all paperwork for an individual production, along with the copy of the script in which you will record blocking and cues. Chapter 4 discusses the prompt book and prompt script in detail.

URINETOWN
Revised Character/Scene Breakdown

ACT ONE		Scene 1: Public Amenity #9														Scene 2: UGC Offices							
		1	2	3	4	5	6	7	8	9	10	11	12	13	14	14	15	16	17	18	19	20	21
Austin Hernandez	Officer Lockstock	+x	x	x	x	x	x-	x	x	x	x	+x	x	x									
Emily Bourland	Penelope Pennywise	+x	x	x	x	x	x	x	x	x	x	x	x	x	x-								
Justin Cooke	Bobby Strong	+x	x	x	x	x	x	x	x	x	x	x	x	x	x-								
Kaylyn Forkey	Little Sally	+x	x	x	x	x	x	x	x	x	x	x	x	x	x-								
Andrew Kelly	Caldwell B. Cladwell															+x	x	x	x	x	x	x	x-
Katie Bakalars	Hope Cladwell			+x	x-												+x	x	x	x	x	x	x-
Lindsay Van Norman	Josephine Strong	+x	x	x	x	x	x-																
Kevin Fanshaw	Hot Blades Harry	+x	x	x	x	x	x	x	x	x	x	x	x	x	x-								
Cassie Pacelli	Little Becky Two Shoes	+x	x	x	x	x	x	x	x	x	x	x	x	x	x-								
Jill Iverson	Soupy Sue	+x	x	x	x	x	x	x	x	x	x	x	x	x	x-								
Alex Attardo	Tiny Tom/Cop	+x	x	x	x	x	x	x	x	x	x	x	x	x	x-								
Jhardon Milton	Robby the Stockfish/Cop	+x	x	x	x	x	x	x	x	x	x	x	x	x	x-								
AJ Porter	Billy Boy Bill/Cop	+x	x	x	x	x	x	x	x	x	x	x	x	x	x-								
Matt Matuseski	Old Man Strong/Ace/Cop	+O	O	O	O	O	O	O	O	O	O	O	O	O-									
Kelsey Taunt	Mouthy Mable	+x	x	x	x	x	x	x	x	x	x	x	x	x	x-								
Lizzie Knothe	Joanie-Girl	+x	x	x	x	x	x	x	x	x	x	x	x	x	x-								
Rhys Wolf	Mr. McQueen			+x	x	x	x-+-									+x	x-		+x	x	x	x	x-
Michael Birr	Senator Fipp			+x	x	x	x-+-									+x	x	x	x-				
Quinn Masterson	Officer Barrel			+x	x	x	x-					+x	x	x-									
Brady Langer	Dr. Billeaux/Cop																		+x	x	x	x	x-
Laura Paulson	Mrs. Millenium																		+x	x	x	x	x-
Allison Langer	Cladwell's Secretary																		+x	x	x	x	x-
		#2 Urinetown				#3A It's a Priviledge to Pee								#4A P2P R		#5 Mr. Cladwell							
	score pages	5–27				31–52								53–57		61–77							

x Onstage, +x Enter, x- Exit, +x- Enter/ Exit, G Ghost of self
Additions and changes may occur during the rehearsal process

Figure 3.9 The character/scene breakdown for *Urinetown*—a musical with designated scenes. (Note that the footer has been cropped out for image clarity, not omitted from

The *Urinetown* character/scene breakdown shows you how to incorporate this additional information. It will affect both content and format. Because the actors and director work primarily from the libretto, those page numbers are located on the top. And because this musical has defined scenes, they are clearly delineated with the same cell merging and shading we saw in the play breakdown.

Music-specific information is found at the bottom of the chart. Just as we did for scene details, cells are merged to help distinguish individual songs, identified both by song number and title. Score pages are included, and, by placing them below the song titles, they are easy to read and not lost in the chart.

Notice what happens when a song is short. A single cell is far too small to say "#4 Privilege to Pee Reprise." Rather than repeating the libretto page numbers solely for the sake of making the song title fit, the stage manager has abbreviated the title. It is short enough to fit and logical, because the reprise follows the original song. But because the stage manager cannot guarantee that everyone follows his or her thinking, the song number provides a reference that everyone will understand.

MULTITASKING TIP

The SM can use the character/scene breakdown to make rehearsals more efficient for all. In the following chart, you can see that Senator Fipp exits early from Scene Two and does not appear in the song "Mr. Cladwell."

If your director schedules a large block of time to work on this scene, Fipp may not be needed for all of it. This could allow the actor to attend a short costume fitting if your shop and rehearsal times are the same, or to work on lines or music for another scene in a second room.

Not all musicals have the traditional book format. Consider a musical like *Rent* with no formal scenes within the acts. In this case, the script divisions—and likely the rehearsal schedule—will be based on songs. The *Rent* example in Figure 3.10 shows the songs now in a place of prominence at the top of the chart.

Because there is only one row devoted to text-based subdivisions of the play, the page numbers in libretto and score have also been placed closer together. Separating them at the top and bottom of the page isn't necessary in this instance. But there are formatting tricks still at work. The score page line is in italics, giving it visual distinction from the libretto page line. And further clarity comes from centering the page numbers so that they are not directly in line with the row below.

RENT

Revised Character / Scene Breakdown

Act One

Song / Score Pages / Libretto Page columns:

Song	1 - Tune Up A		1a - Voice Mail #1		2 - Tune Up B				3 - Rent						4 - Xmas Bells #1	5 - You Okay, Honey?		6 - Tune Up Reprise
Score Pages	1-2		3		4-7				8-25						26	27-31		32-33
Libretto Page	1	2	2	3	3	4	5	6	6	7	8	9	10	11	11	11	12	13
Justin Cooke — Mark	+X	X	X	X	X	X	X	X	X	X	X	X	X	X	(X)	(X)	(X)	X-
Zachary Keenan — Roger	+X	X	X	X	X	X	X	X	X	X	X	X	X	X	(X)	(X)	(X)	X
Brandon Harris — Tom Collins					+X	X	X	X	X	X	X	X	X	X-	X	X	X	X-
Paul Hibbard — Angel									+X	X	X	X	X	X	X	X	X	X-
Lance Newton — Benny						+X	X	X	X	X	X	X	X	X-				X-
Samantha Pauley — Mimi									+X	X	X	X	X	X-				
Hope Parow — Joanne										+X	X	X	X	X-				
Katie Bakalars — Maureen									+X	X	X	X	X	X-				
Mark Sopchyk — Gordon/Rest Man/Season Solo/Cop/Ens									E	E	E	E	E	E				
Sarah Shervey — Ali/Ensemble									E	E	E	E	E	E				
Lindsay Van Norman — Pam/Seasons Solo/Ensemble									E	E	E	E	E	E				
Elizabeth Metz — Sue/Ensemble									E	E	E	E	E	E				
Austin Hernandez — Steve/The Man/Ensemble									E	E	E	E	E	E				
Jake Voss — Homeless/Junkie/Ensemble									E	E	E	E	E	E				
Laura Tracy — Homeless/Ensemble									E	E	E	E	E	E				
Donnie Mezera — Blanket Person/Junkie/Ensemble						+H-			E	E	E	E	E	E				
Margaret Teshner — Homeless/Ensemble									E	E	E	E	E	E				
Dan Liska — Homeless/Bells Solo/Ensemble						+H-			E	E	E	E	E	E	+H-			
Matthew Matuseski — Paul/Vendor 1/Pastor/Ensemble									E	E	E	E	E	E				
Shannon McDonald — Vendor 2/Mrs. J/Moon Backup/Ens									E	E	E	E	E	E				
Christine Walth — Coat Vendor/Mrs. Cohen/Ensemble			+MC	MC-					E	E	E	E	E	E				
Nicky Hilsen — Alexi D/Moon Backup/Mimi Mom/Ens									E	E	E	E	E	E				
Andrew Kelly — Mr. Jefferson/Cop/Mr. Grey/Ensemble									E	E	E	E	E	E				
Amy Nelson — Roger's Mom/Cop/Ensemble									E	E	E	E	E	E				

X Onstage, +X Enter, X- Exit, +X- Enter/ Exit, (X) Onstage no lines
Other initials indicate ensemble character - Ensemble may be added to additional scenes

DISTRIBUTION

The character/scene breakdown is a document you are likely to distribute both electronically and in hard copy. This means you will need to keep both sets of distribution rules in mind.

Production team members are overrun with paper, and, while the breakdown will be a useful document, it is not something they will look at every day. Sending it out via email or posting it on a show website will help ensure they can find it when they need it. So remember the electronic rules and consider the following:

- You've put a lot of time into finding the proper balance between text and white space, and between a title font with personality and a body font with legibility. But what if the recipients don't have your fonts installed? Will the document still be legible?

- Every computer will default to its own printer settings, not the settings of the printer attached to the document's creator. Your formatting work can easily get lost. Will the accessibility of the information be affected by a change in the available print area?

The PDF is the best choice for this document. You can guarantee that everyone will receive the information as you intend. And as a bonus, it doesn't matter if the computer is Mac or PC, new or old.

A third factor supporting the PDF: *usability*. The character/scene breakdown is not an interactive document. You don't actually want anyone other than the SM team to make changes on their own. It's too complex a document to have multiple versions being independently edited. The PDF (with version number and date) creates a snapshot of what you know on the day it is created. Once changes have happened in rehearsal, you can update the document and email or post a new version.

But remember that your actors are much more likely to read something you put in their hands. They will want a printed version. This makes it much easier for them to study it in conjunction with their script. So once you are done with the chart and think you have found a good font at a good size, appropriate shading, and well-balanced rows and columns, print out a page and send it through the copier. If it still communicates the information as effectively as the original, you have found a winning combination.

MEETING WITH THE DIRECTOR

Once the stage manager has completed the first round of theatre and script investigation, it is time to meet with the director. You are now ready to ask show-specific questions and find out about the director's preferences and rehearsal needs. Even if you have a prior working relationship with the director of your show, it is advisable to carve out time for this meeting. You will always have a few questions to ask, and this also provides an opportunity to discuss if anything should be handled differently from previous productions.

If you have not worked with this director before, then this, in a way, is a second job interview. The director may not have been involved in your selection. You have the job, and you want to keep it! Beginning the working relationship with clear communication and mutual understanding will pave the way for successful interaction as things get more complicated.

With that in mind, review your notes and prioritize the information you need right now. Over the course of your career, you will develop a standard list of questions to be answered, which can serve as your starting point. If you do not have such a list yet, use the following information to create one.

SHOW INFORMATION

General thoughts. Before launching into your list of questions, allow the director to talk about the show in general terms. The focus of the director's comments can tell you which characters, scenic elements, or moments in the play he or she considers the most important. This can guide you later on as you schedule time for rehearsing that scene or consider how to word a note in a report.

Specific details. Get clarification about the questions in your production analysis. Now is when you can discover if the gunshot should be live or recorded, and if that has been discussed with the production team yet. Are there aspects of the show that will be different from other productions and necessitate rehearsal time, or items not immediately clear when reading the script? Do you need information to help you complete your character/scene breakdown? Do you need information about audition materials?

Current needs. Is the director waiting for information from any member of the production team that you can help acquire? Which pieces of your preliminary paperwork would the director like to see? To see before distributed to others?

REHEARSAL PROCEDURES

Rehearsal hours. In an academic setting, this would be the general rehearsal hours (if not standardized) and any planned deviations from that schedule. In an Equity setting, this would include preferences for the short or long day, if allowed under your contract.

Overall plan for rehearsals. Will the director begin with a read-through of the show? Will there be any days devoted to table work? How does the director approach blocking—putting a show quickly up on its feet or taking time for exploration before setting the movement? When should the actors be off-book? When does the director hope to see actors working with props? If this is a musical, how will the need for music, staging, and choreography rehearsal time be balanced?

Breaks and time. Will the director create a detailed schedule for the process or communicate priorities and let you work out the details? Does the director have a preference for five- or ten-minute breaks? How should you notify him or her when the break is due: a reminder slightly in advance or stopping rehearsal and calling it on your own? If a scheduled rehearsal is running past its allotted time, should you let the rehearsal continue or alert the director?

Actors' Equity Association specifies the length of the breaks given to actors while in rehearsal—five minutes after 55 minutes of work or ten minutes after 80 minutes of work. An exception exists when running the show. Performers may complete a full act before stopping, receiving a 15-minute break if the act exceeded 80 minutes long. Many academic theatres use these breaks as a guideline for handling stops in their own rehearsals as part of their efforts to train actors and stage managers for professional work.

The room. Does the director have preferences for how the room is set up? If the complete groundplan cannot be taped on the floor, is there an area best omitted or condensed?

Guests and visitors. Are rehearsals closed? Are there any specific periods of time when even production team members might be asked not to stop by?

Special needs. Are there specific items the director likes to have in rehearsal? This could range from dramaturgical reference materials to a favorite snack food on stressful days.

Allow yourself sufficient time for the meeting, and choose a location free from distraction. You hope to receive the director's full attention as you ask questions, and you certainly don't want to be distracted yourself by the surroundings. At the end of the meeting, be clear about your next steps. If you promise to get information for the director or provide copies of your paperwork, do so promptly. If the director needs to provide things for you, determine if a reminder is warranted. Some directors may request a call or email—especially if they are working on multiple shows. Others may find this just a bit too micromanaging. And if you cannot tell what is needed, there is never harm in sending a quick email after the meeting to thank the director for making time for you and reiterating how much you are looking forward to the show. Even without listing the things you are waiting for, this may be enough of a reminder!

MEETING THE PRODUCTION TEAM

If the director does not have all the answers you need, or if there are details requiring input or clarification from the designers, you can repeat the aforementioned scenario and request time to meet with members of your production team. Be sure to find out if there is a production meeting scheduled in the near future. If so, these questions can simply become agenda items or follow-up questions after the meeting ends.

If there is no production meeting scheduled soon, and you get the sense that important decisions still need to be made, check with the production manager or your supervisor/advisor. You might need to call for a meeting, send a group email, or take other actions to unite the players sooner than was intended.

THE PROP LIST

After meeting with the director and designers, the stage manager should have answers to the show-specific questions generated during analysis of the script and can now generate and distribute paperwork to the team. First up is the prop list. Your prop list should contain both the relevant information from the script and the details about this individual production, so it is worth waiting until you can satisfy both of these objectives before sending it out.

KEY USERS

- Director and SM team
- Scenic designer and assistants
- Props master
- Costume designer or assistant if there are relevant items

What it contains

- Page number
- Item
- Details about who uses it and what happens to it

Why do it?

- To provide a complete listing of the furniture and actor-handled items in the show
- To identify overlap items (such as umbrellas) so they can be claimed by the correct department
- To facilitate budgeting in the props department by noting consumables or specialty items
- To set up a method for updating these details throughout the rehearsal process

Before setting out to create your prop list, the stage manager should find out if the theatre has a preferred format for the document. In a department or company with multiple productions at a time, the props personnel may find it simpler to have all lists conform to a single setup, so that their work can focus on seeing the details and not learning how to navigate the page. If this is the case, you are wise to use the provided format. If none is provided for you, or if that sort of consistency is not relevant, then the organization of the information is up to you.

In either case, this is again a detail document. The stage manager's goal is to provide a comprehensive accounting of the items needed for the show. The list will be updated regularly throughout the process, so that it always contains the most up-to-date information.

The simple format shown in Figure 3.11 provides a method for recording all of the needs of the production. It contains a few theatre-specific columns, but ones that are worth considering as good general additions. Column three provides a place for a quick reference as to whether

RENT

Preliminary Prop List

Page	Prop	C	Character	Notes	R	A
FURNITURE/SCENIC ITEMS						
	(2) large tables			3'-6" x 8', danceable Also used as hospital beds		
	1 small table			For Benny & Mr. Grey in restaurant		
	2 square tables			4'x4', capable of seating 4 people, used in restaurant		
	(23) chairs			Some are restaurant only, TBD		
	Pay phone			On casters if possible		
	Burn Barrel					
1	Electric guitar		Roger	Fender- practical		
1	Guitar amp		Roger	practical		
1	16mm camera		Mark			
1	Tripod		Mark			
1	Old Rock & Roll posters	*	Roger	Roger's picture- gigs at CBGB's & the Pyramid Club, torn down		
2	Telephone		Mark	Phone & answering machine		
2	Phone receivers		Various	For "parents" who call, number TBD		
4	Small leather pouch		Mark			
4	(Duplicate) weighted leather pouch		Collins			
4	(2) clubs		Thugs			
4	Cel phone		Benny			
7	Old manuscripts		Mark			
11	10 gallon plastic pickle tub		Angel	Played like a drum		
11	Drumsticks		Angel			
13	Prescription bottle of AZT	*	Roger	Depending on staging, may need consumable pills inside		

NOTE: "C" denotes consumable- props with asterisk will need replenishing

Figure 3.11 The preliminary props list for *Rent*.

or not a prop is consumable. This can aid a props department in accurately budgeting for the item, and the SM team in making sure there are adequate quantities available.

> A **consumable** prop is one that will be used up during a single performance. This may refer to food or drink eaten each night, but can also identify a piece of paper that is ripped up, a candle that is lit on stage and may not survive the entire run, or anything else that would need to be restocked.

The theatre for which this prop list was developed also likes to be able to track progress on the document. The R and A columns provide check boxes to mark when a suitable rehearsal item is provided, as well as when the actual show prop is acquired.

For a show with multiple locations, it may be useful to provide some further subdivision on the prop list. While a show like *Cat on a Hot Tin Roof* takes place in a single locale, *Twelfth Night* features several settings. Rather than including the setting to which each prop belongs in the notes column, a location subheading provides that information for a set of props, allowing the notes column to contain other information.

It is also important to note that the choice to work in this level of scene-related specificity necessitates being consistent. Although II-2 has no prop requirements initially, in this instance it is clearer to list the scene with no props than to omit it and leave the props personnel wondering if the scene is prop-free or was inadvertently omitted. Similarly, because the furniture pieces were repeated for each location—but not identically—it was worth noting that. The use of italics draws attention to the fact that these are repeat items and not additional requirements.

WORKING WITH THE PROP LIST

The samples noted here are preliminary versions of a prop list, prepared before rehearsals begin. Given the range of personnel who will need a copy, neutral choices in font and layout are made to maximize readability on any computer. But because this is an interactive document, it is not shared in PDF form. Doing so would preserve the formatting details, as this technique did for the character/scene breakdown, but it would make it more difficult for others to update it.

Now that technology has made this possible, many theatres have transitioned from emailing the prop list back and forth to creating it in a shared software system like Google Docs. As long as everyone who needs to use the list has access, then all edits can be done to a single version of the document in the same place. This has greatly reduced the chances of two people independently updating separate copies of the list at the same time and creating more than one official version. Another option is to keep editable versions of the prop list in a cloud-based storage area like Dropbox. This provides the same multiple-user access, but without the formatting limitations found in the Google package.

Twelfth Night
Preliminary Prop List

Page	Prop	C	Character	Notes	R	A
I-1 Orsino's Palace						
3	(2) lounge chairs and side table		furniture			
3	Musical instruments		TBD	Depends on casting		
4	Letter		Valentine	From Olivia to Orsino		
I-2 Illyrian Coast						
5	Coins (gold)		Viola	Gives to Captain		
I-3 Inside Olivia's house						
8	Table		furniture	To set down food and wine		
8	One (1) wooden chair with no arms		furniture			
8	Food	?	Toby, Andrew	TBD- may not be eaten		
8	Wine	*	Toby, Andrew			
8	Cups or Mugs		Toby, Andrew			
I-4 Orsino's Palace						
	Repeat lounge chairs & table					
I-5 Inside Olivia's house						
14	(2) high-backed chairs with arms		furniture			
14	shrine		furniture	To Olivia's deceased brother		
14	Photo		dressing	On shrine- Olivia's brother		
14	Candles	*	dressing	On shrine- lit		
14	Flowers		dressing	On shrine		
24	Ring		Olivia	Given to Viola- costumes?		
II-1 A Lodging in Illyria						
24	Bench		furniture			
24	Coat Rack		furniture			
II-2 A Street Near Olivia's House						
II-3 Inside Olivia's House						
	Repeat table, wine and cups (no chair)					
27	Food	*	TBD	Set on table with wine		
28	Sixpence		Toby	Given to Clown		
II-4 Orsino's palace						
	Repeat lounge chairs & table					
34	Towel		Orsino	Comes out of pool		

NOTE: "C" denotes consumable- props with asterisk will need replenishing

Figure 3.12 The preliminary props list for *Twelfth Night*.

AUDITIONS

Auditions for a show are a period of both information distribution and discovery for the stage manager. You will be relaying key production details to your potential cast and collecting information both formally and informally about them. Often this is the stage manager's first simultaneous test of verbal and written communication skills on a production. Many of the key traits of a successful stage manager will be needed—organization, flexibility, clarity, and quick thinking.

The stage manager's concerns regarding auditions can be broken down into three major groups: the space, the show, and the schedule. The checklist in Figure 3.13 provides a starting point for planning successful auditions. While not every question will apply to every show, it is a good reference.

It is important to note that some of the checklist questions require action on your part, and others may require answers from or assistance from other theatre personnel. Of course, you will need the director to provide you with information about the sides or to answer questions related to the setup of the room and the ideal flow of the day. But other questions, particularly space-related ones, are equally important to be asked in advance. Never wait until the day of auditions to go exploring. It is always better to know in advance that signs can be affixed to the wall only with a specific kind of tape or that it requires calling a security guard to open rooms.

> **Sides:** Excerpts of the script chosen by the director for the actors to read at auditions. Typically one to two pages in length, the SM will label the sides with the appropriate character names and make enough copies so that one group of actors can read them in the audition room for the director and other groups can practice the material outside.

As you collect and create information to be posted at the audition site, be sure that you are communicating approved details. There might be a reason your director prefers your calendar to list a more general time for rehearsals rather than specific adjustments for individual days; there could be someone pre-cast whose name has not been released because the contract is not yet finalized; there might be an important question to be posed to actors that will help solidify a pending costume question.

When working on an Equity show, the stage manager will encounter additional rules regarding principal and chorus auditions, handling of nonunion actors, and specific requirements for the spaces themselves and the way notices are posted. Guidelines can be found in the agreements governing each category of AEA contracts.

AUDITION FORM

The stage manager's primary tool for capturing information about the potential cast is the audition form. Like the prop list, many theatres have specific documents they prefer to use. In an academic setting, this is often standardized paperwork that may include releases you are required by the university to collect. In a professional setting, actors represented by agents who schedule auditions for them may not fill out a form at all but simply provide a resume and headshot.

AUDITIONS CHECKLIST

THE SPACE

☐	What is the procedure for locking/unlocking the audition space? Will you have keys?
☐	Are there special considerations for accessing the room in the evening or on weekends?
☐	Does the space have adequate signage to help actors find the room?
☐	Can you post additional signs?
☐	Is there an area which can serve as a check-in spot?
☐	Is there an area for actors to wait? To warm up?
☐	Is the lighting sufficient in the rooms?
☐	Is the temperature of the rooms comfortable? Adjustable?
☐	What is the floor surface of the audition room? Is this acceptable for what you need to accomplish?
☐	Does the room have mirrors?
☐	Does the room have a piano or a CD player?
☐	Are there sufficient tables and chairs?
☐	Does the director have preferences about how the room is set up?
☐	Can you leave the rooms set up from one day to the next?
☐	Are basic office supplies available to you (pencils, staplers, tape, etc)? A copier if we run low on forms?
☐	Will you have access to any basic first aid supplies in case of injury?

THE SHOW

☐	Does the theatre have a standard audition form?
☐	Are there show-specific questions to be added?
☐	Does your theatre require any additional paperwork?
☐	Do you have a basic summary of the show and available roles? If not, is this something you should create?
☐	Do you have your basic overview calendar?
☐	Do you have information about the scenes/songs actors have been asked to prepare?
☐	Will there be additional sides for callbacks?
☐	Is there a camera available for actors who may not bring headshots?
☐	What are the components of this audition process? In what order will they happen?
☐	Will you be asked to read with the actors?
☐	Who will be in the room with the director?
☐	Does the theatre or director have policies regarding youth auditions?

THE SCHEDULE

☐	What is the overall time for the auditions?
☐	How long will individual slots be?
☐	Will actors sign up in advance or upon arrival?
☐	Does the director have preferences for building breaks into the process?
☐	If the audition spans meal time, are there considerations for scheduling around and/or acquiring food?
☐	What are the date, time and location of the callbacks?
☐	When will casting decisions be made?
☐	How will actors be notified?

Figure 3.13 A basic checklist for any set of auditions.

If you are creating the audition form, focus on collecting several necessary types of information: basic contact and descriptive information about the actor, answers to show-specific questions, and details about schedule and potential conflicts. Figures 3.14 A and B demonstrate a way to capture the necessary facts in a two-sided form. The stage manager may not have much time to review the forms during the audition day, but, if possible, you should get them back from the director prior to callbacks. That way you can determine if any of the information provided was unclear—or omitted—and get a second chance to obtain those details before casting begins and missing information is problematic.

The formatting needs of the audition form are simple: present the information requests clearly and provide sufficient room for the replies. Actors should know what is being asked, and the director should easily find the answers. The concept of white space is perhaps the most important formatting principle in this situation. Take a second look at the section of the sample form where show-specific details for *Urinetown* are sought. The two questions to be answered may be in bold, but the space around the questions contributes to the legibility as well. Reducing the white space might make room for the résumé information at the bottom of the front side, leaving a larger area on the back for the director's comment box. That could seem like a useful choice. But consider the importance of those show-specific questions. One is related to the start date of rehearsals and the other to a remount of the show. The answers to both of these questions will impact many more people than just you and the director, and obtaining clear and accurate information up front is a priority.

WHAT THE STAGE MANAGER CAN LEARN

Over the course of the auditions, the stage manager will learn a great deal. Of course, you will meet your potential cast, but you will discover not just who they might be but also how they work. Actors who are early, prepared, and specific with their questions will strike a contrast to those who arrive late, forget their sides or music, or ask the same question multiple times. This does not tell you anything about the quality of their performance but may be an indicator of necessary strategies for assisting those actors with memorizing lines or remembering rehearsal call times.

The stage manager can also learn about the director. If you have not worked with him or her before, this is perhaps even more valuable information than you acquire about the actors. Does the director hold to the set schedule? What is the response to a gentle reminder that the day is running behind? Did you receive very little information up front and are now asked to prepare multiple sides on the spot? What happens if you are running ahead?

ANOTHER FIRST IMPRESSION

The stage manager should recognize that auditions also provide the actors and director with their first opportunity to see you in action. Your ability to organize the day will be seen as an indicator of how rehearsals will go. And while it is important to be friendly and helpful, it is equally important to be neutral and professional. Can you answer questions while still maintaining confidentiality about details not yet released? Can you respond effectively to schedule changes, whether prompted by whimsy or genuine necessity? Can you troubleshoot unanticipated problems? Can you display empathy for a disappointed performer without taking sides?

Particularly as a new stage manager, it can be easy to get pulled into the chaos of a large cattle call or to let your excitement about being "in the know" affect your comments. Your efforts to set the right tone now will pay off throughout the production.

AUDITION INFORMATION FORM

NAME	
Local Address	
Phone	Email

Affiliation	UW-L Student		Viterbo Student	Faculty/Staff	Other
Academic Status (circle one) 1st Year		2nd Year	3rd Year	4th Year	Grad Student
Major			Minor		
Height		Weight		Hair Color	

Are you willing to alter your physical appearance (i.e. color or cut your hair) for a specific role?
Yes _____ No _____. If "no", please explain.

Do you sing? _____Part? (Soprano, Alto, Tenor, Bass) _____

Dance Experience _____

Do you play an instrument? _____What instrument(s)? _____

IMPORTANT DETAILS ABOUT URINETOWN

The show will rehearse during the summer from May 31-June 29. Rehearsals are generally Monday through Friday in the evening. Costume fittings and similar activities will be scheduled during the day. The show will perform June 30 – July 10.

Please answer the following questions:

1. **Would you be available for early rehearsals during the week of May 23?** YES NO

    If yes, please indicate whether afternoon or evening would work best for you _____

2. **Would you be available for a fall remount of this show September 8-11?** YES NO

    The remount is not certain at this time, but would be on those days if it happens

Do you currently have a full or part-time job? _____(including campus employment)
   o If "yes" please indicate your likely summer work schedule on the back of this sheet

Are you willing/able to re-arrange your schedule to accommodate rehearsal? _____
   o If "no" please explain:

Please fill out the information on the back side too! Thanks!

Please **attach resume** or provide a brief history of previous roles.

ROLE   PLAY   THEATRE

SUMMER SCHEDULE INFORMATION
Please mark out any class or work commitments that you will have.

	Monday	Tuesday	Wednesday	Thursday	Friday	Saturday	Sunday
8am							
9am							
10am							
11am							
12noon							
1pm							
2pm							
3pm							
4pm							
5pm							
6pm							
7pm							
8pm							
9pm							

Please list **ANY** potential conflicts with summer/fall evening rehearsals (job, weddings, etc.) This does not disqualify you automatically from casting! But it is much easier to work around a conflict that we know about in advance.

_____

_____

_____

DIRECTOR'S NOTES

Callback for: Cast as:

Figures 3.14A and B A sample audition form.

THE CONTACT SHEET

At the conclusion of auditions, the stage manager will be ready to create the final set of paper-work during this pre-production time: the contact sheets. You will develop separate lists for the cast and production team, ensuring easy communication with these personnel throughout the rest of the show.

Next to the calendar, the contact sheet is perhaps the most distributed piece of paperwork. Certainly everyone whose name appears on it will need a copy. But distribution is likely to extend beyond the immediate participants. The theatre business office may need the information for handling contract and payroll details, the costume shop may want a copy for contacting an actor to cancel a fitting outside of rehearsal time, or the publicity office may wish to phone or email participants to request participation in interviews or other PR events. Most of the time such requests and scheduling will pass through stage management, but occasionally there is a reason for independent communication.

When collecting information for the contact sheet, consider what will be most needed. Mailing addresses, for example, might be useful at the conclusion of a show, but you are unlikely to contact people by mail during rehearsals. An exception to this may be actors staying in company-provided housing at a professional theatre. But although addresses may be useful in this case, it would be temporary local information rather than permanent details. If the stage manager creates the contact sheet using spreadsheet software, information might be recorded now but then hidden when printed and distributed if not currently relevant.

Privacy will also be a factor in the inclusion of information. In an academic setting, a faculty director may wish to have only an office phone number in print. The director can always decide to share a home number or cell-phone number with specific individuals. Actors who have a need to maintain privacy for personal reasons might provide the stage manager with a phone number but request that the stage manager list his or her own number opposite that actor's name on a contact sheet. Attempts to reach the actor could still be successful, with the stage manager passing along messages or providing that number on a case-by-case basis, depending on the actor's situation. Use your discretion and respect the needs of your company members.

TO POST OR NOT TO POST?

For reasons of privacy discussed here, it is rarely advisable to post a contact sheet with personal information online or on callboards in the theatre. Once this information is public, it is impossible to control who has access to the numbers or to keep someone from using them inappropriately. Consider distributing only in hard copy or via email, or posting such documents to a show website only when password-protected access is possible. This can lessen the chance for information to be misused.

FORMATTING THE CONTACT SHEET

As was true for the prop list, a simple chart or table format serves the contact sheet best. This keeps information organized and gives you control over individual cells. It is this author's preference to list personnel in alphabetical order by last name, thereby removing any implied hierarchy. (Why is the assistant lighting designer listed above the costume designer? Why is Ensemble Member C listed before Ensemble Member B?) I also prefer to order the columns so that name, role, phone number, and email address appear in that order.

Twelfth Night	CAST CONTACT SHEET		
	Version 3 11/2/10		
	*Unless Noted, Area Code 608		
Suzanne Clum	Musician	333-555-1212	actor1@provider.net
Brian Coffin	Lord 1, Sailor 2, Officer 3	555-1212	actor2@provider.net
Justin Cooke	Orsino		
Allyssa Dunn	Olivia		
Kevin Fanshaw	Antonio, Feste understudy		
Claire Ganshert	Viola		
Jacob Gustine	Sir Toby Belch		
Donald Hart	Lord 2, Officer 4		
Alden Hedges	Feste		
Austin Hernandez	Valentine, Sailor 3, Officer 1		
Andrew Kelly	Malvolio		
Shelby Krarup	Musician		
Matthew Matuseski	Sebastian		
Tim McCarren	Sir Andrew Aguecheek		
Donnie Mezera	Fabian		
Amy Nelson	Maria		
Luke Prescott	Curio, Sailor 1, Officer 2		
Lindsay Van Norman	Olivia Attendant 2		
Jake Voss	Sea Captain, Priest, Antonio understudy		
Emily Ware	Olivia Attendant 1		
Walter Elder	Director		
Laurie Kincman	Stage Manager		
Melissa Heller	Assistant Stage Manager		
Quinn Masterson	Assistant Stage Manager		
COSTUME SHOP			
BOX OFFICE			

Electronic callboard: http://www.uwlax.edu/theatrecallboard/twelfth_night.htm

Figure 3.15 A sample actor contact sheet. Note that phone numbers and email addresses have been removed for privacy reasons.

The sample contact sheet provides a basic layout and also identifies another specific format-ting preference of this author. Although three of the four columns are left-justified, the phone number column is right-justified. Observing the two sample phone numbers demonstrates why. If only a few members of a company have an out-of-town area code, this formatting allows that area code to be slightly more prominent in this setup. This can be especially helpful if the stage manager's office phone requires dialing a variety of access numbers. (My current office phone requires one method for internal calls, a second for off-campus and local cellular calls, and a third for long-distance numbers.) As a stage manager, if it is your preference to always include the area code, or if your phone is less convoluted than mine, this detail will be less essential for you.

Another important consideration is the need to include additional numbers beyond the cast or staff. The sample is a contact sheet distributed to the cast. For their convenience, the cos-tume shop and box office phone numbers have been included at the bottom along with contact information for the director and SM team. On a production contact sheet, the stage manager might include shop numbers, fax numbers, or even the theatre's mailing address if that will be necessary for nonresident staff arranging for equipment to be mailed or shipped.

Because this theatre maintains an online callboard, the web address is also included at the bottom. And as with all other paperwork that may need to be updated during rehearsals or performances, a version number and date can be found.

THINKING ABOUT THE SM TEAM

As an exercise in multitasking, try the following task:

1. Pull out your favorite *Where's Waldo?* cartoon and find all the Waldo images in five minutes.

2. While doing that, turn on the *Rent* soundtrack and accurately sing along to "La Vie Boehme."

3. And because you are the ambitious sort, do this in a restaurant, and also count how many times the server in your area refills someone's glass of water.

   Sounds crazy, right?

Well, it's not much crazier than trying to write down blocking, follow along with the script, keep an eye on where the props are going, and help the actress in the next scene lace up her corset all at once. Both sets of tasks are much easier when undertaken by a team.

If you are lucky enough to be working with one or more assistant stage managers, it will be crucial to the show's success to use your ASMs wisely and empower them to help document everything that is going on. As you reach the end of your prep period, you will know which aspects of your production might be the trickiest or the most complex. Use that as a guideline to develop a "divide and conquer" approach for the SM team so that all the necessary tasks get done each day, and no one goes too crazy in the process. Of course, the stage manager needs to keep on top of everything and to check in with all production areas. Delegating responsibility is not the same as abdicating it.

By sharing focus on the show, each member of the team can accept responsibility for tracking one set of details and following up on questions in that area. The team as a whole can tackle large projects and the daily setup, and meet regularly outside of rehearsals to share information. By the time you reach the theatre, everyone needs to be an expert in all parts of the show. But during rehearsals, it is very difficult for one person to learn it all at the same time. And if you ever need to work simultaneously in more than one room, each member of the SM team should be knowledgeable enough to be effective.

Particularly in academic theatres, it can be easy to see the ASM as someone with little experience who can be relegated to sweeping the floor and setting out props. That is a big mistake. The assistant stage manager is your ally in this process. Before rehearsals begin, the SM should get the entire team together to talk about the production and to divide responsibilities. It often makes sense to ask one ASM to focus on prop details and another to concentrate on costumes. They can be on the lookout for rehearsal report notes specific to that area and take the lead in creating paperwork for those technicians. Once you move into the theatre, the ASMs will assume responsibility for running the deck and overseeing the crew. Getting them solidly involved in the show from the beginning ensures they will be invested in the production.

AEA contracts specify the amount of prep time given to the assistant stage manager. It is often not a full week like the SM, but even a few days provides the opportunity to learn one another's working styles, get up to date on the production details, and create a plan for the show.

NEXT STEPS

In addition to the meetings and documents featured in this chapter, the stage management team will typically undertake several other tasks during this phase of the process. These include taping out the groundplan on the rehearsal room floor, setting up the room itself to best facilitate the work, collecting rehearsal props and costume pieces, and preparing the prompt book. (These items are discussed in detail in the next chapters.)

At the conclusion of the stage manager's pre-production time, he or she should be prepared to enter rehearsals and begin capturing and sharing the details of the show.

CHAPTER 4

The Prompt Book

Maintaining the script and all documentation of your production in a single location is not just a good idea. It is a primary responsibility of the stage manager, and one specifically articulated by Actors' Equity Association. The following language is excerpted from the CORST Agreement, but nearly every rule book contains a similar paragraph within the section outlining the duties of the stage manager:

> *Assemble and maintain the Prompt Book, which is defined as the accurate playing text and stage business, together with such cue sheets, plots, daily records, etc., as are necessary for the actual technical and artistic operation of the production.*[1]

The prompt book contains the official production script along with charts and lists both created by and distributed to the stage manager—everything necessary to run the show. In a professional setting, the book is the property of the theatre after the production closes, either as an archival reference for other shows or as the primary resource for future productions of the play done at this theatre or by this director.

ORGANIZING THE PROMPT BOOK

In order to keep all of this paperwork accessible, the book benefits from good organization. Investing in a sturdy binder and several sets of dividers allows you to quickly flip to a piece of information (Figure 4.1). Another rationale for detailed subdivisions is to be sure the show could happen without you. Whether the absence is due to vacation, illness, or transfer, a second stage manager should be able to pick up your prompt book and find everything necessary to understand the production. Omitting paperwork because you have a copy on your laptop or clumping scenery, props, and costumes paperwork together in a single "production" section of the binder can make extra work for someone else.

Figure 4.1 Labels and scene tabs.

When organizing your prompt book, think about how often you might need access to the information while in the rehearsal hall. You will frequently be asked questions about the upcoming schedule, or need to phone an actor who is running late. Keep those sections near the front of the book. Archival copies of rehearsal reports or meeting minutes can be filed in the back.

When I create a prompt book, I think about the information in three groups: quick-access details including the script, production information for each department, and archival documents. Within those three groups I separate individual categories.

PROMPT BOOK TABS

My books include the following sections in the order shown here. If a production does not include a particular component, I don't print a tab for it for that show.

Contact Sheets

Cast Information

Schedules

Character/Scene Breakdown

Blocking and Calling Keys

Script

Run Sheet

Show Paperwork (Preset List, Shift Plot, Costume Plot)

Scenery

Props

Costumes

Lights

Sound

Video/Projections

Publicity

Dramaturgy

ASM Information

Crew Information

Meeting Agendas & Minutes

Rehearsal Reports

Performance Reports

Fittings

Dialect Sessions

Blank Forms

AN ARCHIVE, BUT NOT A HISTORY

Keeping on top of the details of your show will mean updating many pieces of paperwork over the life of the production. There is no need to keep every version of every document in your binder. During the rehearsal period, I typically keep the current and immediately previous versions accessible in hard copy. That allows me to quickly look back should there be a problem with an update or if the team suddenly has to revert to the "old" way of doing something. Once performances begin, the binder needs only the most up-to-date documents. If your theatre policy or personal preference is to hold on to more than that, I recommend retaining the other versions in a folder on your computer.

WORKING WITH MULTIPLE BOOKS

A complex show will require a lot of documentation, and a four-hour play can have a very long script. I have seen many new stage managers lugging a five-inch binder in and out of the rehearsal hall—some sort of physical manifestation of all the work they have to do! But unless you are desperate to build an upper-arm workout into your day, there is no need for this. When setting up the prompt book, the stage manager can separate some information into its own binder. Often it makes sense to keep the script on its own—along with copies of those fast-access items from the front of the single-book setup. (When I work in two books, I prefer to have those documents in both locations, so that the paperwork book is complete on its own but I can still access phone numbers or breakdowns quickly.) For a musical, you will have a secondary script that can be several hundred pages by itself—the score. In most instances, the score can also live in a separate binder.

PREPARING THE PROMPT SCRIPT

The small, bound edition of the script distributed to the actors is very impractical for the stage manager. The text is tiny, and room for notes is extremely limited. During pre-production week the stage manager creates a more useful version, set up to capture the blocking and cueing information to come.

Unfortunately there is no magic trick to transforming the printed script into one that works for you. You will need some dedicated time at the photocopier. The process includes several steps: enlarging the script, setting the margins, and copying a sheet onto the back side for recording blocking.

1. Identify the ideal enlargement ratio by testing a full page of text. Acting editions are typically printed on a 5" × 7" page. An enlargement around 115 percent generally works well.

2. Position the enlarged text so that you have adequate margins on all four sides. This means centering the script between the top and bottom of the page and shifting it so there is approximately a one-half-inch margin on the side in which you will punch holes. This results in an enlarged margin on the opposite side that you can use for cues.

3. Copy the script. Make each page identical by using the automatic settings on the copier or by creating a mat to place on the glass into which you can lay each page from the original.

4. Select a backing sheet that will allow you to notate blocking and choreography. Include a small groundplan on this page.

5. Copy the backing sheet on the reverse side of each enlarged script page, making a few extras for the end of acts.

Although it might seem counterintuitive at first, the most effective setup for the prompt script is to place the backing page in relation to your dominant hand. This means a right-handed stage manager would place the script page on the left and the backing page on the right. The large cue margin falls on the outer left side. Such a setup allows the stage manager to quickly record blocking during rehearsals without having to reach across the binder rings while writing. The SM can use his or her left index finger to follow along with the dialogue. Most cue placement work will occur outside of rehearsal time when, the stage manager can easily shift the book over to avoid leaning on the rings. And reading cues on the left is just as easy as reading them on the right. A left-handed stage manager would select the opposite setup for the same reasons. These layouts are demonstrated in Figures 4.2 and 4.3.

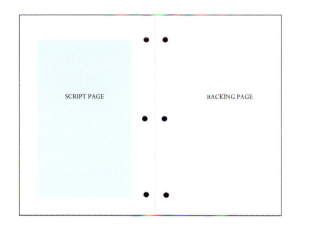

Figure 4.2 The script setup for a right-handed stage manager.

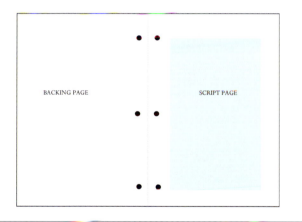

Figure 4.3 The script setup for a left-handed stage manager.

THE BACKING PAGE

Using a backing page allows the stage manager to capture blocking details more efficiently than simply leaving the back side of the script page blank. It requires some additional work and another trip through the photocopier but is well worth the effort.

The two components of a backing page are numbered lines for recording movement and a small groundplan for noting the placement of scenic elements or large ensemble compositions. The backing sheet is a full-size document, taking up the entire reverse side of the script page. Figure 4.4 is the backing sheet I use when working on a play.

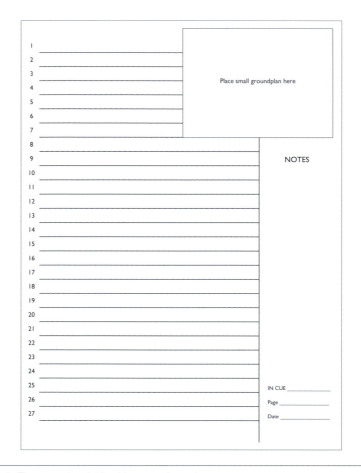

Figure 4.4 The prompt script backing page for a play.

Having lines running the entire height of the page allows the stage manager to record the blocking immediately across from the line of text on which it occurs. The numbers enable you to specifically indentify the spot where the action takes place by writing that number before, after, or directly above the appropriate word. Without lines, the default tendency is to start writing at the top of the page, eliminating this visual link between words and actions.

The stage manager could certainly number entries on the blank page and try to achieve a similar effect. But if the director adds blocking earlier on the page during a subsequent rehearsal, do you renumber? And if you have not left yourself adequate room for the new information, how do you squeeze it in? The backing sheet simplifies the process. Figures 4.5 and 4.6 show the enlarged script and its backing page in action.

The backing sheet is also set up with a small groundplan in the upper-right corner. A director and scenic designer might agree to allow furniture placement to develop organically during rehearsal, within the confines of a specific scene's location on the stage. Such an arrangement would preclude having a complete layout before rehearsals begin. The mini-groundplan provides the stage manager with a quick and visually effective place to record the location of tables, chairs, and other pieces. The SM can glance up at the stage during rehearsal and instantly know if everything is in the correct location without having to scan through the blocking notes for that information.

For plays with multiple locations that are defined in advance, the stage manager can customize the backing pages for individual scenes with the correct plan—or opt to use a blank plan and quickly sketch the items on stage in that scene. When creating your prompt script, choose the option that makes best use of your time and will be the most user-friendly in rehearsal.

The small groundplan is similarly useful for recording the positions of many cast members at once. Just as it was more efficient to draw the placement of a chair rather than to describe it, it is quicker to record the location of many actors at once by placing their initials on a groundplan. The SM can answer blocking questions based on the picture just as effectively—and usually more quickly—than scanning for the uncertain actor's initials.

Because the groundplan is small in size, it is helpful to have one as free of extra markings as possible. Ask the scenic designer or technical director for a blank or unlabeled version that you can reduce for the backing page, or temporarily delete those items if you have the appropriate drafting software and can open an electronic version. As a last resort, you can cover over unneeded information with a correction pen.

A TRICK FOR THE SPLIT PAGE

When acting editions are put together, little thought is given to pagination helpful to a stage manager. If one scene ends with sufficient room left on the page, the next scene often starts a few lines below. This scene might not be in the same location, however.

Once you have created the perfect mini-groundplan for your backing page, make a stack of additional copies the same size. This allows you to add a second, or even a third, plan onto any page where it is needed. My preferred method of attaching the extra drawings is with a stick of removable glue, essentially turning the plan into a Post-it. The glue will hold the drawing firmly in place but without making the page soggy—something you might not realize until you need to write cues on the script side of that page and have a bit of a mess on your hands.

These extra plans are also useful when there is more than one large blocking configuration on a page, and, although the revised groundplan will stay in place until removed, you can peel it off with no damage to the script if the blocking should change.

FABIAN   Here comes my noble gull-catcher.   178
TOBY   ²Wilt thou set thy foot o' my neck?
ANDREW   Or o' mine either?   *180*
TOBY   Shall I play my freedom at tray-trip and become   181
    thy bondslave?
ANDREW   I' faith, or I either?
TOBY   Why, thou hast put him in such a dream that,
    when the image of it leaves him,⁸he must run mad.
MARIA   ⁹Nay, but say true, does it work upon him?
TOBY   Like aqua vitae with a midwife. ₁₀   187
MARIA   If you will, then, see the fruits of the sport, ¹¹mark
    his first approach before my lady. He will come to her
    in yellow stockings, and 'tis a color she abhors, and   *190*
    cross-gartered, a fashion she detests; and he will smile
    upon her, which will now be so unsuitable to her dis-
    position, being addicted to a melancholy as she is, that
    it cannot but turn him into a notable contempt.¹⁴If you
    will see it, follow me.¹⁶
TOBY   To the gates of Tartar, thou most excellent devil   196
    of wit. ₁₇
ANDREW ¹⁷I'll make one too.¹⁸   *Exeunt.*

          20, 21   *

ᴎ III.1 *Enter Viola and Clown [with a tabor].*

VIOLA   Save thee, friend, and thy music.²³Dost thou live   1
    by thy tabor?   2
CLOWN   No, sir, I live by the church.
VIOLA   Art thou a churchman?
CLOWN   No such matter, sir. I do live by the church; for
    I do live at my house, and my house doth stand by the
    church.

---

178 *gull-catcher* fool-catcher 181 *play* gamble; *tray-trip* a game of dice
187 *aqua vitae* any distilled liquor 196 *Tartar* Tartarus, the section of hell
reserved for the most evil
    III.1 Before the house of Olivia 1 *Save thee* God save thee 1–2 *live by*
make a living with 2 *tabor* drum

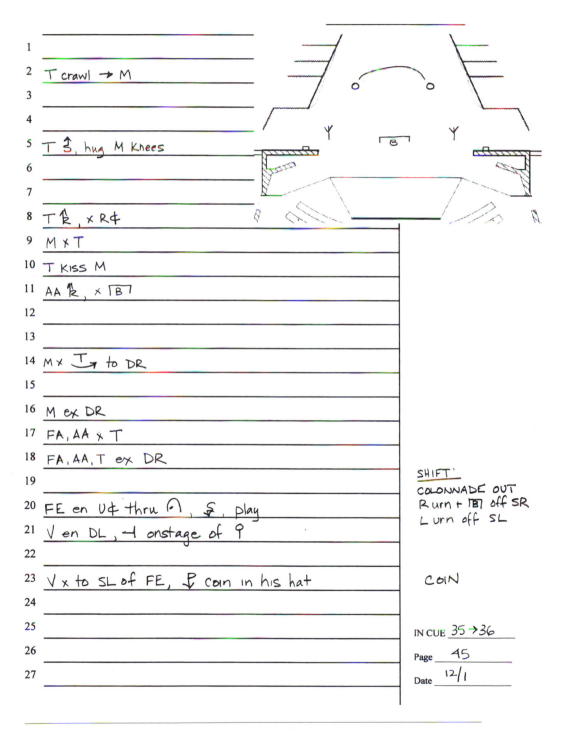

1
2 T crawl → M
3
4
5 T ↻, hug M knees
6
7
8 T ↻, x R↔
9 M x T
10 T kiss M
11 AA ↻, x ⌐B⌐
12
13
14 M x T→ to DR
15
16 M ex DR
17 FA, AA x T
18 FA, AA, T ex DR
19
20 FE en U↔ thru ⌐, ♪, play
21 V en DL, ⊣ onstage of ♀
22
23 V x to SL of FE, ↓ coin in his hat
24
25
26
27

SHIFT:
COLONNADE OUT
R urn + ⌐B⌐ off SR
L urn off SL

COIN

IN CUE 35 → 36
Page ____ 45
Date ____ 12/1

Figures 4.5 and 4.6 The prompt script setup for blocking.

THE SCRIPT FOR THE MUSICAL

When working on a musical, the SM will have two script choices: the libretto and the score. In most instances, the libretto is a good choice and can be formatted exactly like the play script. The libretto offers the stage manager a streamlined version of the show. It contains all dialogue and lyrics, along with headings to note where each piece of music begins.

The score for a book musical, as seen in Figure 4.7, typically contains only the lines that lead into a song or that are spoken during a vamp. This makes it an incomplete document. The SM would not be able to place blocking in relation to specific dialogue, and would have a very difficult time prompting once the actors are no longer carrying scripts.

Figure 4.7 A page of the score for "Look at the Sky" from the musical *Urinetown*. Used with permission of the authors.

If you are hired for a production of *Les Miserables* or *The Who's Tommy*, however, the libretto will fall short. The sung-through musical has no unaccompanied dialogue, and nearly every action will happen in conjunction with music. In order to have sufficient information on the page, you will find the score a better choice this time. Because a score page is inherently more visually complex than a script, the SM should keep it at full size. (In many instances, you will actually reduce the score to get it to fit on a standard sheet of 8.5" × 11" paper.) You will also place cues in a different manner, so the large outside margin is not necessary.

The musical stage manager will be noting both blocking and choreography, necessitating a backing sheet with a different format Figure 4.8 is my current choice when working on a musical. Most productions have a dance captain responsible for writing out individual steps and counts. The SM's choreography notes focus on formations and movement patterns, most effectively captured in visual form. I refer to these notes as "football diagrams" due to their

Figure 4.8 The backing page for a musical.

resemblance to the on-screen sketches done by commentators as they analyze plays for the viewers with a set of *X*s, *O*s, and arrows.

By reducing the width of the lines and adding a series of boxes, the backing sheet can capture this new information. A series of groundplans is not typically the best idea, because some of the configurations you are noting may not take up the full stage. A blank box gives you the flexibility to have a wide or narrow focus.

If you are placing the backing page opposite the score, you might want to reduce the number of lines and increase the space between them to better correspond to the number of systems on the page. Because the score provides both vocal and instrumental detail, an individual page makes less progress through the show. It is not uncommon for a single page of typed lyrics in the libretto to correspond to four or five pages in the score, if not more.

THE HYBRID SCRIPT

Unfortunately, the choice between libretto and score is not always so simple. Consider the song that contains several verses of lyrics and a dance break (one or more bars of instrumental music that is choreographed). The stage manager cannot skip taking dance notes simply because there is no accurate written accounting of that part of the song in the libretto.

The SM could use this as justification to work entirely from the score, but you end up with a much longer prompt script, many more page turns throughout the show, and constant visual complexity. A better option is to create hybrid script pages for these sections. By combining the libretto and score, you can accumulate all the information you need.

A hybrid script can take two forms—writing counts into the libretto to more accurately represent the music, or combining the libretto and score into a single script.

Figure 4.9 is a page from "Look at the Sky" from the musical *Urinetown*. The song has no major dance break, but the words at the end of several lines are held for multiple counts, followed by additional bars of music, before singing resumes. The lighting designer for this production cued the song to follow the musicality, requiring the SM to anticipate the beginning of a new verse in order to call changes correctly.

If the stage manager has a strong musical sense, that anticipation might be instinctual. But keeping in mind the function of the prompt script to be a complete and accurate detailing of the show, instinct may not help another SM. And even an instinctual stage manager might try calling the cue in one or more slightly different locations during tech to achieve the exact effect intended by the designer.

By writing in counts, the SM can record the correct location as precisely as if it fell on an individual syllable of a word. The score provides the stage manager with the information about counts, and it can be easily transferred to the libretto page.

Long instrumental sections of music can get confusing when represented through only a series of numbers. The stage manager can get trapped into staring at those numbers to follow along, easily getting lost if he or she looks up at the stage. The song "Snuff That Girl," also from *Urinetown*, fits our original hybrid criteria by having several verses of lyrics along with a 56-bar dance break. That would require writing a lot of counts!

38   URINETOWN

BOBBY
[1]AS THE WORLD TURNS TO FACE THE SUN AND START
ANOTHER DAY,
IT SUDDENLY
OCCURS TO ME

LX 98   THAT MAYBE WE CAN FIND ANOTHER WAY. 234
LOOK AT THE SKY,
FULL OF HOPE AND PROMISE.
IT'S A SHINING IDEAL.
HOW I REEL

LX 99   WHEN I LOOK AT THE SKY 234   [2]234

PENNY
Now, who's first?

JOSEPHINE STRONG
[5]I am!

BOBBY
Ma![9]

PENNY
LX 100   We'll take your fee, now, Mrs. Strong. The improved fee, that is.

BOBBY
[31]DAILY WE MAKE THEM PAY THEIR NICKELS, DIMES, AND
QUARTERS–

JOSEPHINE
But this is all I have, Ms. Pennywise. [13]

BOBBY
DAILY WE BREAK THEM 'CAUSE WE HAVE TO FOLLOW ORDERS.

LITTLE SALLY
[16]Haven't you enough Mrs. Strong?

BOBBY
[17]AND WE KEEP FILLING MONEYBAGS WITH BROKEN
LIVES AND DREAMS,
BUT WHAT'S IT FOR?
I CAN'T IGNORE

LX 101   THESE BLACK, IMMORAL PROFIT-MAKING SCHEMES. [2]34
[44] LOOK AT THE SKY,
HIGH ABOVE THIS MADNESS.
HERE BELOW, FEEL OUR SHAME.

Figure 4.9 A page of "Look at the Sky" from the musical *Urinetown* in the libretto. Used with permission of the authors.

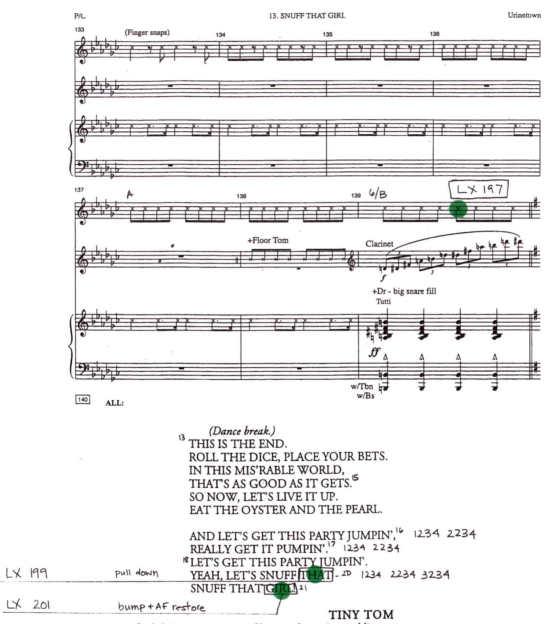

(Dance break.)

[13] THIS IS THE END.
ROLL THE DICE, PLACE YOUR BETS.
IN THIS MIS'RABLE WORLD,
THAT'S AS GOOD AS IT GETS.[15]
SO NOW, LET'S LIVE IT UP.
EAT THE OYSTER AND THE PEARL.

AND LET'S GET THIS PARTY JUMPIN',[16] 1234 2234
REALLY GET IT PUMPIN'.[17] 1234 2234
[18] LET'S GET THIS PARTY JUMPIN'.
YEAH, LET'S SNUFF THAT –[20] 1234 2234 3234
SNUFF THAT GIRL![21]

TINY TOM

Let's bring our message of hate to the entire world!

LX 199   pull down

LX 201   bump + AF restore

PROPS

COSTUMES

OTHER

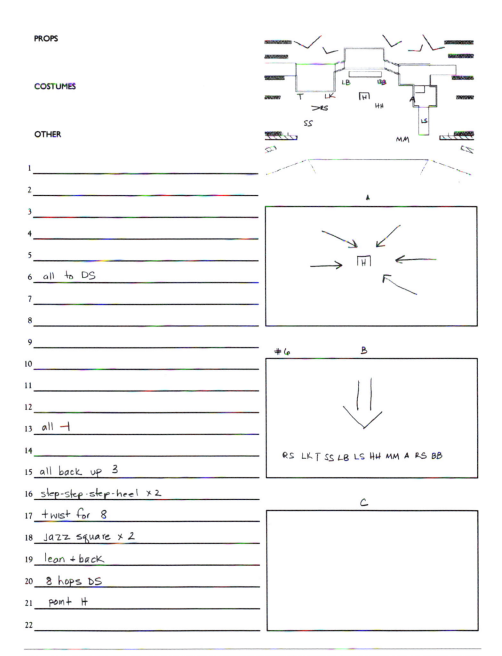

1 _____

2 _____

3 _____

4 _____

5 _____

6 all to DS

7 _____

8 _____

9 _____

10 _____

11 _____

12 _____

13 all —|

14 _____

15 all back up 3

16 step-step·step-heel × 2

17 + twist for 8

18 jazz square × 2

19 lean + back

20 8 hops DS

21 point H

22 _____

Figures 4.10 and 4.11 Hybrid prompt script pages for "Snuff That Girl" from the musical *Urinetown*. Both libretto and score used with permission of the authors.

This time the SM opted to copy and insert full score pages for the dance break, switching back at the end of the choreography as seen in Figures 4.10 and 4.11. A split page provided a transition from the score to the libretto. Some additional quality time at the photocopier presents the final two verses in half of a page as opposed to five. The combined information facilitates accurate placement of cues in relation to both music and lyrics.

When working on a book musical, the stage manager may start with the libretto, automatically recognizing the need for score pages for the overture or entr'acte ahead of time. It is not always clear where other hybrid pages will be needed. Fortunately, you will rehearse every scene in the play more than once before tech! If you find that a libretto page is incomplete, try writing in counts or taking choreography notes on a separate page for the day. You can always take some outside time to make a new page after the fact, transfer the information, and be ready to refine your notes at the next rehearsal.

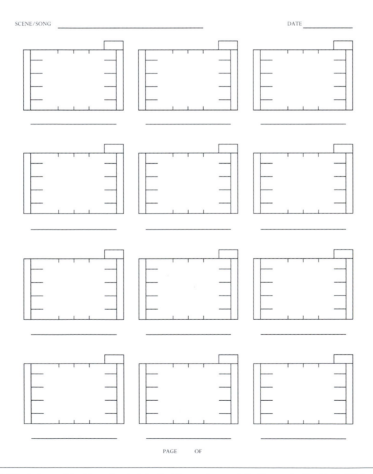
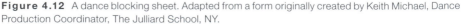

Figure 4.12 A dance blocking sheet. Adapted from a form originally created by Keith Michael, Dance Production Coordinator, The Julliard School, NY.

DANCE, DANCE, DANCE!

When putting together a prompt book, I select a single backing page that will work for the entire script. The only exception I consider is for dance. Because my professional background includes work as a stage manager for modern and ballet companies, I can take dance notation quickly and with good detail—more than can fit into the boxes on my musical backing sheet. Therefore I always have a few dance-only sheets on hand (the same pages I use when working on a dance concert). Sometimes I will insert them into the script as a replacement option, and at other times I will keep these pages in a separate section of my book—much like the fact that I will make prop notes in my script but still keep a separate props list. The sample is included here, as it might prove a useful template or a source for adapting your own backing sheets.

The dance-only sheet in Figure 4.12 is constructed with a series of rectangular boxes. Lines along the right and left sides represent legs and allow notation of the wing through which a performer enters. Marks along the top and bottom indicate center and quarter lines. The small box above the top-right corner, a place for stopwatch times during a dance concert, makes an excellent location for rehearsal numbers from the score. A single line below the box provides a spot for a quick description or nickname for that portion of the choreography.

READY FOR LAUNCH

The prompt book is the most important communication tool of the production. All of the charts the SM creates are designed to provide insight into a specific set of details. Lists of cues from the design team will reflect setup and changes for a single production area. The prompt book, and particularly the script, is the only location where a comprehensive look at the show is available. Taking the time to clearly organize your book, and to create a script in which you can quickly and accurately record blocking and cues, is a key component to your success on the show. Once that book is complete and stocked with the information you have collected and shared during the pre-production phase, you are ready for rehearsals to begin.

CHAPTER 5

Rehearsals

The adventure truly begins at the start of the rehearsal period. Your work organizing initial details and establishing rapport with actors and production team members will now pay off as the show comes to life. The stage manager's overarching goal is to keep everyone on the same page—facilitating discoveries in the rehearsal hall and sharing those discoveries with personnel not in attendance at the time.

REHEARSAL TASKS

- Prepare and distribute daily and weekly schedules.
- Record blocking in the prompt book.
- Help the director and actors understand specifics of the designs.
- Schedule costume fittings, dialect sessions, interviews, and other activities outside the rehearsal hall.
- Generate daily rehearsal reports.
- Update pre-production paperwork.
- Participate in production meetings.
- Begin creating paperwork for the crew.

FIRST REHEARSAL

The first day of work on a production will be part rehearsal and part business meeting. Reading through the play is combined with imparting information about the theatre, this specific rehearsal process, and the union, if you are working on an Equity production.

The day often begins with a meet-and-greet: an opportunity for cast members to get to know one another, members of the production team, and representatives of the theatre in an informal setting. This social time is typically followed by an introduction to the production. The director will share his or her thoughts about the script and vision for the show, and members of the design team present details of their work through renderings, models, or research images.

It is common to have guests at this first rehearsal. Personnel from the marketing department often wish to meet the actors to help personalize publicity requests later in the process. Senior staff such as a theatre's artistic director might attend to welcome the company to the theatre as a whole. Outside producers may even fly in from out of town, especially for a production with aspirations to travel beyond its home theatre after this run ends.

As part of the preparations for the first day, the stage manager should find out in advance who will be in attendance and what support they will need for presenting information. This can include a table for the model, display boards for drawings, or a surface onto which to project computer images. Designers who cannot attend this first rehearsal may send information to be shared on their behalf. The SM should also make sure there is adequate space for everyone, securing additional tables and chairs for the first day if necessary. Even though the guests may not be with you every day, it is important for them to feel welcome and included today.

The stage manager distributes many of the items created during prep week to the actors today. Cast members will need a copy of the contact sheet, the character/scene breakdown, and the preliminary rehearsal calendar. Depending on the policies of your theatre, the SM may also hand out biography and emergency medical forms, details on parking, ticket policies, or general rehearsal guidelines if working in an academic theatre.

The SM will need an opportunity to review this information, collected into an actor packet, with the cast. When working on an AEA production, the stage manager can also use the time for conducting union business, including the election of a deputy and taking any necessary votes about breaks, span of day, or other work details required by your specific contract.

WHAT IS A DEPUTY?

The Equity deputy is a member of the cast elected by his or her fellow actors to ensure that the union rules are followed during the production. On a weekly basis, the deputy will report details regarding hours worked, safety conditions, filming activities, and any grievances filed by or about AEA members. Some of these details will simultaneously be reported by the stage manager. The purpose of a deputy is to provide the union cast members with an avenue for sharing potential violations of union rules.

On an Equity production, only union members are permitted to be in the room while discussions and elections take place. And even on a nonunion show, this actor information may be of little interest to other attendees at your first rehearsal. A thoughtful stage manager will arrange the day so that those not involved with this cast business can easily excuse themselves.

A sample first-day schedule might look like this:

1. Meet-and-Greet
2. Introductions, Director, and Designer Presentations
3. Read through Play
4. Cast Meeting

   General Schedule

   Theatre Callboard/Schedule Updates

   Character/Scene Breakdown

   Theatre Policies

   AEA Business (if applicable)

Such a schedule allows everyone to participate in the show-related orientation without having to come and go from the room multiple times or sit through details not pertaining to their work. Specific times would be identified for each activity, and breaks would be inserted according to the director's preference or the AEA requirements.

An alternative could be placing the cast meeting after the design presentations, so that those who wish to hear the play read will have an identified time to return—using the business meeting time to check in with their shops or offices, read email, or enjoy a second cup of coffee (a rationale for having any meet-and-greet snacks set up outside the room!).

WHAT DO YOU LEARN FROM A READ-THROUGH?

The stage manager can collect several key pieces of information from the first trip through the script, including a preliminary running time and the pace of individual scenes. Pace is particularly important when considered in conjunction with your character/scene breakdown. You have already started identifying scenic and costume changes, with the available time quantified in pages. Pace will tell you how long you *really* have—which might be more or less than you anticipated.

TABLE WORK

Before getting the show up on its feet, it is important for the cast to understand the text. The second phase in your rehearsal process will focus on analyzing the script. This is certainly a necessity when working on Shakespeare or one of the Greeks, but even contemporary scripts can benefit from this exploration of the words. If your production has a dramaturg, he or she will be present for these days to help the director and actors. The dramaturg serves as a production researcher of sorts, collecting background and source information for the company and often creating materials for the audience to help them understand the context of the show. On a new play, expect the playwright to be present.

The amount of time spent on table work will vary from show to show, depending on the wishes of your director. Some productions may devote several days to this type of exploration, while others may only schedule a brief discussion following the first read-through. The stage manager should ask about table work during the initial meetings with the director to know if this will be a part of the rehearsal process.

The stage manager's communication work during this time is about gathering information. You should make note of tricky pronunciations to pass along to understudies and to use when prompting. And if you do not have a dramaturg, you can collect questions about script references that may be posed to the production team through the rehearsal reports.

To facilitate this process, the SM team should ask about acquiring reference aids—source materials, dictionaries, or lexicons. Depending on your production situation, this might be a question for the production manager, a faculty advisor, or a staff member in the literary or education department. It is also helpful for the SM to provide additional notepads, pencils, and highlighters for the actors, so they can successfully take notes during this time.

Table work may also be the start of cataloging script changes. An unedited performance of *Hamlet* can run up to four hours. Most modern productions do not include every word penned by Shakespeare. If the original script distributed to the cast and production team did not include the cuts for your show, the stage manager will need to document the changes as a starting point for further edits to come.

The sample page of line changes for this production of Shakespeare's *Twelfth Night*, reintroduced as Figure 5.1, shows how the stage manager can share both major and minor changes. We first saw this table in Chapter 2 when exploring color and white space. Now we can examine its content. The document provides very specific references to the act, scene, page, and line being altered. Line numbers are helpful for any show in verse. A contemporary text is unlikely to have this information, so the column can be eliminated. The affected text is identified and the change specifically called out. A notes column provides a place for narrative commentary on the edit.

When identifying a change, it is important to be both specific and consistent. You might opt to categorize text that has been removed with the term *cut*, *delete*, or even *omit*. Supplemental words might be an *add* or an *insert*. Your specific choice is less important than the use of the same term throughout the document.

The line-change document will be updated several times throughout the rehearsal process. As discussed in Chapter 2, the use of color can help identify new information in subsequent versions and allow you to record all notes in a single document organized in line order.

If you are working on a new play, line changes may lead to replacement pages in the script. This might be a task undertaken by the SM team, the assistant director, the dramaturg, or the playwright. Before rehearsals begin, the stage manager should inquire where the responsibility for new pages lies. This ensures that once rehearsals begin, there is a plan for who will keep track of the changes, who will type the updates, how new pages will be distributed, and on what timeline. When working on a new play or musical, expect to receive changes from the playwright or the composer/lyricist. Edits on an existing work may be generated by the director or dramaturg. In most instances the stage managers will be responsible for copying and distributing the new pages.

Twelfth Night
Line Changes
Updated 11/18/10

Act	Scene	Page	Line(s)	Character	Action	Words	Notes
II	5	43	117-118	Fabian	CUT	Sowter will cry upon't for al this, though it be as rank as a fox	Malvolio's lines continue from "Softly, M.O.A.I" to his next speech beginning "M- Malvolio…"
II	5	43	121	Toby	CUT	The cur is excellent at faults	Line now ends with . "… work it out?"
III	1	45	2	Viola	CHANGE	TABOR to MUSIC	
III	1	46	9-10	Viola	CUT	or, the church stands by thy tabor, if thy tabor stand by the church	Line now ends with "… dwell near him"
III	1	46	11-13	Feste	CUT	To see this age! A sentence is but a chev'ril glove to a good wit. How quickly the wrong side may be turned outward!	Line now ends after "You have said, sir."
III	2	52	29	Andrew	CUT	I had as lief be a Brownist as a politician	Line now ends after…"for policy I hate."
III	2	53	42-43	Toby	CUT	although the sheet were big enough for the Bed of Ware in England,	Line now skips from "… lie in thy sheet of paper" to "set 'em down."
III	2	53	48	Toby	CUT	at the cubiculo	Line now reads "We'll call thee. Go."

Figure 5.1 A page of line changes for a production of *Twelfth Night*.

Don't forget that you will need to transform these new pages to match the rest of your prompt script. Try to arrange to receive updates so that you have time not only to send them through the copier as-is for the actors, but also to make the size and margin adjustments for your script. In the unlikely event that someone besides stage management is handling distribution of new pages, I recommend that you handle the prompt script's specialized formatting yourself.

MUSIC AND DANCE REHEARSALS

When working on a musical, the table-work phase is often replaced or reduced by dedicated time for learning music and choreography. The stage manager can take advantage of this time to take dance blocking in smaller chunks and to become familiar with the score.

Not every stage manager has a background as a musician, but the music rehearsals give you a chance to pick up key details that will help you throughout rehearsals and performances. The SM can follow along to improve his or her own ability to read music. The musical director will often point out useful clues to help the singers find their notes and rhythm. These same clues can help you as well. Figures 5.2A and 5.2B introduce you to the essential information contained on a page of the score.

The stage manager can also take this time to transfer details such as rehearsal numbers from the score into the libretto. If you are primarily working from the libretto, having rehearsal

NAVIGATING THE SCORE

Whether or not the stage manager knows how to play music, he or she can learn a great deal about how a song will sound by looking for clues in the score. On the opposite page is an excerpt from the Piano/Conductor score for the song "Look at the Sky" from the musical *Urinetown*. Follow the numbers to discover how much information is available.

OVERALL PAGE STRUCTURE

A sheet of music contains one or more groups of five-line staffs known as a SYSTEM (1). The system contains the vocal parts (1A), the orchestra parts (1B), and the piano parts (1C) that are played or sung simultaneously. If more than one person is singing, there will be multiple vocal staffs. A complex song might have so many individual staffs to include that only one system fits on a page.

Each staff is divided into MEASURES (1D). The construction of each measure is determined by the TIME SIGNATURE (3) printed at the beginning of the song. Our sample is page three of the song, but on page one we would find two numbers: 4/4. This tells us there are four beats in each measure and that a quarter note gets one beat. With this information we know how to count the music. The word "sky" will be held for 4 beats.

Measure numbers that appear in boxes are called REHEARSAL NUMBERS (1E). These indicators represent parts of the song where the music changes-- speeding up or slowing down, adding instruments or singers, or changing from accompaniment to underscoring, for example.

We can even find messages from the composer. V. S. (1F) stands for *volti subito*-- turn the page quickly!

WHO IS PLAYING

The score outlines which instruments play at which time. At the top of the page, the *clarinet and trombone* (5A) and the *bass* (5B) play with the piano. At measure 25, the *drums* join in (5C). The percussionist will play a *sustained roll on the cymbals* at measure 27 (5D). This helps the SM follow along by knowing what to listen for.

PITCH

The KEY SIGNATURE (2) tells the musicians whether notes should be played higher or lower than their normal value. The key can change throughout a song. At the beginning of the page we are in the key of *B flat major*. After measure 30, the song changes (2A) to *B major*. The SM can look for key signatures and recognize when the quality of the song will change, even if you do not know how to read the specific notation.

PACE

The speed of a piece of music is its TEMPO. Like the key, it can change throughout a song. As this page begins, the song returns to the original pace indicated by the notation *Tempo I* (4).

VOLUME

Clues about how loud or soft to play can be found in the DYNAMIC MARKINGS. (6A) *Mezzo piano* (*mp*) indicates this section is "medium soft." (6C) *Forte* (*f*) is "loud." Volume can gradually get louder with a *crescendo* (6B), or softer with a *decrescendo* (6D). Absent this kind of notation, the change would be instant.

WORDS VERSUS NOTES

When dialogue occurs during a song, the lines (7) will be printed above the vocal staff . The fact that these words are spoken rather than sung is reinforced by the fact that instead of notes, the vocal line contains only (7A) rests. These particular rests are *whole rests*, which last an entire measure each.

Figures 5.2A and 5.2B "Look at the Sky" from *Urinetown* used with permission of the authors. Explanatory narrative created with Dr. Gary Walth.

numbers will allow you to communicate more effectively with the music personnel by speaking in their vernacular. During a subsequent rehearsal, the director might want to review the staging for the end of a song. Rather than providing a lyric, the SM with rehearsal numbers can ask the pianist to "start at bar 47."

BLOCKING

Once the cast has an understanding of the words on the page, it is time to put the show up on its feet. Blocking is a crucially important phase of the process. Defining the physical shape of the show will provide answers to many prerehearsal queries, and also generate new questions on a daily basis.

Blocking is defined as the movement of the actors on, off, and around the stage—interacting with one another and the elements of the set. The stage manager documents this movement in detail, noting both what happens and when it occurs.

PREPARING THE REHEARSAL ROOM

In both professional and academic settings, the rehearsal period typically overlaps with scenic construction. The actors work either in a separate room, or in some cases in the theatre during nonbuild hours. In order to make this time productive, the stage manager communicates the details of the set by reproducing the groundplan on the floor of the rehearsal hall with special cloth spike tape and acquiring rehearsal furniture pieces. In conjunction with the model or renderings of the set posted in the room, this will help the actors and directors to understand the end product.

The SM will need to consider the size and setup of the rehearsal room when determining the best spot for taping out the set. Within the context of the director's preferences (learned during that early meeting during pre-production week), consider the following:

1. **Side-to-side location.** Ideally you will have enough room to tape out the entire set and still have room on both sides for actor entrances, prop tables, and furniture storage. If your room is not wide enough, think about how to position offstage items to lessen their visual presence while the director is watching the actors.

2. **Front-to-back location.** Downstage of the groundplan, you will need to set up tables for the director and SM team as well as chairs for others. If possible, you also want some empty space between the downstage edge of the tape and those tables and chairs so it doesn't feel like you are sitting on the set. The SM also strives to place the groundplan so that there is room upstage of it for actors to cross from stage right to stage left.

3. **Doors.** Doors are least distracting when located behind the director and SM so that actors entering the room aren't instantly "on stage."

4. **Architecture.** Do you have columns, air vents, or other structural room elements? You cannot move these items, so think about how they can be the least impactful—even if that means placing the groundplan slightly off-center in the room.

No room is perfect! Focus on minimizing obstacles and maximizing the working space. If your room is not wide enough, can you utilize the front corners of the room for the prop tables? If the room is not deep enough, take a look at your set. Is there space between the back of the set and an upstage curtain or cyclorama? If it is not an acting area, consider reducing this space to get adequate real estate at the front of the room. If you have multiple obstacles and may need to eliminate part of the set when taping it out, talk with the director after looking at the room so you can agree on a compromise.

One way to facilitate this conversation is to provide visual support. Get a piece of acetate or clear plastic and draw the outline of the rehearsal room on it (in the same scale as the groundplan), marking doors, columns, and other structural elements. Then you can slide the clear outline over the groundplan to find the most functional layout for the room. If you work regularly for the same theatre, you can save the acetate for future productions. What works for one show may not work for the next.

In order to tape the groundplan onto the rehearsal room floor, the SM team takes specific measurements of the size and location of scenic elements. The stage manager begins by locating the **center line**—the imaginary line running upstage to downstage in the center of the theatre—and the **plaster line**—the imaginary line running stage right to stage left on the upstage side of the proscenium arch. Using these two lines as X and Y coordinate axes, the team can find the distance from the axes to the corners of platforms or edges of walls. Once measured, the SM team can plot these points on the floor and connect the points with tape to mark out the location of both permanent and moving units.

Figure 5.3 is a full-stage image of a production of *The Farnsworth Invention* by Aaron Sorkin. The set consisted of a series of steps and platforms, which remained on stage for the entire show. Tables, chairs, and other furniture pieces moved throughout the play to indicate a variety of locations.

Figure 5.3   The set for *The Farnsworth Invention* at the University of Wisconsin–La Crosse. Scenic design by Mandy Hart.

Translating this design onto a rehearsal room floor would focus on noting the size and location of the permanent pieces along with the front edge of the stage, which defines the downstage area. The director could block scenes on individual platforms by staying within the taped lines. It is not important to the process that ultimately the actors would be raised above the stage floor. Figure 5.4 shows you how to tape out those important scenic elements.

For this production, the specific location of individual furniture pieces on the platforms was left up to the director, making it impossible to tape them out in advance. But that tape would not really be helpful. The actors need actual tables and chairs in order to rehearse. A rectangle the size of a desk would not encourage interaction with the desk or any props placed on it, or allow the director to stage the transitions to move it around the stage. As the director sets furniture placement, the ASMs can mark the locations on the rehearsal-room floor with the same spike tape. Should the actual tables and desks become available later on, the spikes can be adjusted to the size of the new pieces. The SM team can then measure the location of those spikes by the same method used to re-create the ground plan and transfer them to the finished set, so the furniture ends up in the same spots.

The large set of stairs would present a challenge. Obviously no one will build you a set of temporary stairs in your rehearsal hall, so the tape will have to suffice. But the stage manager can facilitate some interaction. If the director asks an actor to sit on a step, the SM team can place a chair or cube in that location. This way, even though the actor may not be literally walking up stairs when crossing upstage, he or she can still find the physicality of a speech delivered while sitting down.

Not every show is this simple, however. When planning for a show with multiple scenic units—particularly if more than one piece plays in the same location—the stage manager should adapt the method for taping out the set. Accurate blocking and furniture placement will depend on a clear understanding of the scenery on stage at a given time.

Our second set of sample groundplans is for a production of Shakespeare's *Twelfth Night* in the same theatre. In this instance, separate locations were defined by using specific scenic units. Some pieces, such as the main gate or trees, were used more than once, but other pieces were flown or carried in for only a single locale. Even without the labels in Figure 5.5, having all those lines on the floor at the same time has the potential to be confusing. Because the stage manager's goal is to communicate the design clearly, the actors need a bit more help than for *The Farnsworth Invention*.

Color comes to the rescue in the same way it has done thus far in paperwork (Figure 5.6). By taping out each unit in a different color, the actors can more easily focus on only part of the detail on the floor at any given time. (If no units overlapped in use, each location rather than each unit, could get a single color.) When working on a scene in Olivia's garden, for example, the actors can be asked to focus on the gate and green colonnade, as seen in Figures 5.7 and 5.9. The urns and fountain could be represented with chairs or cubes, and

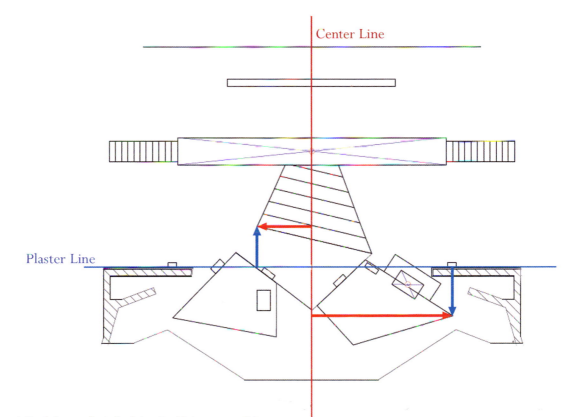

1. Identify the center line (red) and plaster line (blue) on your groundplan.

2. Measure the end points of each scenic unit in relation to those lines (ie: how far upstage or downstage of the plaster line, how far left or right of center).

3. Write down those coordinate measurements.

4. Determine the best place in your rehearsal room to recreate the ground plan.

5. Lay down two tape measures at the center line-- with zero of each on the plaster line. This allows you to measure either upstage or downstage of the plaster line without extra math.

5. Locate the up/down coordinate measurement from the grounplan on your center line tape.

6. Use a third tape measure to locate the coordinate measurement left or right of the center tape.

7. Place a dot to represent that point.

8. Repeat for all necessary points, then connect the dots.

Figure 5.4 Measuring the groundplan for *The Farnsworth Invention*.

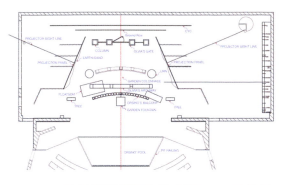

Figure 5.5 A composite groundplan for *Twelfth Night* at the University of Wisconsin–La Crosse. Scenic design by Mandy Hart.

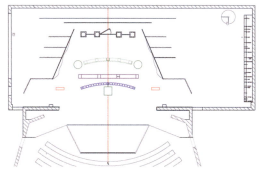

Figure 5.6 The same composite without labels, but with the color used to mark out the rehearsal room floor.

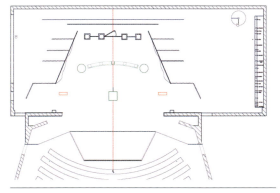

Figure 5.7 The units in use for Olivia's garden.

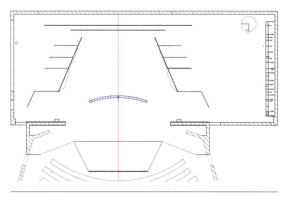

Figure 5.8 The units in use on Orsino's balcony.

Figure 5.9 A production shot of the garden.

Figure 5.10 A production shot of the balcony.

spare music stands make excellent and easily portable trees. When moving to block a scene inside Orsino's compound, only the blue railing found in Figures 5.8 and 5.10 is relevant. Just as was true for the tables in *The Farnsworth Invention*, the cast will need rehearsal furniture to complete the setup, further helping them to temporarily ignore the other colored lines on the floor.

THE BLOCKING KEY

Because the stage manager's goal is to capture the actors' movement with as much specificity as possible, it is important to set yourself up for success before blocking rehearsals begin. To do this the SM needs to decide in advance what abbreviations to use.

These abbreviations will be collected in a blocking key—the Rosetta Stone to your prompt script. The key provides a reference for you, allowing you to be consistent with your use of symbols, but also aids others in understanding your notation. The blocking key contains several categories: areas of the stage and your specific set, actions, props, and character abbreviations. At the end of this section, you will find the blocking key for *Twelfth Night* in Figures 5.12 and 5.13, detailing the collection of all of this information.

The blocking key should be kept in your prompt book at the beginning of the section containing the script. Because I like to have my key out and available while taking blocking, I keep it in a sheet protector so that repeated handling won't damage it. My key also takes two pages, and the sheet protector allows them to be kept together, back to back.

Early-career stage managers may try to write out all movement longhand, but over time you will discover that it is quicker to use a combination of words and symbols. The point of the symbols is to speed up your writing, so you want a system that actually does so.

Figure 5.11 contains the set of the blocking symbols I have developed over time. Many were originally introduced to me by mentors early in my career, and I have adapted them to suit my own style and the needs of shows I have stage-managed.

The top three rows include symbols for common actions. Most are constructed on a very simple principle—the first letter of the action combined with an arrow head indicating direction. Row four is a set of notations for location. These can be used to show where one actor or item is in relation to another. Again, the symbols are simple: arrows or a simple combination of dots and lines, making them easy to write and to understand.

The next few rows demonstrate an approach to noting props and furniture. These symbols are more pictorial than the actions or locations, but similarly simple in their design. You could, of course, draw a more complex lamp or stool, but the time spent on an intricate drawing would defeat the purpose of having it.

The bottom row in the chart shows how to combine symbols. The circle from the top of the lamp is joined with the table to indicate a table lamp. This allows you to distinguish between

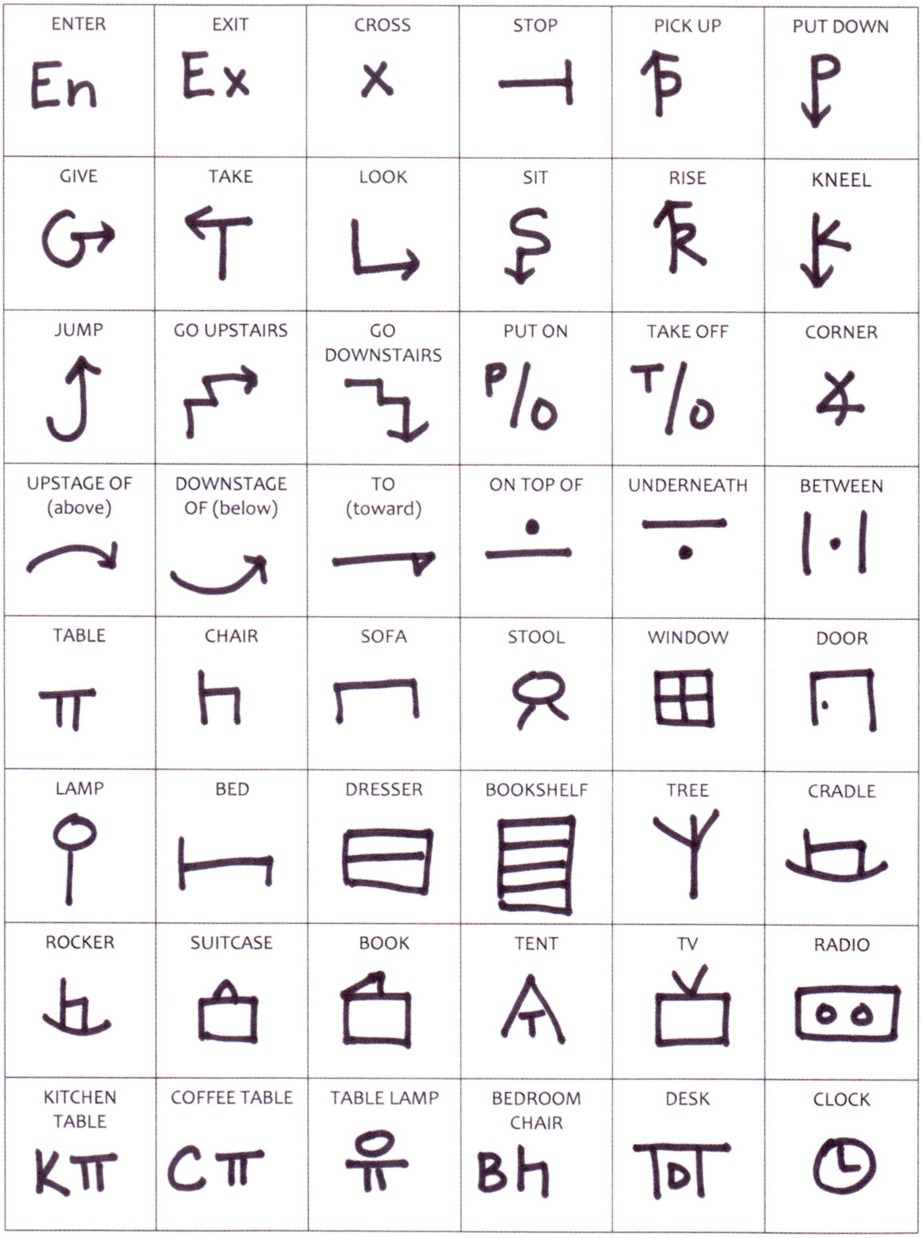
ENTER
EXIT
CROSS
STOP
PICK UP
PUT DOWN
GIVE
TAKE
LOOK
SIT
RISE
KNEEL
JUMP
GO UPSTAIRS
GO DOWNSTAIRS
PUT ON
TAKE OFF
CORNER
UPSTAGE OF (above)
DOWNSTAGE OF (below)
TO (toward)
ON TOP OF
UNDERNEATH
BETWEEN
TABLE
CHAIR
SOFA
STOOL
WINDOW
DOOR
LAMP
BED
DRESSER
BOOKSHELF
TREE
CRADLE
ROCKER
SUITCASE
BOOK
TENT
TV
RADIO
KITCHEN TABLE
COFFEE TABLE
TABLE LAMP
BEDROOM CHAIR
DESK
CLOCK

Figure 5.11 Blocking symbols.

a table lamp, a standing lamp, or even a sconce (which might be that circle within a rectangle indicating a wall). Differentiating similar items is also easy. Look at the kitchen table and coffee table. With the simple addition of a letter, the furniture pieces are distinct. Once you have found a set of symbols that work for you, it is easy to adapt them to the needs of a specific production. You might not always have a kitchen table and a coffee table, but this strategy will assist you in creating a key for any show.

The next component of your blocking notation will be the elements of the set. In this instance, the terminology you use is not entirely your creation. Remember the design for *The Farnsworth Invention* with its three platforms. You might refer to them as stage right, center, and stage left; A, B, and C; or even 1, 2, and 3. During your prep work and initial meetings, the director and scenic designer inevitably discussed these items. What language did they use? That is your starting point. If the director refers to the units by their location on the stage, it will always be momentarily confusing if you answer an actor's question about where they were by referring to platform one instead of stage right.

The final set of decisions to make concerns abbreviations for character names. If every actor in your show plays only one role, then basing abbreviations on those names will work. Bob might be noted with a B and Arthur with an A. But if your two male characters are John and Joe, then you need more. Personally, I would abbreviate them as JN and JO, respectively. Why? Because JO will always read as Joe to me, even though *o* is also the second letter of John. And JN looks like John when I glance at it quickly.

If an actor plays two very distinct characters, it might be reasonable to use two separate character abbreviations. But for less-defined ensemble roles, you may find that abbreviations based on actor names are more successful. The blocking key for *Twelfth Night* contains all four strategies working together. Viola and Sebastian are easily identified with a single letter based on the character name. Orsino and Olivia have two character initials. The same actor played the Sea Captain and the Priest, but due to the differences between the roles and their place in the play, two separate abbreviations for the same actor worked fine. But what about the actors who play a combination of lords, sailors, and officers? When looking quickly in your script to answer a question, will you always remember that Luke plays Sailor 2? Or that Curio, Sailor 1, and Officer 2 are the same actor? For these cast members, abbreviations based on their actual names was faster—particularly since most of these characters spoke no lines. The director created the blocking by asking Brian or Luke to take an action, not Sailor 1 or 2, making this another example of working within the language of your production. If you find that you forget who is who when looking at the text, you can write in Luke's initials next to Curio's lines in your book.

Twelfth Night

Blocking Key

Symbol	Meaning	Symbol	Name	
en	Enter	OR	Orsino	
ex	Exit	S	Sebastian	
X	Cross	AN	Antonio	
→▽	To/Toward	V	Viola	
↘↗	Cross Below/In front of	OL	Olivia	
↘	Cross Above/behind	T	Sir Toby	
R	Rise	M	Maria	
S	Sit down	MO	Malvolio	
S	Sit up	AA	Sir Andrew Aguecheek	
K	Kneel	FE	Feste	
P	Pick Up	FA	Fabian	
P	Put Down	SC	Sea Captain (Jake Voss)	
P	Turn	P	Priest (also Jake Voss)	
G→	Give	MI	Musician 1 (Shelby)	
←T	Take	M2	Musician 2 (Suzanne)	
⟋	Lean	EW	Emily Ware	Attendant 1
⊣	Stop	LV	Lindsay Van Norman	Attendant 2
L→	Look	AH	Austin Hernandez	Valentine, Officer 1, Sailor 3
↷	Jump	LP	Luke Prescott	Curio, Sailor 1, Officer 2
⤴	Go up stairs	BC	Brian Coffin	Lord 1, Sailor 2, Officer 3
⤵	Go down stairs	DH	Don Hart	Lord 2, Officer 4
∘—	On top of			
—∘	Underneath			
|·|	Between			
P/o	Put On			

Figure 5.12 The blocking key for *Twelfth Night*.

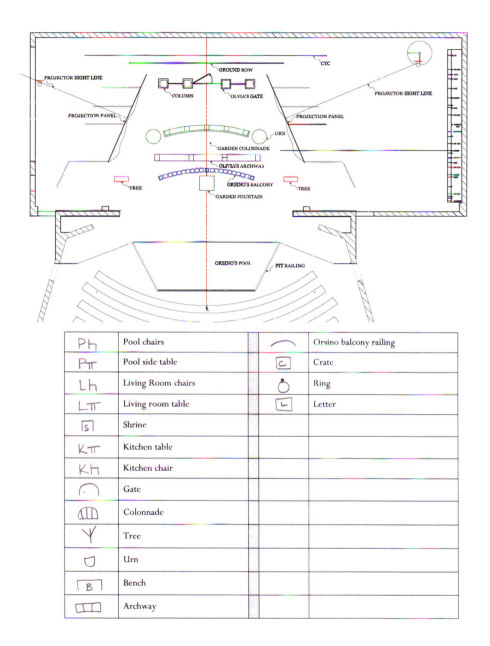

Figure 5.13 The blocking key for *Twelfth Night*.

Symbol	Description		Symbol	Description
Ph	Pool chairs		⌒	Orsino balcony railing
PƬ	Pool side table		C	Crate
Lh	Living Room chairs		○	Ring
LƬ	Living room table		L	Letter
S	Shrine			
KƬ	Kitchen table			
Kh	Kitchen chair			
⌒	Gate			
⊞	Colonnade			
Y	Tree			
∪	Urn			
B	Bench			
⊞	Archway			

PUTTING IT TO WORK

The blocking key and numbered lines on your backing sheet allow you to work precisely, as seen in Figure 5.14. The line number is written by the individual word on which an action takes place, and your use of both words and symbols allows you to quickly describe this action in detail. The point of this specificity is twofold. The stage manager can clearly communicate the intricacies of movement set during a previous rehearsal to forgetful actors or to understudies and also be able to place cues based on specific actions into the prompt script with great accuracy.

MULTITASKING DURING BLOCKING

Even a seasoned director may have difficulty predicting exactly how long it will take to block an individual scene. The daily schedule is an educated guess. The stage manager may find it challenging to schedule costume fittings or other activities that take actors away from the rehearsal room on these days—especially if your costume shop is any distance away. You don't want to arrive at a scene early and have a key actor missing, or be unable to respond to a director's request to add an ensemble member to a nonspeaking moment in a show.

In light of this unpredictability, it is helpful to provide the actors with a nearby area to wait. A second rehearsal space across the hall, or even a green room, will permit actors to work on line memorization or songs or just relax and chat. They are available when needed, but much less frustrated than they would be if forced to sit in the rehearsal room just waiting for hours on end.

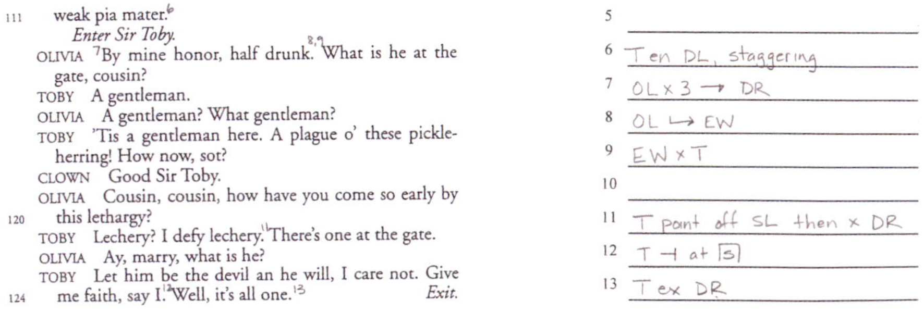

111   weak pia mater.[6]
    Enter Sir Toby.
  OLIVIA   [7]By mine honor, half drunk.[8,9] What is he at the
    gate, cousin?
  TOBY   A gentleman.
  OLIVIA   A gentleman? What gentleman?
  TOBY   'Tis a gentleman here. A plague o' these pickle-
    herring! How now, sot?
  CLOWN   Good Sir Toby.
  OLIVIA   Cousin, cousin, how have you come so early by
120   this lethargy?
  TOBY   Lechery? I defy lechery.[10] There's one at the gate.
  OLIVIA   Ay, marry, what is he?
  TOBY   Let him be the devil an he will, I care not. Give
124   me faith, say I.[12] Well, it's all one.[13]   *Exit.*

5   _____
6   Ten DL, staggering
7   OL x 3 → DR
8   OL ↳ EW
9   EW x T
10   _____
11   T point off SL then x DR
12   T ⊣ at [S]
13   T ex DR

Figure 5.14 A close-up view of blocking notation at work.

THE DAILY CALL

Now that the rehearsal period has begun, the stage manager will disseminate much more detailed information about daily rehearsal activities than available on the overall calendar. General days and times were the appropriate starting point, but now everyone will need more. The stage manager creates and distributes a specific work schedule on a daily and weekly basis. Actors need to know where to place their focus to prepare for the next day's work; the production team will be concerned with what units might be in use in order to be ready for a specific rehearsal prop or costume request—or to determine what *not* to make unavailable for that day. Communicating these plans requires both written and verbal strategies.

At the end of one day's rehearsal, you hope to announce to the cast the plan for the next day, emphasizing anything that has changed from previous information. That schedule may include actors not present at the time, so you need a way to reach them as well. Many theatres maintain a rehearsal hotline—a telephone number on which the next day's schedule is recorded as the outgoing voicemail message each night. Written communication of the schedule might take the form of a document posted on your callboard and/or a show website or emailed out to your cast.

The sample daily call from *Footloose* found in Figure 5.15 is a good example of the potential intricacies of a single day of work. This would never fit onto a general calendar. It also did not exist at that time. Wednesday's schedule was the product of several days of notes from the director, musical director, and choreographer.

In written form, the call makes use of columns, allowing the actors to visualize how the activities overlap. The music sessions fit within the same time blocks set up for the director and choreographer. By merging cells to line up the time blocks, making use of sufficient white space, and placing commentary in italics, the actors have a way to navigate the plan.

I was the stage manager for this production, and can honestly say I am glad that my indirect way to reach my cast was a website and not a telephone hotline. It would be tricky to make this much information clear over the phone! My schedule was posted directly on the actor information page, with a hyperlink to a PDF file of the schedule in case someone wanted to print it out or was having problems viewing the columns (for example, on a mobile device).

But had the phone been my only option, I would have taken the following approach:

1. Begin by announcing any fittings scheduled for the day before getting into the schedule—so that information wouldn't get lost.

2. Read the details for one location and then the other rather than going in time order and addressing both rooms at once.

3. Start with the scene work and choreography column, because it is less complex.

4. Concentrate on articulation and keeping my pace even.

REHEARSAL SCHEDULE

Wednesday June 13

Scenework & Choreography (in Toland Theatre)			Music (in the Choir Room)		
6:30-7:30 pm	Willard, Ren	Assorted Scene work	6:30 pm	Wendy Jo, Urleen, Rusty	#1, 4, 6, 7B, 11, 18
			7:00 pm	Posse (Beyer, Cornwell, Lake)	#10
			7:10 pm	Wendy Jo, Urleen, Rusty, Beyer, Bush, Cook, Cornwell, Escher, Lake, Schneider, K. Wolf	#1, 4, 9, 16A
7:30-8:00 pm	Chuck, Lyle, Travis, Ariel	Assorted Scene work	7:30 pm	Willard, Garvin, Jeter, Bickle	#13, 13A
			7:45 pm	Ren	#3, 9, 12C
8:00-9:30 pm	Rusty, Wendy Jo, Urleen, Ariel, Willard, Ren, Garvin, Jeter, Cowboy Bob, Travis, Beyer, Black Cornwell, Fanshaw, Lake, Schneider *(in other words, everyone at the Bar-B-Que except Erica and David)* Travis to arrive at 8:40 pm	Let's Hear It For the Boy	8:00 pm	Black, Willard, Garvin, Jeter, Bickle, Chuck, Lyle, Travis,	#1, 4, 9, 16A
			8:25 pm	Chuck, Lyle, Travis	#2, 7B
			8:40 pm	Travis	Go to Toland!

Figure 5.15 A daily rehearsal call.

5. Make sure I preceded the schedule with an introduction similar to this: "The following is the *Footloose* schedule for Wednesday, June 13. Please listen carefully, as we have lots of small overlapping work sessions planned. Grab your pencil now! If you have any questions, please call Laurie at 333-555-1212 for clarification."

This would prepare the actors to hear a lot of detail and allow them to have my phone number jotted down right on the page with the schedule. I had, of course, provided it several other times, but why not save a confused actor an extra step?

At the beginning of the rehearsal period, you are likely to have simple schedules—full company calls for introductory sessions, and days divided into large segments for table work. Blocking and scene work days will be more complex. The director may wish to work with select groups of actors for more-defined periods of time. As you approach technical rehearsals, the schedule will simplify again as the work turns to repeated runs of the show followed by notes, requiring the full cast.

CONFLICTS

One of the trickiest aspects to developing a rehearsal schedule can be finding a balance between the director's wishes and the actors' availability. Absences may occur less frequently in a professional setting, but you can still have a cast member with a previously scheduled appointment or last-minute emergency. Academic stage managers find themselves handling many more conflicts. The ideal actor for a role might also play in the orchestra, which rehearses on Monday nights. Another might have a class on Tuesdays until 8:00 p.m. Both actors will clear their conflicts for tech week and performances, but may not be able to do so for the first four weeks of work on the show. The director agreed to this unavailability during casting but will still be frustrated by rehearsals that become unproductive due to absences. Two-way communication helps to ameliorate the problem. Be sure you have a complete list of actor conflicts. Consult that list carefully when helping to create the schedule. Sometimes the solution can be found in suggesting a new order for a given night so that everyone can be present. At other times you may need one of your ASMs to walk the role and write down any notes or blocking to give to an actor before the scene is next run. Keeping the director informed and getting missing actors caught up quickly allows work to be successful every night.

FITTINGS

The stage manager will be asked to schedule actors for costume fittings—times to visit the costume shop to try on costume pieces as they are built or altered. In a professional setting, the shop hours may be simultaneous to the rehearsal hours, requiring the stage manager to weave these appointments into the rehearsal schedule. In an academic setting, it is more common for fittings to happen during the day and rehearsals to take place at night. The stage manager will still schedule the appointments, helping the actors to find the best blocks of time within their class or work obligations.

Once scheduled, fitting reminders should be available to the actors. This might take written form on a callboard, website, or individual appointment slip filled out at scheduling time (much like the reminder card you get when scheduling a doctor's visit). You can also provide verbal reminders on the rehearsal hotline.

If your costume shop is responsible for building more than one show at a time, the stage manager may need to coordinate fittings across several shows so that only one person arrives at a time to see the same designer or staff member. The costume shop will request fittings a day or so in advance, allowing each stage manager time to consult their rehearsal schedule for potential slots, check with other stage managers, confirm times with their actors, and then communicate the combined fitting details to the costume personnel.

Your department or theatre may have a form for scheduling fittings. If not, you might choose to develop something to simplify the process for yourself. But it may be just as easy to type up a list of costume fittings similar to a rehearsal schedule. As long as the information is clearly presented for all users, the choice is yours.

THE FIRST RUN-THROUGH

The stage manager should help to develop a schedule during blocking days that allows both for new work and for the occasional review prior to the first attempt to stumble through the show on its feet. Your director might prefer spending the final portion of each day reviewing work or waiting to run several scenes at the end of the week. Review is ideal for two reasons: (1) actors will memorize blocking more effectively if given the chance to walk through it multiple times, and (2) understudies can take their notes in more manageable chunks. On professional productions, understudies are not always called for rehearsal if they do not also have a role in the show. Understudies who are members of the primary cast may not always be free to attend blocking sessions if called for other work at the same time. In both instances, this allows them to get information in concentrated doses.

But whether or not you've done any review, the first full run of the show is a major event. The SM team can confirm blocking and prop/costume tracking notes and obtain an updated running time for the show.

It is important to set up the room so that rehearsal props and furniture pieces can be moved efficiently, whether done by actors or the ASMs standing in as the crew. The stage manager should also anticipate the return of some of the first-day guests—particularly in-town designers. If you have moved the extra tables and chairs out of the room, now is the time for their return. You are striving for an efficient, functional work space for everyone.

THE REHEARSAL REPORT

At the conclusion of each rehearsal day, the stage manager will prepare a report to be distributed to the production team and other staff members as required by your theatre or department.

Recipients

- Director and SM Team
- Designers and Assistants
- Production Manager
- Shop Heads (as appropriate)
- Production Stage Manager (if theatre has one)
- Faculty Advisors (academic productions)

What It Contains

- Details of the day's work, including breaks
- Overview of the next day's schedule
- Absences, latecomers, and visitors
- Questions for individual production areas from the director or SM
- Discoveries about scenery, costumes, props, or any other physical element of the show
- Notations of any accidents or injuries
- General information for the full team

Why Do It

- To provide an accounting of what is happening in the rehearsal room
- To alert production team members to needs or requirements for individual items
- To share the director or stage manager's questions

The rehearsal report is the most important communication tool for the stage manager. It is a direct line from the rehearsal room to the rest of the production team, and the most effective method for distributing a large amount of information to a diverse audience. It can be sent as easily to guest designers in another state as it can be to staff members across the hall. The rehearsal report is considered an official document of the production, particularly for Actors' Equity or insurance issues.

As such, the stage manager should treat the report as formal communication, employing the three key rules first introduced in Chapter 1—to be tactful, timely, and specific.

The rehearsal report should thoroughly address each category of information. If you have no questions or information for the sound department on a certain day, it is better to write that you have "no notes today, thank you" rather than to leave that section blank. This reassures the sound designer that he or she has no notes—and not that you have forgotten to include them.

One characteristic of the blocking period is its distinction as the time when the most props are added to a show. It is also true that some of these props will be cut once you reach scene work and the actors are no longer carrying scripts. So should you wait to make requests for additions to the prop list in case they go away? *No.* The props department will be unable to accurately plan their time or budget if you request a long list of items late in the process. The scenic designer will be unable to share concerns with the director or to discuss compromises about a specific prop if he or she doesn't know about it. And if a request cannot be fulfilled, then everyone's time is wasted in rehearsal by miming an item that will never come.

Notes should also be written as specifically as possible. If your director requests a baseball cap for an actor, then you are omitting details by writing a note asking just for a hat. Conversely, it is not up to you to make artistic decisions. If only a hat was requested, it is not your job to determine a baseball cap is the best choice.

It can be awkward to write a note you feel will be unpopular or that delivers bad news. But that does not mean the stage manager should not write it. Pre-production time spent learning about the elements of the design will provide you some context to know if requesting a change or asking a question could prompt an emotion-filled response, but the stage manager's job is to communicate nonetheless. You might opt to combine written and face-to-face communication by conveying general details in the report and following up in person the next morning. You need to provide the information so that a conversation can happen—even if that conversation is an argument.

"THE DIPLOMATIC HAND GRENADE"

In their book *Difficult Conversations*, authors Douglas Stone, Bruce Patton, and Sheila Heen describe delivering a difficult message as the equivalent of tossing a hand grenade. No matter how hard you try, tact may not truly soften the blow. They stress dealing "creatively with problems while treating people with decency and integrity." Transforming your message-delivery role into the opportunity for a conversation is much more constructive.[1]

REHEARSAL REPORT

Production: Twelfth Night
Date: Friday October 29
Stage Manager: Laurie Kincman
Assistant Stage Managers: Melissa Heller, Quinn Masterson
Guests: Colleen Schulz
Call Began: 7:00pm   Breaks: 7:45 (5), 9:00 (5)   Ended: 9:30 pm
Late: none   Absent: Austin Hernandez (excused)

Rehearsal Breakdown		
Time	**What**	**Who**
7:00 pm	Block II-1	Sebastian, Antonio
7:50 pm	Block III-2	Sebastian, Antonio
8:05 pm	Block II-2	Viola, Malvolio
8:40 pm	Block II-4 to p. 37	Orsino, Viola, Feste, Coffin, Hart, Prescott

Next Rehearsal Monday November 1		
Time	**What**	**Who**
6:30 pm	Block I-3	Toby, Maria, Andrew
7:30 pm	Block II-3	Toby, Maria, Andrew, Malvolio, Feste
8:30 pm	Block II-5	Toby, Maria, Andrew, Malvolio, Fabian

Scenery/Technical Direction (Mandy and Ron):

25. Will the gate be pinned to the deck after it flies in? (We are not asking for this—just wondering if we should allow time/personnel for it)

Props (Mandy and Laura):

26. Please ADD a rucksack for Sebastian in II-1.

27. Please ADD a change of clothes for Sebastian to pack into the rucksack. It will be preset on the bench when brought on.

28. Several people are now blocked to sit on Orsino's poolside table (only one at a time, though)

29. Please ADD money (bills) for Valentine to pay Feste in II-4.

Costumes (Michelle):

Please see prop note #27 regarding clothing for Sebastian to pack

30. Sebastian and Antonio's overcoats for II-1 will be preset on the coat rack when it is brought onstage.

31. Antonio's overcoat should have an inside breast pocket for his wallet

32. Walter would like Antonio's disguise for III-3 to include dark sunglasses.

Lights (Nick):

33. III-3 is currently blocked to occur far downstage right on the apron in front of the proscenium arch

Sound (Brent):

No notes tonight, thank you.

Miscellaneous:

34. Suzanne Clum and Shelby Krarup will be the Musicians in the production. There will be no third musician

Thanks everyone,
Laurie Kincman, SM

Figure 5.16 A rehearsal report from *Twelfth Night*.

ANALYZING THE REPORT

The sample rehearsal report from *Twelfth Night* in Figure 5.16 allows us to examine the document both for format and content. General details requested by the theatre appear at the top, including personnel, date, and attendance information. The next section outlines the schedule in summary form. Because this is not a document for the actors, you can present the facts simply—and in this case in a slightly smaller font size to minimize the amount of space it takes up. The most important sections of the report are those for individual production areas, so they should be the most prominent components of the page.

Other general document design principles from Chapter 2 in action include the following:

- A layout that presents the information legibly in the least number of pages

- Just enough white space to keep the text accessible

- A commonly available font, consistent with the one used for other show paperwork

- Minimal use of color and shading

REHEARSAL REPORT TEMPLATES

If your theatre does not have a format for rehearsal reports, the one provided here is a good start. If you have been asked to present the information in a specific way, however, you should do so. When beginning work for a new company, ask the production manager or a fellow stage manager about existing forms you should use. Often they exist in a common folder on a computer available to the stage managers, so that you can easily acquire the necessary templates to fill in for your production.

Looking at the report for content, a stage manager can find several useful strategies at work. The necessary formal tone is in place, set by the use of full sentences with correct grammar and punctuation. Questions and comments are concise, including all information from that night's rehearsal, without embellishments. Additions are requested with a *please*. And every area of the report is filled in, even if there are no notes.

CLARITY AND COMPLETENESS

The props notes from this particular evening include both additions and clarifications. The additions are obviously important but so is the detail provided about the poolside table (note #28). As the scenic designer and props master search for the most aesthetically pleasing furniture piece, it will be important to know it needs to bear weight. If the first-choice piece might not do this on its own, the team can now plan to reinforce it, look for another option, or initiate a conversation with the director about the necessity of that blocking. Similarly, the costume section includes specifics about where a coat pocket is best located for the blocking and an addition to a disguise for later in the show.

NUMBERING NOTES

Throughout this report, you will notice that most notes have a number. Numbering facilitates directing attention to a specific detail—either sending the same production area back to a previous report or directing a different area to a note with shared implications. A good example of this can be found at the beginning of the costume section. It is reasonable for the costume designer to want input into this prop clothing. Even though an actor will not wear it, it belongs to a specific character and should fall within the design concept for his look. If the rucksack had been added as a filled item (meaning the contents would never be seen on stage), then props could handle this alone. But because the clothing is seen, both areas should know about the note.

The stage manager should expect that production personnel will read notes in their individual sections thoroughly, general notes quickly, and other area notes not at all. Without a reference to the prop note, the costume designer could easily overlook the information. And by directing the designer's attention to a specific prop note, time is better used than if he or she was asked to search through the props section for the relevant item (not difficult on a night with only four prop notes, but what if there were more?).

The "please see" note does not need its own number, because it is not new information. It is the equivalent of the italicized commentary a stage manager might include on a chart or in a schedule. Personally, I also omit numbers when the note is a thank you. I do this to keep some control over the number of numbers. Thoroughness in reporting is essential, but there is something a bit overwhelming about opening a report to find it begins with note number forty on day five!

PRESENTING THE PROBLEM, NOT OFFERING THE SOLUTION

One of the toughest things to master as a stage manager is learning when to step in. If a prop or scenic piece should malfunction during a performance, of course the SM's problem-solving skills take over, and your job is to find a way to temporarily repair or replace the item so the show can go on. But during rehearsals, when you have the full staff working on the show, that is not your responsibility.

The stage manager can communicate if a piece of music is shorter than the transition for which it was written, if a table is too heavy to be carried by the actor tasked to do so, or if an actress in a long skirt has been blocked to run up a flight of stairs. That information is exactly the type of detail you should include in a rehearsal report. However, it is not your job to inform the costume designer that the skirt should be shortened, or to pull a lighter table for the show yourself. By presenting the problem, the stage manager allows the correct area to work on the solution—whether that is an easy substitution or a compromise reached after discussion in a production meeting.

Particularly in a rehearsal report, which is written and widely distributed, the SM should be careful not to imply that a colleague has made a poor choice or done an inadequate job. If your solution is requested, you will be asked for it. This might happen in follow-up conversation in person, where you can utilize your skills at reading body language to help gauge how much "help" to provide if asked.

The exception to the unsolicited suggestion rule might be during a production meeting if the personnel involved have reached an impasse. The SM can read the room and offer the "I know this might be a crazy idea, but could we…" comment. Your idea might work. Or it might restart the conversation and lead to a different outcome. The change in setting makes all the difference!

DISTRIBUTING THE REPORT

We have seen tact, timeliness, and specificity at work within the report itself, but the issue of time applies equally to distribution of the report. Daily reports obviously need to be sent out every day, and the stage manager should do his or her best to keep to a schedule. Complete the report at the end of the rehearsal, send it on its way, and then go home. Production team members will get used to receiving information at a certain time, and may not always keep checking for their notes.

This is particularly true in an academic setting when you are communicating with both students and faculty. A student stage manager may be concerned about a test the next morning and want to study for a few hours before typing the report, or want to go have some fun before tackling more work. If you fall asleep, get home later than intended, or simply forget, appropriate areas may not get your report before working on a project directly affected by your notes from the night before. Their class or work schedules might permit reading email only at the beginning and end of the day. If that beginning is 8:00 a.m., and your report arrives at 1:00 p.m., the information may be missed.

This author also strongly recommends finding the review method that works best for you. As part of the formal presentation of information, the report should be free of easy-to-find spelling errors or missing words. Notes need to be coherent. Your first effort to get the words on the page may not be as successful as you think.

I know myself well enough to realize that I proofread hard copies more successfully than written words on a computer screen. So once the report is done, I print a single copy. And I often read complex sentences and potentially unpopular notes out loud. If there are no changes to be made, then I already have a report for my prompt book. I can print any additional copies, distribute the report electronically, and call the task complete. But if I find errors, I have an opportunity to catch them before sending the information out into the world. I would rather waste a sheet of paper than appear sloppy or uncaring.

In today's electronic age, the rehearsal report is typically emailed out to production team members. By choosing common fonts and relatively simple formats, you can ensure that the report will look the same when opened on any computer. If you find that your reports are accessed over a wide variety of electronic devices and jumbled formatting is compromising legibility, you might consider distributing a PDF copy as first discussed in Chapter 2.

The stage manager may also be asked to post one or more copies in specific locations around the theatre. Follow these policies, but keep them in mind while preparing the report. Personally, I do not like posting reports —not because they are secret, but because the potential exists for others to read the information out of context. Consider the following hypothetical situation: The stage manager needs to inform the costume shop that the director has considered the options shown to him earlier in the day and has decided he would prefer for Actress X to wear the sundress rather than the shorts and T-shirt. A seemingly harmless note. But what happens if the report is posted in a common area where that actress can read it? Perhaps she won't think much of it. But she could just as easily infer that the director thinks she looks fat in shorts and her body problems are better hidden by the dress. Of course, your note said nothing of the kind, nor did any portion of the conversation between the director and designer concern that issue. This is a scenario existing solely in the actress's head—but one you cannot predict or control. Loss of context opens the door for outside interpretations. If I were posting a report with that note in a public place, I would alter it slightly to say that the director had decided the dress will work well with no reference to the other option. The decision has been communicated just as successfully, but with less opportunity for misunderstanding.

PRODUCTION MEETINGS

During the rehearsal period, your production team will gather regularly for meetings, allowing everyone a chance to discuss multi-area issues, schedules or budgetary concerns, and to get clarifications on information from your reports. The meeting might be run by the stage manager, the production manager, or even the director, depending on the tradition of your theatre. You will also find differences in formality regarding an agenda. Some meetings will work from a previously distributed list of topics, and others will unfold more organically.

The stage manager should come to production meetings with an agenda, even if one is not distributed or required. Preparing an agenda gives you the chance to look back through the previous week's reports—identifying unanswered questions or group topics—and to think ahead to upcoming events that might impact the production team. The agenda can function as a checklist for you to ensure all those items get discussed. If a conversation turns into a very specific discussion of small details that do not affect everyone, the list provides the SM with some backup to suggest finishing that discussion in a "meeting after the meeting" with only the necessary participants, as there are still multi-area questions needing attention during the actual meeting time.

The sample agenda in Figure 5.17 was prepared for a production meeting just two weeks prior to the beginning of tech rehearsals. The stage manager itemized the pressing issues for the show along with important events in need of confirmation.

Twelfth Night

AGENDA: November 10

Director- Walter

Top of show- designers thoughts on using shrine without gate?

Intermission after III-3

Scenery and Props- Mandy

Time to set a height for the pit with Orsino and Malvolio

Live flame concerns for candles on the shrine

Ripping up the challenge letter

TD- Ron

Status of pit repair

Costumes- Michelle

Confirm PR photo on Thursday at 6:00

Confirm Toby coat test right after photo

Scheduling a quick change rehearsal

Lights- Nick

No current questions

Sound- Brent

OK on headsets?

Music- Alden

No current questions

SM- Laurie

Paper Tech next week at 11- lovely to get cues Friday or Monday!

Replaced lost crew member

Discuss use of dry tech time on Sunday

Figure 5.17 The agenda for a production meeting during the rehearsal period.

MEETING MINUTES

Often the stage manager is asked to record minutes from production meetings. Taking these minutes is not about stenography—the important components are to present decisions made during the meeting for those who were not in attendance, and to remind everyone about upcoming action items. You don't have to capture every word uttered in the room.

When organizing meeting minutes, it is helpful to summarize discussions under the relevant production area—no matter who initiated the conversation. For example, during the meeting for which our sample agenda was prepared, the director was the first to ask about the status of the problem with the stage elevator. But, as this was ultimately a technical direction issue, the notes were summarized in that section of the minutes.

Minutes should be distributed within 48 hours of a meeting—sooner if possible. Because most production meetings take place on a weekly basis, the action items and schedule reminders are typically short-term. If too much time transpires between the meeting and the distribution of the minutes, the details may no longer be relevant.

SCENE WORK

Returning to the phases of rehearsal, the first run-through of the show will be followed by further exploration of the play. The work shifts from "what" rehearsals concerning logistics to "why" rehearsals concerning intention and motivation. Actors have a thorough grounding in the physical shape of the play and can now begin exploring details of their character.

Character work on a scene often requires a larger segment of the rehearsal day than was allocated for blocking it. Scene work may also be done out of order, so that an actor can explore the arc of a character through the play more concisely. In contrast to the blocking rehearsals, the stage manager may more easily identify opportunities to schedule costume fittings, dialect sessions, and other events that make actors temporarily unavailable to the director.

Scene work usually coincides with the line-memorization deadline because these rehearsals are more successful once actors are no longer carrying scripts. In addition to the added scheduling, the SM team will now take on responsibility for prompting (feeding lines to actors if they forget them) and taking line notes during this phase.

DONE TAKING NOTES?

The blocking may not be changing, so should the stage manager take notes in the prompt script during character rehearsals? *Yes!* Particularly if you will be maintaining the show or rehearsing understudies, document the discoveries taking place. The ability to refer to the director or the actor's own words will help legitimize your feedback later on.

LINE NOTES

Line notes are a tool to help actors memorize the script accurately. Although technically a form of written communication, they are a bit less formal. The goal is to achieve specificity, even though you are writing quickly. Using preprinted slips with a series of categories facilitates noting the type of error and indicating the beginning of the relevant line along with the problematic section is sufficient identification. Figure 5.18 provides a sample of a single-note form.

When beginning the line-note process, the SM team should concentrate on major problems—dropped lines, significant paraphrasing, or jumped cues. As the rehearsals progress and the actors become more proficient, the stage managers can correct more minute details. When the stage manager notices a line that is repeatedly misdelivered, it may be useful not only to identify the problematic part of the script but also to indicate what the actor is actually saying. Often the error has already been memorized, and the actor may not be aware of the inaccuracy.

CHARACTER_____			PAGE_____
Dropped Line	Paraphrased	Jumped/Missed Cue	Called for Line
Dropped Words	Sequence of Lines	Pronunciation	

Added:_____

LINE:_____

_____

Figure 5.18 A line note. These notes are formatted four per page, and are copied and cut into the individual slips prior to use in rehearsals.

THE ASM POINT OF VIEW

Two young stage managers offer their perspective on the role of the assistant stage manager in rehearsals.

Holly Burnell: "I know that everyone is relying on me to be on top of my game and relay accurate and detailed information, so I am always on my toes during rehearsals, keeping constant notes and ready to reset a scene at the drop of a hat."[2]

Nicole Smith: "I believe the goal of the ASM is to prepare in rehearsals the transitions of the props, costumes, and scenery to the best of your ability, so the actors, SM team, and director are comfortable with how those elements will work on stage, which will allow their focus to be on the new elements added in tech."[3]

ADDING THE ELEMENTS

As your production approaches technical rehearsals, the shops may be able to provide the cast with actual furniture or access to movable scenic units now built—both to enhance the rehearsal hall experience and to prepare them for the process of pulling the show together in tech. Other useful additions might include rehearsal costume pieces or sound cues.

In some theatres the SM team will pull rehearsal props or costumes from their stock. If you are responsible for collecting rehearsal items on your own, be sure that you familiarize yourself with the drawings and renderings so you can pull accurately. There is a big difference between working in a chair with and without arms. You also would not want to provide an elastic-waist prairie skirt to an actress who will wear a straight, above-the-knee skirt in the show. In an academic situation where actors may provide their own rehearsal items, use this same criteria to recommend what they should bring from home. Ask for help if the SM team (or a cast member) does not have something appropriate at your disposal.

During this phase of rehearsal, the stage manager works to successfully integrate these new elements and increases specificity in the rehearsal notes. Switching from one rehearsal chair to another is of less concern to the props shop than making an adjustment to a show item recently purchased or built.

Whenever a "real" item comes into rehearsal, it is important to make sure the director is aware of this fact. He or she will inevitably give it more serious consideration than the stand-in version. Walk the director through all the new items prior to the start of a rehearsal day. The stage manager should also specifically ask the director for notes about these pieces at the end of the day, so they can be immediately put into the rehearsal report.

If you are working on an Equity production, specific rules regarding shoes come into play. Under most contracts, dancers must be provided with shoes at least one week prior to dress rehearsals. If your show includes any traditional ballet, the shoes must be provided for any rehearsal in which the performers are dancing *on pointe*. The SM will be responsible for reminding costume personnel about this deadline, and then facilitating the pickup, use, and storage of the shoes once they arrive.[4]

Some production elements will never be replicated in the rehearsal room. Just as you will never get a second floor, you are extremely unlikely to execute light cues. The stage manager's method for communicating important lighting changes is through narration. Announcing "blackout" and "lights up" appropriately will help the actors to become aware of how light will interact with their work—even if they do so unconsciously. Similarly, the stage manager can narrate sound cues prior to playing anything in rehearsal. This is particularly important for effects that impact the action: a door knock that prompts a line, an offstage crash or gunshot, or the fading out of music that signals the start of the next scene.

PLANNING FOR EXTRAS

As the SM team prepares to incorporate new elements into rehearsal, take time to think proactively about what you will need to make the process a success.

- Do you need more time to set up? Does this mean overtime that needs approval?

- Do you need dollies to help cart things around?

- Do you need a better sound system in the room than your boom box?

- Do you need to borrow the production assistant from the other show to be on book because both of your ASMs will be moving scenic pieces?

- Do you need to return items to the shops at the end of the night? Do you have keys to do so?

- Can you leave things in the room? Is there a secure place for valuable items or electronics?

UPDATING PAPERWORK

As rehearsals progress, the SM team will add and delete props, make changes to the calendar, and gain new information about actor entrances and exits. Part of successful communication is keeping the relevant documents up-to-date and distributing those revisions to the production team.

Updated paperwork should reflect the new version number and date. Archival documents such as the character/scene breakdown might not need to highlight the updated information, but interactive documents will benefit from some additional formatting to make the new facts stand out.

The prop list in Figure 5.19 is a look at that information after three weeks of rehearsal. New items, first appearing in the rehearsal report, have been inserted. They are presented in blue

RENT
Revised Prop List: 6/12/10

Page	Prop	C	Character	Notes	R	A
~~61~~	~~Drinking Glass~~		~~Mark~~			
64	Quarter		Shannon/Roger			
67	Beepers		Mimi, Angel, Collins, Roger			
67	Pill	*	Mimi	Not in a pill bottle		
74	Mock door		Mark	With padlock & chain		
74	Open bottle of champagne		Roger/Mimi	With liquid		
74	(2) cups		Roger/Mimi		X	
75	Bag of potato chips	*	Maureen			
76	Cel Phone		Maureen		X	
77	Rope		Maureen		X	
78	Bottle of champagne	*	Collins	Will not be opened	X	
78	Small blowtorch		Angel		X	
~~82~~	~~Key~~		~~Benny~~		~~X~~	
84	(1) Champagne glass		Collins		X	
86	Small plastic bag of white powder		The Man	Given to Mimi		
94	White sheet		Multiple	Large enough to cover several people- for "Contact"	X	
111	Small projector		Mark			
111	Milk crate		Mark	Projector sits on it		
111	Dolly		Mark	For projector and crate		
112	$20 bills		Collins		X	
115	Acoustic guitar		Roger		X	

NOTE: "C" denotes consumable- props with asterisk will need replenishing

Figure 5.19 One page from a revised props list.

text to make the additions visually distinct. This makes it easy for the stage manager or props master to look at the list, remember what is new, and make sure there is a representative item for rehearsals. If the list is distributed in hard copy, and your team does not have easy access to color printing, consider another option to achieve this same heightened focus (use of bold, large asterisk outside the left margin, etc.).

Props that have been cut remain on the list, but the text has been struck through. The stage manager could remove the entries, but by choosing this formatting option instead, it is clear that the item is indeed cut and was not accidentally deleted during the updating process.

The SM team should have a consistent schedule for updating paperwork. It is rare that items will need to be redistributed more than once a week. It is also ideal to send out updated documents the day prior to your next production meeting, so that everyone can operate from the same version of the information.

If this prop list needed a version 5, the updating procedure would be as follows:

1. Turn all existing text back to black. In the next issue, it will not be new.

2. Insert all props added since the last version, and add notes to reflect any new information about them.

3. Change the font color for all above items to blue.

4. Update cut props to appear in strikethrough text.

5. Update the revision number and issue date.

6. Redistribute and update the copies posted on any callboards or show websites.

CONCLUDING TIME IN THE HALL

The final days in the rehearsal hall are for refining the work. The stage manager should anticipate running the show multiple times, with each run to be followed by a notes session. Continue to take important character-based notes during this time, and hold on to them for additional assistance during the run of the show.

The SM team is now eagerly anticipating the arrival of crew! We will meet the paperwork distributed to the crew in the next chapter, but it is during these final days when preliminary versions are created and checked to be as thorough as possible.

The stage manager should also make time to visit the theatre as load-in progresses. Adjustments are occasionally necessary as pieces are assembled, and the SM gains the opportunity to alter the rehearsal-room spike tape, so the director can address the blocking before arriving on the set if a big change is necessary. If it is feasible, you also might want to arrange a field trip for the cast. Standing on stage for even a few minutes will enable them to more successfully make their own transitions from tape to platforms, and to start incorporating a sense of the theatre into their final rehearsals in the hall.

If you are lucky, your schedule will permit a day or more to rehearse on the set before tech rehearsals begin. This allows sight-line adjustments and other small changes to happen in advance and could give the lighting designer a chance to see the actors in place as he or she finishes focusing lights and begins to create cues. The assistant stage managers get a preview of life backstage and may find additional duties that need to be incorporated into the crew paperwork. If such a day does not exist on your original production schedule, the stage manager should inquire about the possibility. You may face time or budgetary restrictions that preclude transition days, but you will never know if you don't ask!

CHAPTER 6

Technical Rehearsals

Technical rehearsals are one of the most exciting parts of the process for a stage manager. You are at the heart of the show, essential to the successful integration of all the production elements. With your guidance and expertise, the work of the actors, designers, and technicians seamlessly merges into a complete show.

The beginning of this new phase in the rehearsal process also brings with it new communication challenges for the stage manager. Your overall communication goals to be tactful, timely, and specific remain the same. But you now find yourself doing so on longer days and in the presence of the entire company at once—most of the time while in the dark and with one of your ears covered! The work done thus far has prepared the SM to introduce new personnel (the crew), coordinate multiple activities at once, and be mindful of time and space constraints.

TECH REHEARSAL TASKS

- Set up and label prop tables and map out backstage storage and changing areas.
- Revise paperwork documenting the placement and movement of technical elements.
- Train the crew to execute these moves.
- Learn to call lighting and sound cues.
- Write cues in the prompt script.
- Facilitate necessary adjustments for the actors as they move from the rehearsal hall to the theatre.
- Fully delegate responsibilities to your assistant stage managers.
- Manage the needs of all personnel.

CREATING THE TECH SCHEDULE

In most theatres, the schedule for technical rehearsals will be created by the production manager or technical director, who will apportion the available hours in the theatre to ensure there is adequate time to rehearse, and also an opportunity for the SM team to set up backstage and for production areas to attend to notes within the available hours each day and each week.

On an Equity production, additional rehearsal hours are usually available during the seven days before the first paid audience. Many contracts also allow the option for a longer day in which actors can work for 10 hours within a 12-hour time span, as opposed to the rehearsal period, when you worked seven out of nine hours, or possibly a shortened six-hour day that runs straight through without an extended meal break. Individual agreements outline rehearsal hours and dictate if and how "10 out of 12" days can be utilized. When personnel from other unions are working on the show (such as crew or musicians), the production manager will also balance the provisions of each individual set of union rules to create something that meets everyone's needs.

AEA stage managers may find themselves spending a week or more in technical rehearsals— a detail again dictated in each specific agreement. Academic productions typically have less time, possibly only two or three days. Some theatre departments opt to begin tech rehearsals on the weekend, allowing them to simulate the 10 out of 12 days by working for a longer period of time on a day with no classes, with subsequent tech rehearsals taking place on weekday evenings.

TYPES OF TECH REHEARSALS

Your tech period can include several different types of rehearsals, each intended to unite the production elements and the actors in a slightly different way. No show will need all of these events, but the stage manager should consider what is most beneficial to the process. Take full advantage of those planned for you, and be prepared to ask about useful options not on your original schedule.

Dry tech. A rehearsal without actors focusing on sequences where multiple cues occur at once: a transition where the lights change while music plays and scenery moves onto the stage. Such a rehearsal provides the designers and technicians a chance to synchronize their work without asking actors to stand around and wait. Be sure you have time to train the crew in advance, so the designers don't wait around either.

Cue-to-cue. A rehearsal with actors that skips over sections of the show with no cues. This can maximize the available time in the theatre by prioritizing technically complex moments. When working in this scenario, the stage manager should be sure to know when backstage prep moves or costume changes will take place. Even if no cues are called during these pages, running these sections of text allows backstage personnel to be sure they have adequate time to complete their work. The cue-to-cue can be a tricky choice, however, because it may turn out that a designer does need a cue in a section initially skipped over. Once you finally run the entire show, the SM might get additions—and have less time to practice these parts of the show.

Tech rehearsal. A stop-and-start progression through the entire show, often over multiple days. This is the most common circumstance under which the production elements and actors come together.

Quick-change rehearsal. A chance for actors and wardrobe crew to practice costume changes happening in under a minute. If such a rehearsal is needed, the SM should request time on stage prior to the first day the cast will work in costume. The actor will make his or her exit, get to the backstage location, change costumes, and reenter. The stage manager can rely on a stopwatch to determine if the speed of the change fits within the amount of time taken up by the dialogue or music happening on stage at that time, without calling those actors or technicians as well.

Sitzprobe. Exclusive to the musical, this is the first opportunity for the performers to work with the orchestra. This German term is loosely translated as "sit and sing." The conductor and musical director focus on timing, tempo, and fitting the music into the dialogue—without staging, scenic moves, or other cues. Productions that benefit from having performers on their feet for this work opt for a *wandelprobe* instead.

Dress rehearsal. A run of the entire show with no stops. For some theatres this marks the introduction of costumes. Other productions may allow the actors to work with wardrobe pieces for all rehearsals on stage. On a musical, this is often the transition from piano to full orchestra.

PREPARING FOR TECH

SM LOAD-IN

As noted in the previous chapter, the stage manager should plan to visit the theatre during the final days of scenic construction to get any necessary updates from the designer and technical director. Once the set is in place, the SM team can conduct a load-in of its own. You will identify the best locations for prop tables and quick-change areas, tape out sight lines, check for adequate running lights, and mark any potential safety hazards backstage. If actors move around the stage in the dark, you can strategically place glow tape to identify the edges of platforms, walls, and so on. The spike marks denoting the location of furniture and other scenic items should now be transferred from your taped-out floor in the rehearsal hall to the stage itself.

If you are working on a production with a nonunion crew, there will be few restrictions about working on stage beyond identifying a time to do so. You may be able to share time with other departments as they finish up their work—laying out backstage areas while the painters are at work, or placing glow tape and spike marks while the sound designer sets preliminary levels. The SM should make such a shared time request an agenda item for one of your final production meetings so the technical director or production manager can include this in the tech schedule.

If your production features an IATSE crew, the SM will find some additional challenges in those union regulations. Typically the stage management team is not allowed to do this work themselves (or actually handle the props or scenic pieces). In this case, coordinating a load-in will involve a more careful negotiation so that time can be allotted within the crew's work hours. You may find that you are unable to participate and instead provide a detailed list of needs to the production manager, technical director, or head carpenter on the show, so those duties can be included in the load-in schedule and addressed on your behalf.

> **IATSE** is the International Alliance of Theatrical Stage Employees, the union representing technicians in theatre, film, television, trade shows, and professional shops building scenery or costumes for these art forms. Similar to Actors' Equity Association, union members have specific work rules outlined in their contracts that must be followed by employers. These include schedule and safety issues as well as jurisdictional guidelines about working with production elements.

The stage manager should also think ahead about communication needs backstage. Prior to arriving in the theatre, provide information to the appropriate departments about the setup for headsets and cue lights—essential tools for talking with backstage personnel and triggering scenic moves or actor entrances.

TECHNOLOGY FOR THE STAGE MANAGER

Technological improvements in theatre are not limited to the designers. Today's stage manager has access to several new tools that enhance communication between the stage and the booth.

Cue lights. A light bulb mounted backstage and run to a switch box at the stage manager's desk. Cue lights can be used to initiate scene shifts or actor entrances when it is not possible to have personnel on headset in that area. The stage manager will turn the light on as a warning and off when the move or entrance should happen. Examples of the light and box can be found in Figures 6.1 and 6.2.

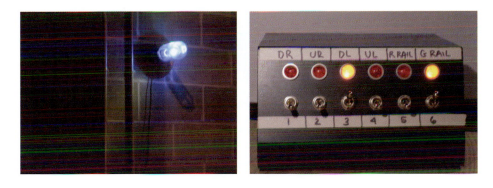

Figures 6.1 and 6.2 A cue light mounted backstage and the stage manager's control box.

Video monitors. The stage manager can use several different types of video monitors to receive detail about the show. A *stage monitor* provides a full from-the-front view of the stage, especially useful if you are calling from backstage or from a partially obstructed location out front. An *infrared monitor* allows the SM to watch the stage during a blackout and see actors and technicians not visible to the naked eye. The *conductor monitor* allows the stage manager of a musical to follow the gestures of the conductor as he cues orchestra members or singers. Figure 6.3 shows both of these monitors in use. Other specialty can provide an up-close view of a particular part of the stage, generally for safety reasons.

Each of these monitors would have a corresponding camera installed in the theatre— above the stage, in the house, or in the orchestra pit. A cable will connect each camera to the corresponding monitor(s). Small, easy-to-install cameras can often be purchased from companies specializing in security equipment, including the specialty infrared camera, which has a series of "emitters" surrounding the lens to enhance its night-vision capability to see people based on body heat. A theatre can often set up a camera and monitor for a few hundred dollars.

Headsets. Although not new, headsets are essential tools to allow the stage manager to talk to personnel backstage while sitting in the house or in the booth. This intercom system consists of a headset at the master control box (the base station), typically located with the SM, and individual intercom boxes with headsets run to board operators, your ASMs, and key locations backstage. Modern intercom systems can be equipped with an interface that permits the use of wireless intercom—meaning that personnel will have the same boxes and headsets but not the tether created by the cable when plugged into an intercom outlet on the theatre wall. (This might sound complicated, but it is much like the improvement that cord-less telephones provided over old phones with a handset connected to a base connected in turn to a phone jack.)

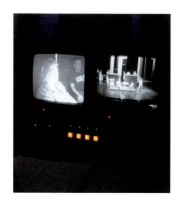

Figure 6.3 Conductor and infrared monitors in action.

If your theatre has a standard setup for this equipment that works for your production, the SM need only confirm these items will be in use. If you have a more complex backstage that requires more headsets than normal or cue lights in show-specific locations, the stage manager should document his or her request well in advance so that the load-in period can include this setup.

The map in Figure 6.4 details the setup for a very complex show. This production featured both flying and automated scenery, projections, and a host of called cues. The stage manager outlined not only standard-use items, but also some emergency backup gear. The technical director engineered the moving wagons to be operated manually should the automation computer ever fail during a performance. But the operators would move to the rear of each unit, leaving the normal control station on stage right. Rather than having to run additional headsets at the last minute, the emergency items were included on the original setup plan so they would already be in place if needed.

Due to the number of cues, many scenic moves and actor entrances relied on cue lights. The SM requested two separate colors for the bulbs. For tight sequences originating in the same area backstage, the stage manager could communicate specifically to both actors and technicians without uttering anything else over an already busy headset.

The map itself makes use of words, pictures, and color to make the specifics as clear as possible. It is the rare show that will need this type of backstage setup, but when required it is in the stage manager's best interest to invest the time up front to articulate requests, so everyone can plan appropriately or find a compromise setup if the initial scenario is not feasible.

DELEGATION

The SM team adopts a divide-and-conquer approach to the vast array of information during rehearsals, sharing responsibility for capturing details about the production elements. Everyone participates in setting up the room for the day, and the stage manager can get up just as easily as the ASM to reset a prop or spike a chair.

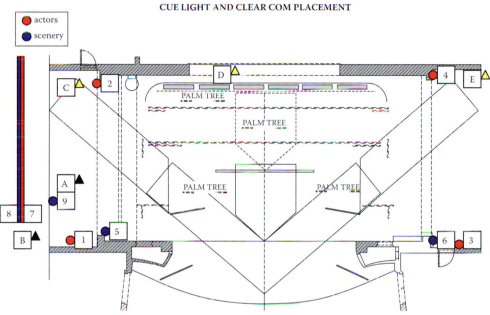

RUM & COKE
CUE LIGHT AND CLEAR COM PLACEMENT

CUE LIGHTS note: maker color indicates lamp color ● actors ● scenery (Except for rail that has both colors)

Circ. #	Box #	SM Label	Color	Perm.
	1		Red	Y
	2	UR	Red	Y
	3	DL	Red	Y
	4	UL	Red	Y
	5	SR WALL	Blue	N
	6	SL WALL	Blue	N
	7	Red rail	Red	Y
	8	Blue rail	Blue	Y
	9	Automation	Blue	N
	10	(Spare)		
	11	(Spare)		
	12	Late seating	Red	Y

CLEAR COM note: ▲ indicates regular use, △ indicates emergency back up (Wireless also in use for ASMs)

Circ. #	Box #	SM Label	Color	Location
	W1	ASM SR		Wireless
	W2	ASM SR		Wireless
	W3	ASM Spare		Wireless
	A	Automation	Black	SR
	B	DS Rail	Black	SR
	C	Emergency UR Deck	Yellow	SR
	D	Emergency UC Deck	Yellow	UL
	E	Emergency UL Deck	Yellow	SL
	F	Lights		Booth
	G	Video		Booth
	H	Sound		Booth

Figure 6.4 A cue light and headset map for a complex backstage setup.

Once you move to the theatre, the stage manager functions at a bit more of a distance: both physically due to your location out front and psychologically as you take responsibility for the big picture. The SM must rely on the assistant stage managers to oversee the deck. Be sure that you are talking with your team about the goals for the day. Share last-minute updates you receive on your way into the theatre. Information is not a commodity. Keeping it to yourself will only slow down the process.

WORKING WITH THE CREW

The day your crew arrives—whether one person or an army of technicians—is a happy event for the SM team. Throughout rehearsals you worked diligently to set up the rehearsal room quickly, facilitate scene shifts effectively, and identify potential problems. By the first tech, all of those details are firmly ensconced in your brains. One of the most significant challenges presented by the arrival of your crew is getting all of this information out of your heads and onto paper. Just as the stage manager wishes to empower the ASMs and delegate responsibility, the ASMs strive to train the technicians to set props and execute scene changes without constant supervision. In order to make that happen, the SM team creates several pieces of paperwork designed to relay all the necessary details to individuals who have never read the play or seen a rehearsal prior to their first day of work on the show.

THE PRESET LIST

The first of these documents is the preset list—a chart that outlines where everything goes at the top of the show. Formatted as a checklist, the preset list allows the crew to place everything correctly on stage and in the wings. Figure 6.5 provides you with a sample of the document at work.

The preset list is organized into sections addressing (1) onstage areas, (2) offstage prop tables, and (3) offstage locations for furniture and other large items. Each entry is listed in specific detail, grouping objects that are placed together.

The document can be set up in portrait orientation because the columns to check off that something has been set for each show can be much narrower than the column listing the items themselves. Choose a reasonable number of performances to include on the page. If you are running a production with an eight-show week, you might opt for eight check boxes and make fresh copies for each week. If your show performs six times over two weekends, you can fit the entire run. Try to avoid needing new paperwork within a show week itself.

On a long-running show, you can also consider making the preset list reusable. Instead of noting the dates, insert day-of-week initials, place the preset list into sheet protectors, and use a dry-erase marker. At the end of the week, you can clean off the list and start over.

The Farnsworth Invention   **PRESET LIST**

	October						
	10	11	12	13	14	15	16
Onstage							
Desk, with (in drawer):							
Clip-on Tie							
Legal Pad & Pencil							
Manila Folder							
Paper & Pencil							
Armless wooden chair with high back							

Bridge							
Stack of Homework							

Stage Right Furniture							
Russian Wagon							
Armless wooden chair with low back							
Conference Table, with:							
Conference Chairs 1 and 2 on top							
Conference Chair 3, with:							
Legal Pad & Pen							
Radio							
Conference Chair							
Two (2) Bentwood Chairs							
Square Table, with:							
Table Cloth							
Martini Glass							
Rectangular Table, with:							
Stock Ticker							
Padded Arm Chair							

Stage Right Prop Table							
Two (2) Champagne Glasses							
Five (5) Rocks Glasses							
Camera							
Four (4) Brown Beer Bottles							
Notebook and Pen							
SF Chronicle Newspaper							

Figure 6.5 A sample preset list.

Only a very minimal amount of shading is used to separate the individual areas onstage and backstage. Since you will be photocopying the preset list for distribution to the crew and SM team, color is of no use. And as is true with all other paperwork, the revision date and page number appear at the bottom.

When identifying the props and furniture pieces, avoid using character or scene names as descriptors. Your crew has just joined the production—it will be a while before they know the show as well as you and can remember the story.

The stage right furniture section of the sample demonstrates this technique. The square table was used by a character named Gifford for a scene in a restaurant. The ASMs know the table this way. But for the crew, describing it solely as a square enhances their ability to set it on the first day, and to put both the square and rectangular tables in the correct spots. This preset list also includes an armless wooden chair, a bentwood chair, a padded armchair, and a conference chair—easily distinguishable by description. (The conference chairs matched the conference table. And we've all seen enough movies and television shows with scenes in a board room to recognize the largest table backstage as that conference table. It's a reasonable exception to the rule.)

The preset list should indicate when items are set together, and one way to accomplish this is to indent. Our square table has a tablecloth and a martini glass. By listing those items immediately below the table and indenting them, it is clear they are a part of the table preset and not placed elsewhere. The same principle is at work for the desk set on stage at the top of the show. Several props start inside the desk's drawer.

Figures 6.6 and 6.7 Labeled prop tables and parking spaces.

For items set on a prop table, take care both to label the table and to use the same terminology found on the preset list. This makes it easy to both set and check. Oversized items will obviously not be placed on a table, but when laying out your backstage area, the SM team will identify storage locations for these pieces that utilize the same labeling consistency. These parking places will be important for managing backstage traffic during the show.

You might notice that the prop table photo above contains more items than appear in that section of the corresponding preset list. That is because our sample is only page one of a three-page

Cat on a Hot Tin Roof

PRESET LIST

ONSTAGE	M	T	W	R	F	SA M	SA	SU
Vanity								

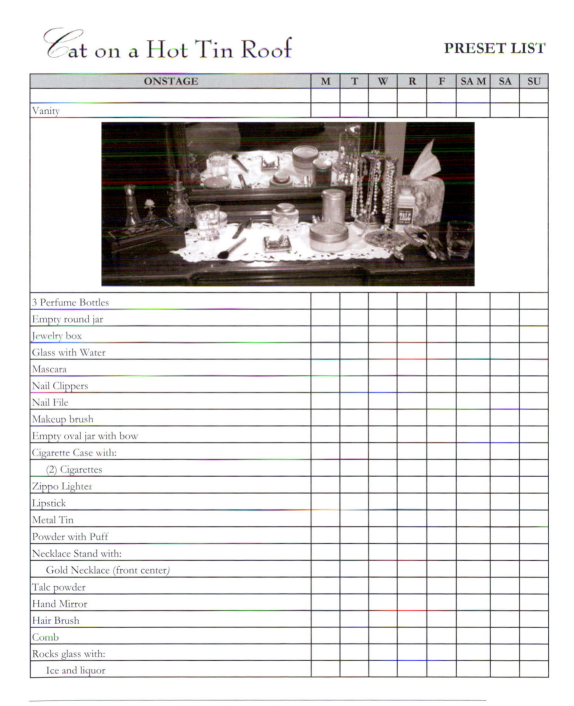

ONSTAGE	M	T	W	R	F	SA M	SA	SU
3 Perfume Bottles								
Empty round jar								
Jewelry box								
Glass with Water								
Mascara								
Nail Clippers								
Nail File								
Makeup brush								
Empty oval jar with bow								
Cigarette Case with:								
(2) Cigarettes								
Zippo Lighter								
Lipstick								
Metal Tin								
Powder with Puff								
Necklace Stand with:								
Gold Necklace (front center)								
Talc powder								
Hand Mirror								
Hair Brush								
Comb								
Rocks glass with:								
Ice and liquor								

Figure 6.8 Using a photo to clarify part of a preset list.

document. It will be rare for sections of the preset list to magically self-paginate. When you need to continue a section of the document to the next page, simply repeat that section's header. Page two of this preset list has "Stage Right Prop Table (continued)" as its first row.

There are times when too much description can work against you. Consider the excerpt of a preset list for *Cat on a Hot Tin Roof* for the top of Maggie's vanity in Figure 6.8. It contains 26 props, each with a very specific placement. Trying to describe both the items and their location solely in words would be overwhelming. By inserting a photo of the vanity top, the crew has both a visual of the completed setup along with an itemized list to check off.

MORE ABOUT PROP TABLES

A well-labeled prop table is actually a communication tool of its own. By specifying areas for each item, you are not only telling crew members where to place them but also telling actors what is there for their use.

When planning the layout for a prop table, the stage manager needs to know both where the prop starts and where it ends up. Not everything will make it back to its home, and your tables may need to provide bonus space for things that start and end on opposite sides of the stage.

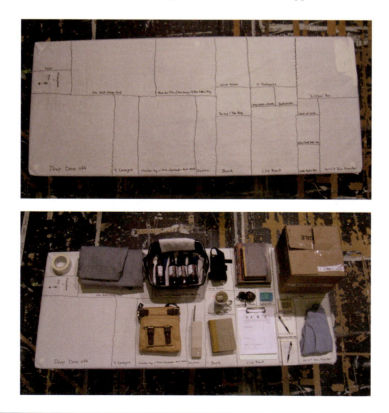

Figures 6.9 and 6.10 A prop table before and after it is set.

The pair of prop table photos in Figures 6.9 and 6.10 demonstrates efficient organization by the ASMs. Each prop has a defined spot. There is also a large block in which nothing is set at the top of the show. Marked "prop drop off," this space exists for those items that switch sides of the stage during the show. If the props were to be used repeatedly, it would be worth providing a labeled space for them on each side of the stage. But for things that will not reappear, a single area is sufficient. If the drop-off block gets full during Act One, the crew can clear it during intermission, readying the spot for Act Two props.

THE SHIFT PLOT

In addition to documenting how to accurately set up for the show, the stage manager needs to detail what happens once the curtain goes up. This is done through a separate document known as a shift plot, introduced in Figure 6.11. Cataloging every move taken by the backstage crew, the shift plot will capture when and how the following activities take place:

- Scenery moving on or off the stage
- Handing a prop to an actor
- Catching a prop from an actor
- Prep work for a scene change
- Fast costume changes that impact the deck crew

This piece of paperwork has the distinction of being both a detail document and one that will be read quickly in low light. This means that the stage manager will need some extra organizational and formatting tools to facilitate successful use of it.

NECESSARY INFORMATION

The shift plot includes a number of columns, each containing a valuable piece of information. These details are collected throughout the rehearsal process and enable the crew to accurately execute all moves in the show.

WHEN? The first two columns denote the order in which shifts occur. The SM numbers each activity or simultaneous group of moves. When more than one shift takes place within a single scene, they can be subdivided to identify a more precise order. Each event also has a time—when it takes place within the act. Times are presented cumulatively until intermission and then start over. Because intermissions can vary slightly in length, it is more precise to contain the running time to the act itself.

WHO? The next column identifies the personnel involved in the move. Actions may be taken by one or more crew members, assistant stage mangers, or even cast members. Although the document may not be distributed to the actors, their activities should still be included. This enables crew members to work with them or around them, and also allows the ASMs to check for their presence. By placing actor moves in italics, there is just enough visual distinction for substitute crew members to see they are not responsible for these tasks.

Twelfth Night

Revised Shift Plot

#	Time	Crew	Lineset	Unit	Move	Spike	Notes
Shift II-3 to II-4: After "Maria Hatches a Plan"							
9A	54:15	Hans	LS 22	Gate	OUT	Red	**RED RAIL**
		Courtney, Anastasia		Kitchen table	OFF		SL
		Meghan		Kitchen chair	OFF		SL
		ASM-L		Pit	UP		to AUDITORIUM level
9B	54:35	*don, luke*		*SR railing*	ON	*Blue* ▲	
		ASM-R		Curved Legs R	PAGE		
		austin, brian		*SL railing*	*ON*	*Blue* ▲	
		Matt		Curved Legs L	PAGE		
		Katie, Ashlynne		Wicker settee	ON	Blue ▲	SR
		Courtney		Wicker table	ON	Blue ▲	SL
		Anastasia		Wicker chair	ON	Blue ▲	SL
During II-4: "Cesario Falls in Love with Orsino"							
	57:00	Katie		(2) towels and robe	HANDOFF		SR to Austin
		Meghan		Self	Go SR		to be ready for next scene shift
Shift II-4 to II-5: After "Cesario Falls in Love with Orsino"							
10A	1:04:00	Katie, Ashlynne	LS 22	Wicker settee	OFF		SR
		Courtney	LS 15	Wicker table	OFF		SL
		Anastasia	LS 6	Wicker chair	OFF		SL
		don, luke		*SR railing*	*OFF*		
		ASM-R		Curved Legs R	PAGE		
		austin, brian		*SL railing*	*OFF*		
		ASM-L		Curved Legs L	PAGE		
		ASM-L		Pit	DOWN		
10B	01:04:30	Hans	LS 22	Gate	IN	White	**RED RAIL**
		Matt	LS 15	Colonnade	IN	White	**RED RAIL**
		Amanda	LS 6	Trees	IN	White	**GREEN RAIL**
		Katie		SR urn	ON		SR
		Ashlynne, Meghan		Garden bench	ON	Green ••	SR
		Courtney		SL urn	ON		SL

Figure 6.11 A page from the *Twelfth Night* shift plot.

WHAT? The next two columns list the specific prop or scenic piece affected. If the moving unit is a flying piece, the lineset number is included. When working on a show with no rail activity, this column can be deleted. The item description is brief, and should match the description used on the preset list and prop table for continuity.

WHAT HAPPENS TO IT? Next, the stage manager will describe the move itself. Specificity and consistency of verbs are key. Flying scenery can move *in* or *out*. Rolling units can move *on* or *off*. A technician can *hand off* a prop or *catch* it from an actor. If an item is moving to a new location but is still in use, it is being *reset*. If it is removed from the stage, the crew will *strike* it. Technicians might *load* a scenic piece by moving it closer to the stage to enable a quicker entrance in the next shift, or *park* it by moving it to a storage location once a shift is complete. Technicians might also need to *page* a curtain to allow actors or scenery to pass quickly through a wing.

WHERE DOES IT GO? Moving units will be traveling to a precise location, and the stage manager should record any spike information available. On a show with a simple deck layout, noting the side of the stage may be sufficient. A more elaborate show will need more detail in this column.

The two sample scenic designs first presented in Chapter 5 illustrate this difference. In *The Farnsworth Invention*, furniture pieces moved on and off specific platforms. Because only a few units ever played on each part of the stage and in distinct locations, the spike column on the shift plot could simply identify on which platform the move occurred. Personnel easily learned which spikes belonged to each piece of furniture and could place them accordingly. During *Twelfth Night*, a stock set of items played in a wide range of locations. Several units were placed in the same area of the stage at different times. In order to ensure that each shift was done correctly, colored spikes were used, and the shift plot references these colors.

Twelfth Night also presented an additional challenge—some shifts took place in light and others during a blackout. The color of the deck was light enough to make glow tape a bit difficult to see when not actually glowing. To manage these conditions, both colored spike tape and glow tape were used. But glow tape does not come in multiple colors. So how do you distinguish between several glowing objects in the same place? Shape. The small pieces of tape were cut in squares, circles, triangles, and other simple forms. The shift plot notes both the color of the spike tape for *a vista* shifts and the shape of the glow tape for those happening in the dark.

WHAT ELSE DO WE NEED TO KNOW? By providing a notes column at the far right, the stage manager has a spot to provide whatever other information is necessary. This might include the manner of cueing or the fact that a prop hand off takes place during a fast costume change. "Notes" is a general enough heading to accept all these details and allow the stage manager to vary the entries as necessary.

PROVIDING LANDMARKS

Even though the shift plot includes running times, this is not quite enough information for the crew, particularly on a busy show. The shift plot is subdivided according to the scenes of the play.

These subdivisions have two characteristics. First, these headings reference the scene that has just ended or that is happening at the time, beginning with the word *after* or *during*. Identifying an activity as happening *before* a certain scene presents the same challenges as describing a prop by the character that uses it. During the early days of technical rehearsals or a performance with a substitute crew member, the stage manager is asking the crew to act based on information they don't have yet. This leads to the unpopular "oops, I was supposed to …" realization once that scene begins.

Subdivisions based on scene numbers are equally useless. An effective shift plot will include scene nicknames based on easy-to-identify plot points. When working on a musical, using identifiers based on song titles can be effective as well.

Crew members will have additional responsibilities at the beginning and end of each rehearsal or performance. The shift plot begins with these pre-show duties, noted in Figure 6.12, and ends with a section to address post-show. Setting props will be one of these tasks. Given the amount of detail and differences in formatting, it would be difficult, if not impossible, to find a common setup for these two documents.

FORMAT CONSIDERATIONS

It should now be clear why the shift plot is described as a detail document. On a busy show, the SM team has a significant amount of information to convey. The formatting work will help do this successfully. The basic requirements can be achieved with either a word-processing table or a spreadsheet.

The landscape orientation best suits the shift plot because it provides enough width to fit all of the columns. Column headings are repeated at the top of each page. A moderately sized font allows everything to fit and still be read easily. In general, a single line of text for each activity is best. Some wrapped text appears in the preshow duties, but those lines will be read in full work light and under less time pressure. Setting up the entire document in portrait orientation would necessitate a smaller font size or much more wrapped text—either scenario making the document more crowded and less accessible.

WHITE SPACE

Each column is slightly wider than the longest text entry in it. And when multiple shifts occur in the same scene, there is an empty row in between them. These techniques are providing the eye a place to rest. To help reinforce which actions happen simultaneously, the shift and time columns for each group have been merged so that the information appears centered in a larger box.

Twelfth Night
Revised Shift Plot

#	Time	Crew	Lineset	Unit	Move	Spike	Notes
Preshow Duties							
		Hans, Matt		Deck	SWEEP		
		Courtney, Anastasia		Deck	MOP		
		Katie, Meghan		Prop tables	SET		see preset list for details
		Courtney		Urns	SET		onstage for fight call
		Meghan		Toaster	SET UP		on counter in green room
		Meghan		Flask	FILL		1/2 with water
		Meghan		Wine bottle	FILL & CORK		1/4 with water
		Hans, Matt	LS 9, 21	Legs	IN		clip to boom and screen
		Hans, Matt	LS 6, 10, 15, 22	All flying units	TEST		End with colonnade left onstage for fight call
		Katie		Shrine	ON	Red //	
		Courtney, Anastasia		Pit Steps	ON		pit is all the way down
		ASM-L		Pit	CHECK		PIT POWER IS ON (light switch lit)
		ASM-L		Fan in pit	OFF		
		ASM-L		Pit remote	MOVE		arrange cable so you won't be run over by railing later!
		Hans	LS 15	Colonnade	OUT		fly out on SM request during fight call
		Courtney		Urns	OFF		strike to preshow spots on SM request during fight call
		All Crew		Glow tape	CHARGE		
		Video		Projector carts	SET		also run video test once plugged in!
At the 15 minute call							
		Meghan		Toast & Juice	PREPARE		make toast, pour juice, deliver to tray on SR prop table
Into I-1: After Opening Storm							
1A	2:20	Amanda		Shrine	OFF		DR cue light

Figure 6.12 *Twelfth Night* preshow duties

SHADING AND COLOR

Only a minimal amount of shading has been used for the subdivision headings. While it might seem useful to employ color to reinforce these rows or emphasize the spike mark detail, this document gets photocopied. Each technician will need one, along with all members of the SM team. The document will also inevitably be updated as tech rehearsals progress. Practicality does not support repeatedly printing this multi-page document in order to use color.

PAGINATION

One final way to manage the information on the page is to keep the sections of the document together. Achieving this means not splitting shifts. Our preset list was functional with repeated headers when one section flowed to a second page. Because the shift plot is used in low light and with little time to stop, turning the page during a scene shift can ever-so-briefly affect the user's concentration and slow him or her down. The stage manager should use the page break options available in the chosen software to keep sections together. At times this will mean leaving some additional blank space at the bottom of one of the pages. Small adjustments to the overall page margins and column widths of the completed plot can help you achieve a balance between many half-filled pages and shifts that don't quite fit.

UPDATING THE SHIFT PLOT

The shift plot with which the stage management team begins tech rehearsals should be considered a well-organized plan A. No one is at fault if extra duties arise, a job takes more crew than you expected, or the production team decides to take a different approach to a transition. Throughout tech the stage managers will keep notes on changes and additions in order to update the paperwork.

Crew members can also make valuable contributions to the updates. Encourage your crew to take their own notes and inform you about other tasks they find themselves undertaking. This does not mean that crew should rework shifts on their own, but the ASMs cannot be everywhere at once. If, for example, a crew member finds himself holding a flashlight during a fast costume change, that should end up in the shift plot. The actor and wardrobe crew will become dependent upon this assistance. If you have a substitute technician on the deck one night and that job isn't written down, no one might remember to ask for the light until the change is in progress and not going as well as normal.

The SM team should provide the crew a revised version of the shift plot by the next time you rehearse that section of the show. If your tech rehearsal schedule is set up to work Act One on Tuesday and Act Two on Wednesday, new paperwork will not be needed until Thursday. The stage managers can enter the first night's changes right away but wait to reprint the paperwork until they have rehearsed both acts and have a full set of changes. When the schedule dictates running the full show each day, updates will be processed more quickly.

THE ASM POINT OF VIEW, PART TWO

Another young stage manager, Kristen Harris, offers her view of life on the deck: "One of the most important things I have found during the tech and preview process is flexibility. As the show is coming together artistically, there are bound to be things that are added or cut, and being flexible during these long rehearsal days allows changes to be implemented seamlessly backstage."[1]

PAPERWORK VARIATIONS

Not every show is as large as the samples presented here. And while these productions benefitted from two sets of paperwork for the deck crew, the stage manager may be able to simplify the work for less-active productions.

When working on a show with no internal prop or scenic moves, the stage manager can adapt the preset list to serve as the sole piece of paperwork. By adding a "pre-show duties" section at the beginning and a corresponding "post-show duties" section at the end, tasks not related to the props can be listed and checked off.

If your crew has shift duties only at intermission, you might still consider a single document. By adding one more sections to the preset list for those intermission tasks, you can successfully detail all backstage responsibilities. The SM's main concern should be efficiency—and a separate document to list only a few tasks may not qualify.

Considering the other extreme, there are times when you may find yourself working on a show where the quantity of flyrail or automation cues prompts you to separate them from the prop handoffs on the deck to make the plots clearer for the individual operators. In this circumstance, working in a spreadsheet such as Microsoft Excel will be your best software choice. The worksheets within an individual document can be linked. The SM can simply highlight and copy all columns of the completed plot, and then paste them into a second worksheet using the Paste Special function. Select Paste Link, and the pages are joined (Figure 6.13). It is then possible to delete all unessential information from the second worksheet to create a customized plot for certain technicians. As long as the stage manager makes all updates to the original master version, the linked pages will automatically contain the changes.

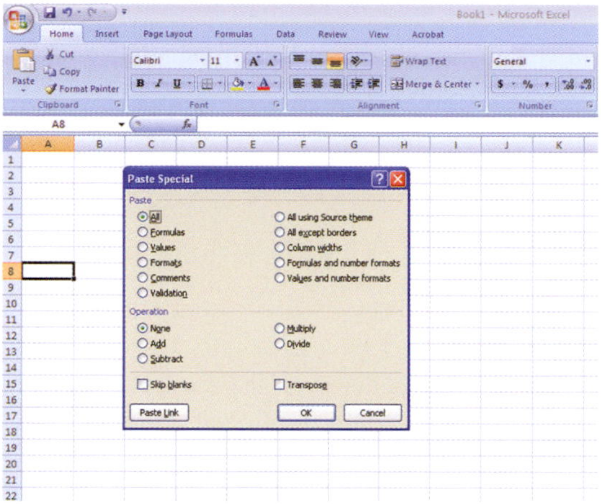

Figure 6.13 A screen shot of the paste special functions in Microsoft Excel.

THE COSTUME PLOT

The last major piece of backstage paperwork is the plot documenting the actors' costume changes throughout the show, seen in Figure 6.14. Like the shift plot, this is a detail document for the show.

The content of the costume plot is similar to that of the shift plot—several different categories of information denoting when and where activities occur. Each change has time markers, and the overall plot will be subdivided by scene. The SM team should use the same subdivisions and the same nicknames to create continuity between the two documents and help the entire crew talk about the show in the same language.

The most significant difference in the philosophy of the two charts is that the costume plot tracks where the actor exits and reenters as well as the change itself. Large scenic units rarely have more than one offstage location due to space, and these locations are clearly delineated in the companion preset list. If you know you are moving the conference table, you know where you will be. Actors are much more flexible! Wardrobe crew members need locations for every change.

WHERE SHOULD THE CHANGE TAKE PLACE?

Fast costume changes are best located as close to the reentry spot as possible. If the actor switches sides of the stage, it is best to travel first and change later. This helps to manage unforeseen delays caused by a problem with the costume. As soon as the actor is dressed, he or she is ready to go—and doesn't have to run around the theatre before entering.

Act I

Run Time	Actor	Exit Location	Exit Character	Exit Costume	Re-Enter Location	Re-Enter Character	Re-Enter Costume	Length (FAST)
During Opening (After Footloose)								
3:45	Lauren Cmernik	SL	Teen	Purple Dress	SL	Rusty	ADD Lavender Sweater	:12
	Cassie Pacelli	SL	Teen	Base Costume	SL	Urleen	ADD Blue Sweater	:12
	Seth Steidl	SR	Teen	Base Costume, NO hat	SR	Jeter	ADD cowboy hat	:12
	Kyle Olson	SR	Teen	Base pants and shoes, club shirt	SR	Bickle	CHANGE shirt to base costume	:12
During The Girl Gets Around								
13:30	Colleen Schulz	SR	Wendy Jo	Purple Blouse/Denim Skirt	SL	Wendy Jo	Base costume	
	Cassie Pacelli	SR	Urleen	Base Costume and Sweater	SL	Urleen	REMOVE Sweater	
After The Girl Gets Around								
A (17:30)	Sarah Shervey	SL	Ariel	Blue Dress, character shoes	SL	Ariel	Jeans, Black halter, **boots**, jacket	:30
B (17:30)	Austin Hernandez	SR	Chuck	Base Costume, NO Jacket or Hat	SR	Chuck	ADD Jacket and Hat	
	Corey Holloway	SR	Travis	Base Costume, NO Jacket	SR	Travis	ADD Jean Jacket	
After Somebody's Eyes								
	Justin Cooke	SR	Ren	Base Costume	SL	Ren	Buger Blast Uniform and skates	
	Derek Sveen	SL	Coach Dunbar	Track Suit	SL	Coach Dunbar	Gym Uniform	
	Seth Steidl	SR	Jeter	Base Costume	SL	Jeter	Gym Uniform	
	Alex Atardo	SR	Garvin	Base Costume	SL	Garvin	Gym Uniform	
	Kyle Olson	SR	Bickle	Base Costume	SL	Bickle	Gym Uniform	
	Anna Mae Beyer	SR	HS Kid	Base Costume	SL	HS Kid	Gym Uniform	
	Kristen Lake	SL	HS Kid	Base Costume	SL	HS Kid	Gym Uniform	
	Bobby Black	SL	HS Kid	Base Costume	SL	HS Kid	Gym Uniform	
30:00	Annelise Escher	SL	HS Kid	Base Costume	SL	HS Kid	Gym Uniform	
	Casey Schneider	SR	HS Kid	Base Costume	SL	HS Kid	Gym Uniform	
	Kaylin Wolf	SL	HS Kid	Base Costume	SL	HS Kid	Gym Uniform	
	Erica Bush	SR	HS Kid	Base Costume	SL	HS Kid	Gym Uniform	
	Cara Cook	SR	HS Kid	Base Costume	SL	HS Kid	Gym Uniform	
	Rhys Wolff	SL	Wes	Base Costume	SR	Wes	ADD Coat, tie and Choir Robe	
	Kelsey Taunt	SL	Lulu	Blue House Dress	SR	Lulu	Black Print Dress and Choir Robe	
	Lily Cornwell	SR	HS Kid	Base Costume	SR	HS Kid	Gym Uniform	
After Burger Blast								
A (47:00)	Justin Cooke	SR	Ren	**Burger Blast uniform**	SR	Ren	**Base Costume w/ Hoodie**	ASAP

NOTE: Length provided for fast changes only. Items in bold require assistance of wardrobe crew.

Figure 6.14 A sample costume plot.

The costume plot is set up to track every time an actor adds or removes clothing. One way to streamline the document is to use descriptive phrases rather than listing each garment separately. In the production of *Footloose* referenced in the sample, most characters had four main looks—a base costume, a gym uniform, clothing for church, and a prom dress or tuxedo. The cast and costume crew had master lists from the designer of the individual pieces for each look—a costume preset list of sorts. Referencing the look in the plot rather than its components required fewer words, helping the accessibility of the information. Of course, if a character is simply adding or removing a single item (a hat, sweater, etc.), that is all the stage manager needs to record. Principal characters like Ariel changed costumes more frequently and at different times than the ensemble members. This made it appropriate to detail her changes differently—the shortcut technique did not apply.

Speed is an important factor in costume changes. The plot is set up to identify those changes considered fast (less than one minute) as well as those that will require assistance.

In plays or musicals where actors portray more than one character during the play, the "character" column helps track that information. Although in this production only some actors played multiple roles, the stage management team set up the chart based on the most complex information needed.

Changes are grouped according to their location, with actors listed in the order in which they reentered the stage.

FORMAT CONSIDERATIONS

The costume plot and shift plot bear several formatting similarities as well. Both are best presented in landscape view, with column size and blank rows set to maximize white space. Running-time cells are merged to unite simultaneous events, and shading is used only minimally to reinforce subdivisions.

The plot header and footer are repeated on each page. For the costume plot, a two-row header best organizes the details, banding together the exit and reentrance facts. Changes do not need to be numbered, because the stage manager will not call them, but the use of A and B helps to point out multiple sets of activities within the same scene.

The discussion of these three major pieces of paperwork should reinforce the importance of delegation within the stage management team. The assistant stage managers are best suited to oversee these activities backstage and to update the corresponding documents during tech. This keeps the SM free to undertake his or her own major projects—managing the big picture and calling cues.

CUEING

PARTS OF A CUE

Every cue has three parts: the preface, the action, and the trigger. The **preface** refers to the element changing along with its sequential number in the show (lights 19 or shift 4A).

The **action** is the word *go*. Occasionally you may also use the word *stop* to announce the end of a manual move. For example, a fog machine might be turned on when the stage manager says "fog, *go*" but turned off when you say "fog, *stop*." Saying "fog end *go*" is clumsy and not quite natural speech. Cues can be **triggered** by a word in the text, an action taken by a performer, a beat of music, or even the end of an appropriate pause.

CUE NAMES

Over time a common vernacular has developed for the prefaces of cues for each production area.

Lights: Any lighting change that occurs by pressing the Go button on a light board. On Broadway and in some dance companies, the word *electrics* is used instead.

Sound: Recorded effects or music

Shift: Scenic moves

Rail: Flying scenic moves, if a separation from deck cues is warranted

Auto: Computer-controlled scenic moves

Effect-specific: Sequences involving spotlights, pyro, fog, haze, snow, or other similar special effects are commonly labeled by the equipment itself.

The advent of projection and video design has introduced new categories of cues and necessitated the development of additional names that have not yet found the same standard across the industry. Video is a clear-enough preface to indicate the start of a movie sequence. Projections are a bit trickier. In the early days, the word tab was used. It referred to the computer key pressed to execute a change. Because projections today are controlled by a wide range of programs, that word has fallen out of use. Some stage managers preface these cues as *projection* or *slide*. My personal preference is the word image. It is aurally distinct (*slide* and *lights* can sound alike) and has fewer syllables than *projection*.

PLACING CUES IN YOUR SCRIPT

The stage manager writes all cues into the prompt script, using the oversized margin created during the photocopying process. Cues are marked as precisely as possible, written on a line that extends to the trigger. Often the stage manager will note visual triggers immediately above or below the drawn line rather than boxing a blocking number. Figure 6.15 is a sample page showing the placement of cues for a transition between two scenes. Additional cue page examples were presented in Chapter 4.

RECEIVING CUES

Cues come to the SM in the form of lists provided by the lighting and sound designers, samples of which can be found in Figures 6.16 and 6.17. The shift plot functions as the scenic cue sheet. Some productions will schedule a **paper tech** to discuss the technical elements. This is a meeting attended by the stage manager, designers, and director. It provides everyone

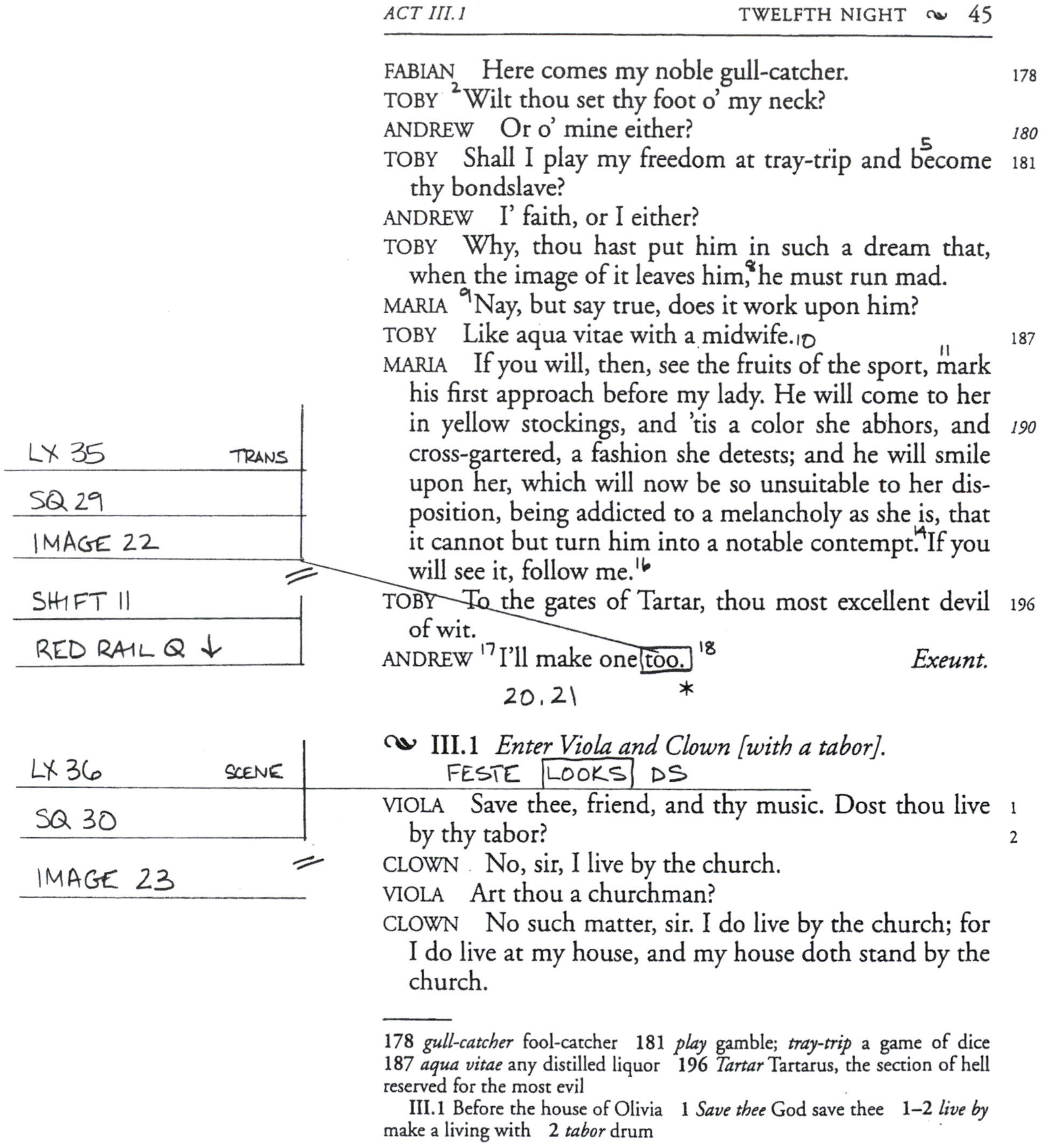

ACT III.1   TWELFTH NIGHT ∾ 45

FABIAN   Here comes my noble gull-catcher.   178
TOBY   [2]Wilt thou set thy foot o' my neck?
ANDREW   Or o' mine either?   180
TOBY   Shall I play my freedom at tray-trip and become   181
    thy bondslave?
ANDREW   I' faith, or I either?
TOBY   Why, thou hast put him in such a dream that,
    when the image of it leaves him,[?]he must run mad.
MARIA   [9]Nay, but say true, does it work upon him?
TOBY   Like aqua vitae with a midwife.[10]   187
MARIA   If you will, then, see the fruits of the sport, mark
    his first approach before my lady. He will come to her
    in yellow stockings, and 'tis a color she abhors, and   190
    cross-gartered, a fashion she detests; and he will smile
    upon her, which will now be so unsuitable to her dis-
    position, being addicted to a melancholy as she is, that
    it cannot but turn him into a notable contempt.[?]If you
    will see it, follow me.[16]
TOBY   To the gates of Tartar, thou most excellent devil   196
    of wit.
ANDREW   [17]I'll make one too.[18]   Exeunt.

LX 35   TRANS

SQ 29

IMAGE 22

SHIFT 11

RED RAIL Q ↓

20.21   *

∾ III.1   Enter Viola and Clown [with a tabor].
    FESTE LOOKS DS

LX 36   SCENE

SQ 30

IMAGE 23

VIOLA   Save thee, friend, and thy music. Dost thou live   1
    by thy tabor?   2
CLOWN   No, sir, I live by the church.
VIOLA   Art thou a churchman?
CLOWN   No such matter, sir. I do live by the church; for
    I do live at my house, and my house doth stand by the
    church.

---

178 *gull-catcher* fool-catcher   181 *play* gamble; *tray-trip* a game of dice
187 *aqua vitae* any distilled liquor   196 *Tartar* Tartarus, the section of hell
reserved for the most evil
    III.1 Before the house of Olivia   1 *Save thee* God save thee   1–2 *live by*
make a living with   2 *tabor* drum

Figure 6.15 A cueing page from *Twelfth Night*.

The Wild Party

WORKING LIGHTING CUE LIST

	Cue	Time	•	Pg. / Sys. / Mes. / Beat	Description	Intels	Spots
Pre-Show	I	5		Pre-Show	House Full & Preset		
Pre-Show	2	5		Pre-Show	House to Half		
Pre-Show	3	3	•	Pre-Show	BLACKOUT		
#1 - Opening	4	5		Pre-Show	Music Stand Lights up, cueing musicians to start.		
#1 - Opening	5	8		I / I / 3 / 3	Add city sky-line & stage glow		
#1 - Opening	6	8		2 / I / I / I	Add deep blue down light		
#1 - Opening	7	8		2 / 2 / 2 / I	Add backlight special CS for Queenie		
#1 - Opening	8	6		2 / 3 / 3 / I	Add spots on Queenie		2 & 3 - Queenie
#1 - Opening	9	8		3 / 3 / 3 / I (she)	Add colors in dim pink	Colors - dim pink full stage	

Figure 6.16 An excerpt of a lighting cue sheet for *The Wild Party*. Used with permission of Sean Michael Smallman, lighting designer.

Sound / Projection Cue List

S	Cue	Page	Type	Called on	Description	Where
Scene 3	27	20	Video	At top of scene	Fast and Furious plays on one screen, living room look on rest	
Scene 3	AF	20	Sound	Autofollow	Strreet noise fades out	
Scene 3	28	20	Video	MAMA:" No you are not"	TV snaps off	
Scene 3	29	21	Video	DAD: "...if you don't mind"	Newscast w/ bombs on TV (@W1)	
Scene 3	30	21	Video	VISUAL as Mama turns off TV	TV off	
Scene 3	31	21	Sound	MAMA: "...stands for hyperactivity"	Blast of rap music from Jesse's room (@2)	
Scene 3	32	21	Sound	DAD: "Turn it off!"	Rap music fades down a bit	
Scene 3	33	21	Video	VISUAL as Dad turns on TV	Video of Pres. Bush (@W1)	
Scene 3	34	22	Sound	DAD: "You worry too much."	Blast of rap music upstairs	

Figure 6.17 An excerpt of a combination sound and video cue sheet for *Distracted*. Used with permission of Sean Michael Smallman, sound and projections designer.

the chance to talk through the entire show before the first tech rehearsal, confirming individual placements and discussing groups of cues that will happen simultaneously. If provided ahead of time, the SM should arrive at paper tech with cues written into his or her script and make adjustments warranted by the discussion. At other times the SM will receive the cues during paper tech, writing them into the prompt script as they are discussed. Despite the value of such a meeting (in either form), not all theatres will schedule one. In some cases the SM might meet individually with designers and in other instances receive only the lists themselves.

SPECIFICITY IN THE SCORE

Identifying a specific note within a piece of music, particularly when there are no accompanying lyrics, requires the designers to use a different technique. Individual notes are referenced by using a set of numbers that identify their location by the page, system, measure, and beat. (This can be seen in the placement notes for the light cues in Figure 6.16. If you need further explanation of these references, please review Figures 5.2A and 5.2B.)

THE STANDBY

Once all cues are placed, the stage manager adds standbys into the script. These warnings alert board operators and other technicians to an upcoming cue or sequence of cues. Standbys should be placed approximately one half-page before the cues begin, allowing time for the SM to warn all necessary operators and to receive confirmation that everyone is ready. For cue-heavy sections of a script, the stage manager groups cues in the standby—warning lights 10–17 and sounds 4–9, for example.

When multiple departments are included in a standby, the stage manager should announce them in a consistent order. This commonly means standing by (1) lights, (2) sound, (3) video/projections, (4) scenic moves, and (5) effects. If cue lights are in use, the stage manager should include them in both the standby and go sequence, placing their notations at the end of the above list.

It is helpful to make the standby distinct from the cues placed into the script. This can be achieved by drawing a box around the standby or even placing it on a small Post-it. Should the stage manager be in problem-solving mode during a performance, the additional visual element will help remind the SM to prepare for the next cue sequence.

CALLING KEY

The final element of preparing the prompt script for cueing is to create a calling key. Similar to the blocking key, it serves as a guide to the symbols and notation used within the script. The SM will not need the calling key at hand during tech; you should be able to read your own pages without help. The key is intended to help other stage managers who might use your script. Figure 6.18 presents my key for a production of *Urinetown*.

The key outlines your method for marking cue placement. This includes abbreviations, symbols for turning on and off cue lights, bracketing cues to be called together, and your method for identifying specific triggers. When working on a musical, many stage managers

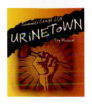

CALLING KEY

ABBREVIATIONS

LX	Light Cue ●	
SQ	Sound Cue ●	
SHIFT	Scenic move ●	(call standby only- ASM gives crew cue to go)
S/B	Standby for one or a series of cues- listed in small yellow post-it, always in above order!	
↑ or ↑↑	Cue lights ON (standby)- one arrow for single cue light, double arrow for multiple cue lights	
↓ or ↓↓	Cue lights OFF (GO)- one arrow for single cue light, double arrow for multiple cue lights	

CUE LIGHT LOCATIONS

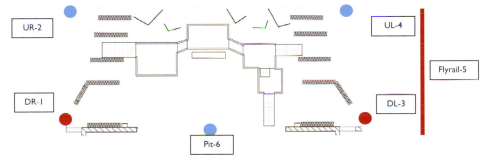

PLACEMENT WITHIN SCRIPT

- A cue drawn to a line of text with a box placed around a single word or syllable means the GO is called on that <u>word</u>

- A cue drawn to a line of text with an X at the beginning or end of the line means the GO is called immediately <u>before or after</u> that line/lyric

- A cue drawn to a line/lyric with no specific box or X but with an action written to the right of the cue means the GO is called on <u>that specific action</u> of the character, which generally occurs during the line or lyric underlined

- A cue drawn to a line/lyric with no specific box or X but with "vox" to the right of the cue means the GO is called to <u>anticipate the vocals</u> in that song or verse (watch conductor)

- A cue drawn to one in a series of numbers means the GO is called on <u>that specific beat</u>- may also be seen as "on 3" or similar notation for calling GO within the measure preceding the vocals

- A cue drawn to the symbol ♪ means the cue is called to <u>anticipate the downbeat</u> of the music (watch conductor)

- Cues which are bracketed together should be called simultaneously with a single GO

- Descriptions of lighting change or sound effect are provided within cue box whenever possible

---

Figure 6.18 A sample calling key.

employ semitransparent colored dots to help highlight specific score placements. The color and location of these dots would also be explained in the key.

WATCHING, READING, AND TALKING

During tech rehearsals the stage manager calls each cue as it is written in the prompt script, taking care to follow notes precisely and to articulate as clearly as possible. This ensures that changes are executed in the exact spot chosen, so that everyone can see if adjustments are needed. A designer might change the length of a cue or request a different placement; a director might ask the stage manager to move the cue in relation to an action on stage. And even without receiving a note, the SM can sense how best to land a cue to make it work as intended. But all these scenarios are dependent upon accuracy with plan A.

During early rehearsals it can be difficult for the stage manager to get his or her head out of the script and look up at the stage. One of the secrets to an effective call is to leave space between the cue preface and the word *go*. This space provides the SM time to listen for an individual syllable or look up to watch for a specific action. When calling a musical, cues within songs will happen at precise locations in the music. The video monitor providing the SM with a close-up view of the conductor will allow you to correctly anticipate these moments, and the space provides you that chance to watch for the appropriate signal.

WORKING ON HEADSET

Nearly every directive from the stage manager during tech will be delivered over headset. Most of the technicians with whom you are communicating will not be able to see you at all, making it essential to speak clearly and to develop a consistent method for warning and executing cues.

When working with new board operators or ASMs, try to find a moment before the first tech rehearsal begins to let them know what they will hear from you and what you expect in return. Describe the fact that you will always insert a tiny pause before the word *go* and emphasize that operators should wait for that word. Clarify the type of confirmation you want after a standby. Typically that will be "lights," "sound," "stage right," or the equivalent. Voices always sound slightly different over an intercom system, and you may not be able to tell who has replied if the response is "okay" or "standing by."

When calling very fast sequences, the stage manager may need to limit the number of words said in order to get all the *go*s in the right place. Explain this to your operators, and remind them of this difference in the standby if you need to. For example, the production of *Footloose* for which I was the stage manager included a tight sequence of cues at the end of the first act—four light cues on each of the final three beats of music and a blackout in rhythm one beat later, followed by the main curtain coming in and then the house lights up for intermission. This entire sequence lasted five seconds. There was no way to say more than the actual word *go* on a single note. I called the sequence by saying "lights 136 through

139— *go, go, go, go* and then throwing a cue light to bring in the main curtain when we were at black. Once the curtain landed, I could announce, "Lights 140 *go*." This worked well and allowed me to be very precise. Under other circumstances the SM might need to drop just the cue number at times to save the syllables. As long as your operators know what you are doing—and you resume using cue numbers as soon as you can—find whatever method lets you talk quickly enough to make everything happen.

THE ART OF IT ALL

The stage manager has everything written down, but the joy of live theatre comes from responding to each individual rehearsal or performance, working in sync with the performers. Susan Threadgill, Director of Production for University Events at the University of Texas at Austin, offered this apt description of the art of calling cues:

> *A stage manager is never "given" his or her cues; there is a dialogue between the stage manager, the director, and the designers to determine when the audience should become aware of the cue; when the cue should resolve; and whether the cue is dependent on the music, dialogue, or action. Because the art form is live, the conditions for the call of the cue could be, and often are, different every night.*

> *A good stage manager adapts to his or her given circumstances on the fly. The conductor is moving slowly tonight and has tacked on a total of two minutes in Act One alone ... change the call to make the cues **work**. The leading actor has entered a bit late and is not clear of the area where the Act Two wall comes to the deck... change the call to make the cue **safe**. The ensemble has risen to new heights in the final scene and needs one half-second more with this phenomenal moment ... change the call to make the cue **right**.*[1]

STEPPING UP TO RUN THE SHOW

The consolidation of all elements and personnel marks the beginning of a transition in authority for the show. Most directors and designers depart after opening, and the stage manager will be tasked with maintaining the collective artistic vision until closing night. Tech rehearsals are designed to let you learn the intricacies of doing just that.

Tech rehearsals also prompt a change in priority from written to verbal communication. You will continue to prepare and distribute rehearsal reports, but you are now interacting with those same individuals constantly throughout the day. Bring the same sense of professionalism and clarity to your conversations that you showcase in your reports. Provide the information you have. Seek details you are missing. Take notes (no one remembers everything). Even when you are stressed, try to remember that you do love your job!

Throughout this book, I have used the words *authority* and *responsibility*. Note that you do not find the word *power*. Power implies control over other people and a hierarchy of who is right and who can act. Remember that theatre is a collaborative art, and being entrusted with the job of bringing everyone together is not the same as being made the boss of them all.

It is also important to remember that not everyone with whom you interact will be able to both see and hear you. Backstage personnel on headset will be informed by the tone of your voice. Staff sitting in the house may see only the expression on your face or the hunch in your shoulders. Your words, actions, and body language are still working in harmony to communicate your thoughts and feelings, whether you like it or not.

If you are overtly frustrated or overwhelmed, everyone will know it. If you exude confusion, you undercut trust in what you say and do—and even in the paperwork you have prepared. Project confidence; breathe; remain calm. Make sure you actually take at least part of your breaks to step out of the theatre for a moment and away from the chaos.

Undoubtedly, it is far easier for me to type these reminders than for you to live them. With experience you will learn to manage your emotions and go with the flow. As a new stage manager, it is common to take everything personally. In Chapter 1 we first discussed the complexity of seeing the difference between someone yelling at you and yelling toward you. When a director or designer is upset, it is easy to assume they are upset with you. Trust in the work you have done so far. Expect that there will be changes. Remember that many times it isn't anyone's fault. As time and money become limited, tensions rise. And as the central point of communication, much of that tension comes your way. Over time you will develop the skill to listen and not automatically react.

In addition to setting the tone, responsibility for the big picture requires the stage manager to keep goals in mind and use time wisely. You have the authority to announce, "Hold, please," and make everything stop. But the stage manager should always evaluate what adjustments warrant that stop. When safety is at risk, or multiple departments need to make changes for a moment to work, time is best spent addressing those issues right now. Moving a piece of set dressing a few inches upstage or calling a ten-count cue a beat earlier can probably be handled with a note and adjusted for the next day.

While you are holding, be sure that work is taking place. If the lighting designer indicates it will take a few minutes to reprogram a sequence, this might be a good time to add a newly requested piece of glow tape or allow the director to give an acting note on the previous scene. Tech rehearsals can be slow—multitasking helps offset that trait. And when work resumes, the stage manager should make sure everyone is back in place and then clearly announce where the scene will pick up.

REHEARSAL REPORTS DURING THE TECH PERIOD

The stage manager continues to prepare rehearsal reports during the tech period, but the content changes. It is not necessary to catalog adjustments made to the show during rehearsal itself. Most production teams also gather briefly at the end of each night of tech. These short production meetings provide the opportunity for feedback and questions that were not possible while everyone was working. The SM does not need to document this entire discussion either.

As your days are getting longer, your reports in general are getting shorter. This is both appropriate and convenient. Members of each production area will be present during tech rehearsals, taking their own notes or at times fixing problems right in the moment. The SM team can certainly use the extra time to update paperwork and script notations before the next rehearsal.

The notes in the tech rehearsal report primarily focus on information acquired without everyone present. This could be news of a broken prop—discovered at the end of the night as a crew member put it away. It could be a comment the director forgot to pass along during the postshow meeting, or one that came from a cast notes session not attended by the designers. It could also be a request based on a problem-solving session the SM team had time for only after everyone else was gone.

On occasion, though, the SM may be asked by a production area to repeat a note given during the day. This might be to ensure that it does not get forgotten, or because it is a job for a member of their department not in attendance. Be sure to follow those requests and include the information. And if you are unsure if a note was given earlier, cover your bases and write it down.

After the final dress rehearsal, the company is ready to add the final component to make the show complete—the audience.

CHAPTER 7

Performances

Figure 7.1 The stage manager's view during performances.

The audience is an essential component of theatre. Performing in front of a live audience is what makes our art form different from television or movies and keeps the experience new and fresh every night. Each time the house lights dip to half, the entire company takes a leap together—hoping that everything will unfold as planned, and that all the work will pay off.

The audience on night forty deserves to see the same show as those in attendance on opening night. The stage manager is responsible for maintaining the artistic and technical components of the production, so this will be possible.

PERFORMANCE TASKS

- Maintain the director's vision.
- Ensure that the artistic and technical components of the production remain accurate and consistent.
- Work with front-of-house personnel to look out for the audience.
- Incorporate understudy, substitute, and replacement cast and crew members into the production.

PREVIEWS

In many professional settings, the first nights in front of an audience are part of the rehearsal process. Preview performances exist to allow the company to "test" the production and make adjustments based on the reaction of patrons. Evening previews can be followed the next day by additional rehearsals to refine a technical moment, clarify an onstage relationship, or, in some cases, to make major changes to lines or blocking.

The stage manager must help the entire company to work with extra efficiency. The time allotted for rehearsals during the preview weeks of an AEA contract is traditionally much less than other points in the rehearsal process. Areas of the show in need of work are selected precisely, and adjustments must be communicated very clearly, so that everyone understands how these new elements weave into the show as a whole.

STOPPING DURING PREVIEWS

Technically, because the preview is a rehearsal, the stage manager could stop the show so that an error can be corrected. Practically, the culture of stopping during a preview is very specific to an individual theatre. Some companies will welcome moments to stop and reset to remind the audience this is still a rehearsal. Others will treat the presence of any audience the same and resist stopping for anything besides a true emergency. The SM needs to understand the point of view of the theatre's artistic leadership in order to accurately assess how to proceed when complications arise.

REFINING YOUR ROUTINE

The presence of any audience places a time constraint on preshow activities. If things run behind during tech rehearsals, you might get under way later than originally planned. And while this might be an unpopular experience for the production team, no one else is left waiting. Audiences are generally allowed to enter the theatre 30 minutes prior to the performance—meaning that all setup must be completed by that time.

The stage management team facilitates this goal by developing an order for preshow activities once dress rehearsals begin. Identify tasks that can happen simultaneously, as well as the overall order of all jobs. The SM and ASMs take responsibility for overseeing specific portions of the setup to ensure not only that everything gets done, but also that it happens in the most efficient manner possible. These include tasks performed by the crew as well as the stage managers themselves. In some professional theatres, this will include taking over tasks previously completed by members of the design team, such as conducting the dimmer check with the light board operator.

In an academic setting, or one with nonunion crew, the development of the preshow routine will primarily be determined by the SM team. When working with union crew, the stage manager will partner with the head technicians to coordinate tasks within the contractually defined responsibilities of individual technicians and the allotted preshow work time. By the time you reach previews and performances, this routine will be set and allow both backstage and front-of-house needs to be met.

RUN SHEET

The stage manager should document the overall flow of the preshow activities, creating paperwork that would help a substitute SM to be in exactly the same places at the same times. The run sheet shows how divided responsibilities fit together, and how the preshow section of the shift plot fits with actor time on stage before the house opens.

FORMATTING AND CONTENT

The run sheet is not a document to be widely distributed and does not need a significant amount of formatting. The sample found in Figures 7.2A and 2B is a simple list, specifically for the SM, containing two types of information: the time and what happens. Stage managers looking for more structure in the list or wanting a place to check off completed activities could either utilize a formatting style reminiscent of the preset list, or place the run sheet in a sheet protector and use a dry-erase marker to cross off jobs as they are completed each day.

Recently I have also seen stage managers load their duties into smart phones or tablets, giving them the ability to mark an activity as complete by touching it on the screen. This makes for a very portable list, but it will not be useful for a sub. If you opt to work with an electronic device, I recommend keeping a printed copy in the prompt book as a backup.

Very basic headings break the duties down into those happening before the show, during the show, and after the show. The times are included for both evening and matinee performances to prevent the SM from repeatedly stopping to translate from day to evening when looking at his or her watch.

Note that the content of the entries does not presume previous knowledge. This is particularly important for academic productions. Not everyone may know where the light switches are located, who needs to attend fight call, or which ASM will call missing crew members. The goal of the run sheet is to provide as much specificity about how to get to the start of the

Twelfth Night

SM RUN SHEET

PRESHOW

5:15 pm /11:45 am   Arrive at theatre

Turn on house, work, and grid lights from touch panel backstage (SR or SL)

Unlock doors:
-back of house left and right
-stage door left and right
-lower house door left
-dressing rooms, makeup room, laundry room
-storage room: open and place stage weight in door
-green room
-room 70

Unlock booth and turn on lights

5:45 pm /12:15 pm   Check for crew arrival. Ask Cara to call anyone who is late.

6:10 pm/12:40 pm   Check in on video setup & make sure dimmer check is happening
Check glo tape onstage and replace any missing pieces
Check cue lights
Confirm headset check is complete

6:15 pm/12:45 pm   Check sign in sheet for actors- Ask Melissa to check for missing folks & call anyone who is late.

6:25 pm/12:55 pm   Be in house for rail check. Pay special attention to amount of stretch in ropes on LS 6 (trees)

Be prepared to make a slight adjustment if hitting the out spike means flying the bottom of the tree hardware above the first electric. (Trees will catch and not come in correctly during the show if this happens)

6:30 pm/1:00 pm   Stage Open

6:35 pm/1:05 pm   Make sure fight call setup is onstage: colonnade, 2 urns, bench

6:40 pm/1:10 pm   Fight Call: Antonio, Sebastian, Fabian, Andrew, Viola, Toby
Sword fight and fist fight
** keep ASM and rail on standby to fly out colonnade/strike urns after sword fight

6:55 pm/1:25 pm   Close stage
Final check of onstage preset
Make sure pit power is on

Go into Lights 1 and Sound .5

7:00 pm/1:30 pm   Open House
Announce half hour dressing rooms

7:15 pm/1:45 pm   Announce 15 minutes in dressing rooms then check in with ASMs

---

Figure 7.2A The stage manager's run sheet for *Twelfth Night*.

7:20 pm/1:50 pm	Check in with House Manager then head to booth
7:22 pm /1:52 pm	Call 5 minutes over cast call mic and headset
7:27 pm /1:57 pm	Call Places over cast call mic and headset
7:30 pm /2:00 pm	Begin show (or when receive "house is closed" from house manager) Crew on headset to start- lights, sound, (2) ASM, (2) projections operators

Top of show places:
> SR- Orsino, Prescott, Hart, Coffin
> SL- Olivia, Hernandez

INTERMISSION

At 8 minutes in	Call 5 minutes in dressing rooms then check in with ASMs
At 10 minutes in	Check in with House Manger- head to booth
At 13 minutes in	Call Places
At house closed	Check for places, all crew back on headset

Part Two Places:
> SR- no one
> SL- Toby, Andrew, Fabian, Maria

POST SHOW

At house empty	Announce house is closed and ask for work lights & call Sound 46

Go down to deck and check in with ASMs and crew
-prop notes
-consumables check

Go down to dressing rooms to check with actors & costume crew

Pit back up to auditorium level, fan off, power off

Lock all doors that were unlocked at beginning of show

Collect stuff from booth, turn out lights, lock door

(Make sure center projector in booth has been turned off!)

Go to office: write report, email it to production team, and post on theatre callboard in hallway and online on show website

Figure 7.2B The stage manager's run sheet for *Twelfth Night*.

show as the script does in how to execute the cues. This, at times, might include a narrative explanation of why something happens, if the reason is not obvious. The italicized note below the check of the flying scenic pieces is an example of this.

OPENING NIGHT

Opening night marks a new phase for your production. It is the point at which reporters can attend a professional production and review the work. It also begins the final set of guidelines within an Actors' Equity contract, outlining new rules about when actors need to arrive at the theatre and how much rehearsal can take place each week. (Yes, there is still rehearsal!)

The opening night audience will be different from any other group of patrons you are likely to see during the run. In addition to the press, the house is filled with friends, family, and fans. They will applaud often, laugh loudly, and inevitably give you a standing ovation at the end of the night. While this enthusiasm is welcome, it often impacts the rhythm of the show in a unique way. The SM should always be sensitive to the dynamics of an individual audience. But it is important to recognize that although tonight you may wait longer than ever before to call the scene-change cue at the end of a big song, this is not a permanent change simply because you have reached performances.

The opening performance may begin with curtain speeches or other acknowledgements requiring an alteration of cue sequences. The SM should think ahead to be sure these special events can happen successfully. Does the preshow music fade directly into the "turn off your cell phones" announcement, which itself fades directly into the first sound cue? You might need to coordinate with the director and designers for a temporary adjustment so there can be silence for a speech at some point. Is there adequate visibility in the preshow light cue for someone to stand on stage? You might also require a one-night-only lighting or follow spot addition. It is best not only to get verbal confirmation that adjustments have been made, but also to have the operators go through those sequences to ensure they are correct. And once someone removes these extras from the show after opening, make sure to review the sequences on night two as well to make sure they are really gone!

WORKING WITH FRONT-OF-HOUSE

The arrival of the audience brings the stage manager a new partner for overseeing the show—the house manager. The house manager is the liaison between the audience and the production, and is responsible for the order and safety of the patrons.

In order to do this job successfully, the house manager needs to know about the nightly schedule as well as elements of the show that could affect members of the audience. These include physical aspects of the production that could exacerbate a patron's medical condition or content issues that could impact his or her enjoyment of the play. This same information may be requested by the box office staff in order to successfully answer questions from ticket buyers.

The stage manager might convey these details verbally by meeting with the house manager or box office manager prior to the first night the audience will be in the theatre. Describe the relevant production elements with conciseness and specificity—remember that the house manager is as new to the show as your crew was only a few days or weeks ago. Answer questions thoroughly, and consider walking through the theatre during the meeting if you have a particularly audience-impactful setup.

Other theatres may request written documentation in order to provide the same information to all staff members and volunteers who will interact with the audience. Figure 7.3 is a sample of a front-of-house information sheet that can be used to capture a wide range of production facts.

Much like a rehearsal report, the front-of-house information sheet contains organizational and time information at the top and devotes the bulk of the document to specific details in a series of categories. The first set of questions addresses general concerns relating to the overall performance. These details allow the house manager to know about interaction between the stage and audience areas of the theatre. Some items are general information that could impact any venue, while others may be more important to a specific theatre configuration. The existence of a scene change during a blackout, for example, has little impact on patrons of a proscenium-style theatre. But an audience member sitting in a thrust space could try to step out into the lobby at the exact moment a large furniture piece is en route to the stage down the same vom. Knowing this detail allows the house manager to make an informed decision about the best location to station ushers inside the theatre during the show.

The second and third categories focus on production-specific details. These include the physical components of the design such as fog, gunshots, or strobe lights, along with content considerations such as profanity, smoking, and adult content. There is little the house manager can do about these aspects of the play or musical, but, with information, he or she can be prepared for audience members who leave early, complain at intermission, or demand refunds.

FORMAT

The front-of-house information sheet is designed to present the information cleanly with streamlined formatting considerations. As with other paperwork discussed in this book, the form is set up to capture the broadest range of information. A performing arts center with multiple performance spaces might not want individual layouts for different venues. Details have specifically defined and labeled boxes, placed on the page in sections devoted to each category. Individual questions can be concisely answered yes or no, and space is provided for supplemental details or explanations. Questions not applicable to an individual theatre can be marked as such. White space sufficiently separates each category, and the prominence of the show title allows users to easily differentiate this sheet from the one belonging to other productions. A busy theatre might wish to further distinguish individual venues. The lack of shading on this form would allow the use of colored paper with no loss of accessibility.

NAME OF SHOW

FRONT OF HOUSE INFORMATION SHEET

Opening Date:	Closing Date:	Theatre:
Director:	SM:	ASMs:

RUNNING TIMES

Act One	
Intermission	
Act Two	

GENERAL

	Y/N	NOTES
Latecomer Seating Hold		Length of Hold:
Actors Enter through House		
Actors Travel into Audience		
Audience Members Onstage		
ASL Interpreters Scheduled		
Scene Change(s) in Blackout		
Obstructed Views		
Preshow Fight Rehearsal		

EFFECTS

ONSTAGE Gunshots		
OFFSTAGE Gunshots		
Fog/Smoke		
Strobe Lights		
Flash/Smoke Pots		
Other Loud Sound(s)		
Other Effects		

CONTENT

Characters Smoke Onstage		
Characters Drink Liquor Onstage		
Drug Use Depicted		
Violence Depicted		
Nudity		
Profanity		
Sexual/Suggestive Content		

Additional Notes/Information:

Figure 7.3 An information sheet for front-of-house and box-office personnel.

THE PERFORMANCE REPORT

The stage manager continues to provide daily updates about the production after opening. Like the rehearsal report, the performance report is an official document of the production and maintains the link between the show and its artistic and technical personnel.

RECIPIENTS

- Director and SM team
- Designers
- Production manager
- Shop heads receiving rehearsal reports
- Theatre personnel with new run-of-show responsibilities
- Executive personnel (if requested)
- Production stage manager (if you have one)
- Faculty advisors (academic theatres)
- House manager (some theatres)

What It Contains

- Details of the day's show
- Upcoming performances
- Technical problems fixed before or during the show by the crew
- Unresolved technical issues needing attention
- Information about illnesses or injuries
- Front-of-house details as requested

Why Do It

- To document the events of the performance
- To provide updates or make requests regarding technical problems
- To report audience size, patron issues, or other requested house information

The performance report should maintain the formal written communication style of the rehearsal report. Although information may be categorized differently, the same care should be used to tactfully and specifically relay all details. It is unlikely the relevant team member

PERFORMANCE REPORT

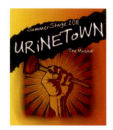

Production: URINETOWN

Date: Saturday July 9

Stage Manager: Laurie Kincman

Assistant Stage Managers: Shelby Krarup, Erica Perrin

House Open	7:00 pm
Curtain	7:31 pm
Act I	1:05:45
Intermission	16:30
Act II	53:52

Next Performance Sunday July 10		
Time	**What**	**Who**
12:15 pm	Call to Theatre	Cast and Crew
2:00 pm	Curtain	All

Actors or Crew Late:

Sabrina Diehl (absent-excused). Duties covered internally by Nick Martin.

Notes to House Manager:

No notes tonight, thank you

Problems or Repairs:

15. COSTUMES- The shoulder seam on Kelsey's dress has ripped again. Kris is coming in early tomorrow to repair it.

16. COSTUMES- The lining inside Lockstock's jacket has a large rip on the left side. Kris was unsure how to tackle this problem.

17. SOUND- Alex's mic picked up a strange interference during the first scene. He was switched to a different transmitter when he exited after "Privilege to Pee."

18. FACILITIES- The upstage-left emergency lights came on for no reason at 7:25. They were reset by the crew after a few minutes and did not come back on during the show.

Accidents or Injuries:

Laura was feeling ill tonight but was able to perform in all her scenes and songs.

Additional Notes:

Nothing else tonight, thank you

Thanks everyone,

- Laurie Kincman
Stage Manager

Figure 7.4 A performance report from *Urinetown*.

was present for the performance. Providing context for technical notes allows staff members to work effectively to solve any problems that took place. Did you try a repair that was unsuccessful? Will the temporary fix hold for a few shows but then need further attention? Have you exhausted the supply of backups?

CONTENT CONSIDERATIONS

The sample performance report in Figure 7.4 provides a format for the relevant details for the run of the show. Requested organizational information again appears at the top, presented in largely the same manner as it was during rehearsals.

The schedule overview component includes the first significant change in content. Everyone receiving the document knows there was a performance last night. It is not necessary to list out the calls. Of more concern is how smoothly the performance ran. A late opening of the house might indicate work on a technical issue or problem in the box office. The same rationale prompts including the length of the intermission. Directors pay particular attention to the running times of individual acts—large unexplained variances from the original pace of the show will prompt concern, and the stage manager should not be surprised to hear from the director if this is an ongoing event. These times also contextualize any potential feedback from audience members regarding their overall experience. A reminder of the next performance concludes the time section, serving as a reminder of the deadline for any potential work needed on the show.

The meat of the report is again devoted to the presentation of specific details. The requested information for this theatre includes a more prominent accounting of absences and late arrivals, front-of-house issues, and any technical notes. If your theatre requests the information be presented in a certain way, you should defer to the provided format, as you did with rehearsal paperwork.

At this point in the process, it is not essential to subdivide the technical notes and acknowledge when there is no information for each designer or shop head. Problems and concerns can be addressed in a single section of the report, with care taken to prominently identify the department who is receiving a note. If you prefer to maintain individual department areas in your report, use your rehearsal report as a template and adjust the other areas of the document (such as the schedule and run times) to capture the new information to be recorded.

The *Urinetown* sample includes several different kinds of technical notes: problems resolved during the show, a note that can be addressed by the crew the next day, a note beyond their capability, and an unusual facilities issue needing attention from personnel outside the production team. The SM wants to include this range of detail in the report. It might seem unnecessary to document problems that were solved, but a pattern of mic problems lets the sound-department head foresee a larger potential issue, if one exists. Continual mending of the same costume piece might warrant replacing it in the future. And if no proactive response is needed, department heads are made aware of the hard work being done by the crew.

Some theatres also request that performance reports include such other information as the ticket count for the night, any special guests in the audience, or even the weather (especially in outdoor venues). This sample could easily be modified to include another section for these details.

FORMATTING THE REPORT

Because the performance report serves a similar function to the rehearsal report, it is logical that it contains many of the same formatting principles. The formal tone is maintained by the continued use of complete sentences and correct grammar. The report is typed in the same commonly available font as other show paperwork, and in this case also continues to use a graphic from the show to provide a quick visual identifier as to which show this report belongs. The numbering of notes continues, but resets back to one.

The reader's eye is guided by two techniques—adequate white space within each section of the report, along with the use of capital letters to highlight the technical areas receiving notes. (This is the trade-off for not including individual sections for each department.)

DISTRIBUTION

The final parallel between the rehearsal and performance report is distribution. The report should be sent promptly following each show to all production team members. In the case of a two-show day, the SM should investigate theatre policy about sending a report during the dinner break versus sending two reports at the end of the night. Due to the shortened amount of time before the next performance, it is not always feasible for staff to read email, get to the theatre, and complete any repairs before the evening show. In many instances you will be able to set up a system that "no news is good news" between performances. Urgent problems are often best communicated through a phone call. The SM might be able to receive all necessary information verbally, or at least instructions on how to start a repair while the needed staff member is driving in. Be sure that you know what you will do before the first weekend is upon you, and be sure that your production team is on the same page.

The avenues of distribution should match your rehearsal report. If you have been sending it via email, continue to do so—with any adjustments to the recipient list warranted by personnel changes. If you also post copies, do this as well. You may think that no one will look at a posted report in between the Saturday evening performance and the Sunday matinee. Perhaps you are right, but perhaps not. As always, it is best to have the information available, should anyone need it.

CHANGING PERSONNEL

Opening night typically marks the departure of the director, along with designers who are not resident to the theatre. Although these team members remain connected to the show by continuing to receive reports, they will not be able to provide any hands-on attention to problems that arise. The stage manager might need to expand his or her communication circle to include theatre personnel not previously associated with this show who take on new responsibilities during the run. For example, daily oversight for the lighting created by a guest designer might be a task for the theatre's resident lighting assistant.

It is wise to talk in person with the new team members before simply adding them to your email distribution list. You can establish a more personal connection and bring a new contact up to speed with the history of production elements in their area. Do you have ongoing problems with a piece of equipment and anticipate frequent notes for continued repairs? Is there a cast member who has recently been ill and whose understudy has not yet had a costume fitting? By providing some advance context for your reports, the new personnel will more easily be able to support the show's needs and save you from providing lengthy explanations later on.

MAINTAINING THE ARTISTIC INTEGRITY OF YOUR SHOW

Now that the director has left the production, the stage manager assumes full authority for maintaining its artistic components. Even if the director does not leave the theatre company itself, he or she often begins work on a new show and will not give your production primary focus.

Artistic maintenance of the show is first achieved by continuing to call cues accurately. There is a difference between responding to the ebb and flow of live performance and deciding now is your chance to "fix" a cue you never liked. The latter is not your job.

Occasionally you may find that a moment in the show grows over the course of the run and warrants a design adjustment. If, for example, an auto-follow cue is now consistently cutting off the applause at the end of a song, the SM reports this change and requests assistance. The designer can then ask that the board operator make a programming adjustment (extending a wait time, making the second cue manual, etc.). Your observation is apt, and clear communication that respects the designer's work will lead to a solution.

The stage manager also looks out for the work done by the actors. Your task is to watch the performance with the director's vision in mind, giving notes when required to keep everyone on the same page. This means looking out for added business or ad libs, altered blocking, changes in pace to individual scenes, or anything else that impacts the rest of the cast and the overall show.

Giving notes to the cast can be a tricky endeavor. Not all performers will be receptive to your observations. Although you have been part of the show since day one, the SM plays a very different role during the rehearsal process. You did not create the blocking or the character, and your feedback can sometimes come across as an indicator that the actor is doing something wrong.

So how does the stage manager approach this situation? Be proactive. You know this job is coming, so do everything you can to position yourself for success. Actively listen to notes sessions during rehearsals. Notice how cast members react to receiving line notes or late arrival calls. Consult the director for specific things he or she would like you to look out for. And if you are a new stage manager, consider asking the director to share this information with the cast during one of the final notes sessions before opening, so it is clear that your authority on the show includes this duty.

And once the run begins:

1. **Remember that anyone can have an off day.** Unless it is an issue of safety, apply a "one for free" filter to your notes.

2. **Recognize that shows do grow.** Is the change within the parameters established during rehearsal? Has the actor simply become more comfortable with an aspect of their character and found something new that the director would encourage if present?

3. **Prioritize technical aspects of the performance.** Is the actor now crossing farther stage left than originally set and walking out of light? Has the actor changed the timing of her entrance, causing a blocking problem for someone else on stage? Performers may more easily accept those big-picture observations from your position out front.

4. **Consider timing when delivering notes.** Your feedback will be better received at the end of one night's performance than it will be at the fifteen-minute call the next day. Providing the actor time to think about the note will be less intrusive to their process.

5. **Show the actor respect.** If you need to deliver a note that concerns the quality of a performance, do not do this in front of a full dressing room. Consider delegating part of your postshow routine to your ASM so you can be available to talk with the actor as he or she leaves. Or pop your head into the dressing room and ask that the actor find you on the way out so you can "ask a quick question." This avoids potential embarrassment or the implication in front of the rest of the cast that an actor is doing a poor job.

6. **Ground your feedback in the show.** Now is the time to use those artistic notes you took during character rehearsals and run-throughs. By employing the director or actor's own words, it will be clear that you are not trying to take the production in a new direction.

7. **Find out if you have backup.** In the case of an actor who might be negatively impacting the show but with little interest in receiving your notes, do you have options? Is the director close enough to come back to see a performance if needed? Is the theatre's artistic director available in an extreme situation? Looking out for the show also means knowing when you need help to do what is best for everyone.

In general, verbal notes come across as less autocratic than written notes. The SM will also be able to use his or her skills reading body language to gauge how the feedback is received. You might have three notes to give. Perhaps the performer can only handle one tonight. Or perhaps the change has been prompted by another actor. Verbal notes also provide the opportunity for a conversation to take place.

Most Equity contracts permit a small number of rehearsal hours once a show opens. The specifics vary with each agreement, but an average of 10 hours per week is generally available—documented in each individual rule book. Brush-up rehearsals can be an effective way to address a physical change that impacts several actors, or to clean up fight or dance scenes in need of more concentrated work than the preshow schedule allows.

In an academic situation, you are unlikely to have designated rehearsal time after opening, aside from a possible brush-up rehearsal if several days transpire between performances. But in exchange for this, the SM has other options available that do not exist in professional theatre. There is no overtime penalty involved if you need to call one or more actors early to address a problem from the night before; you may have access to the actors during the day and can discuss notes in between classes or over lunch; and the director is often a faculty member and never very far away from the production.

WORKING WITH UNDERSTUDIES

The stage manager's duties during the performance period also include working with the understudies in the cast. Should one of the actors be unable to perform on a given day, the understudy will step in to cover the role. In most instances, the understudies will not have a chance to work on the role during the rehearsal period. These actors attend rehearsals to learn blocking and observe character work, but may never get up on their feet. After opening, the SM will conduct understudy rehearsals to provide them an opportunity to work through their characters and become acquainted with the set.

UNDERSTUDIES VERSUS SWINGS

An understudy is a member of the cast who learns the role of another actor and is prepared to step in should the primary actor be unavailable due to illness, injury, or absence. Understudies can have this "substitute" duty as their sole position in the acting company, or they might be ensemble members learning a second role in addition to their primary work in the show.

In the case of a musical that has a chorus, swings may also be required. A swing is a multi-actor understudy who is asked to learn the roles of several (or all) chorus members of their gender and to be prepared to perform for any one of these actors. A chorus member could also be a partial swing—indicating that he or she has been hired to learn the role of a fellow chorus member for numbers in which they do not normally appear. Each type of AEA agreement outlines specific requirements for understudies and swings, which vary by cast size and type of show within each agreement itself.[1]

Not all productions have understudies. Only certain Equity contracts mandate having such backup for the performers, and academic productions do not always have enough students to cast two sets of actors. If you are working on a show without understudies, it is important for the SM to know what would happen if an actor becomes ill or injured so that such emergency planning could be put into action quickly.

UNDERSTUDY REHEARSALS

On most productions, understudy rehearsals begin during the week following opening night. The stage manager will focus on accuracy with lines and blocking, delivering any acting notes within the same guidelines as those for giving feedback to the primary cast. The intent of understudy rehearsals is to give these cast members a chance to re-create the roles developed by the original actors, in case they are required to perform. Understudy rehearsals are attended by the understudies themselves as well as the SM team but not other members of the cast. Typically they are conducted with only minimal technical support—working with scenery and props but not lights, sound, or costumes, for example. When working on a show with fight choreography singing or dancing, be sure that the understudy rehearsals include the chance to review these elements as well and that the appropriate staff is in attendance—your musical director, fight captain, or dance captain.

CAPTAINS

The **dance captain** is a member of the cast of a musical who is assigned the responsibility of learning all the choreography in a production and assisting the other actors with learning and maintaining the steps. The **fight captain** has similar responsibility for all stage combat, and will run the review of all combat moves before each performance—known as a fight call. On an Equity production, these actors will receive additional compensation for this work.

Non-Equity or academic productions might provide opportunities for understudies to get up on their feet during the initial rehearsal process. The amount of rehearsal time and theatre tradition will guide the SM to know if he or she should pursue building this into the schedule. If this is not possible, then the stage manager should plan to hold understudy rehearsals on the AEA model.

PUT-IN REHEARSAL

Because understudy rehearsals do not involve the primary cast in their normal roles, the SM will need to call a specific rehearsal to work important moments with those actors in the event an understudy is going on. As a rule of thumb, I never ask an actor to sing with, dance with, fight with, or kiss another actor for the first time in front of an audience. The put-in rehearsal will also address tricky physical or dialogue timing, actions that trigger cues, and anything else that could not be replicated during understudy rehearsals.

You will almost never have a full complement of understudies to individually cover each role in a large show. During understudy rehearsals you might need to run a scene twice for an actor covering two roles. You might also send your ASM on to read lines for an uncovered part or to handle a scene shift. The put-in rehearsal allows the understudy the chance to work necessary parts of the show with the correct people and with all the technical elements in place.

The limited work hours available after opening are also intended for these understudy and put-in rehearsals. If you know in advance that an actor will be out, the SM can proactively schedule put-in time. In the case of an emergency, you will most likely be calling actors to ask them to come early to the next performance to address parts of the show.

In most cases, you will call only the actors directly affected by the existence of the understudy to the put-in rehearsal. The exception would be when an understudy for the lead role in a show is slated to perform. Your emergency scenario may not change, but with advance notice the SM might be able to arrange for one day with only the affected actors and a second day to run the entire show so the new lead can feel the full pace of the show—including the times he or she is not on stage. This may also be a significant-enough development to warrant requesting crew, so that the second rehearsal can include all of the cues. Advance scheduling gives you the chance to get any necessary overtime pay approved and to let the crew make themselves available.

UNDERSTUDY DOMINOS

Given the range of relationships an understudy can have to the principal cast, the SM team will want to plot out what would happen should that understudy be required to perform.

Consider *Twelfth Night*, one of our sample productions in this book. If the actor playing Orsino is out, obviously the role will need to be covered. If Orsino's understudy does not have another part in the show, then he will step in as a straight substitution—requiring no other adjustments. But if Orsino is understudied by the actor playing Valentine (a smaller speaking role, but one who appears in scenes with Orsino), then a second understudy will step in for him. If Valentine's understudy is outside the primary cast, then the switching is complete. But if Valentine were to be understudied by one of the lords, then a third set of adjustments will be required.

Such a scenario can quickly get complex, and it can be difficult to think through all the potential ramifications on the fly. When working on a show with understudies, the stage manager's time is well spent to plot out the dominoes in advance, so that as many situations as possible can be covered during understudy rehearsals and the put-in can focus on making the adjustments, not figuring out what they will be. You can also identify absences or dominoes not currently planned for!

Figure 7.5 is a sample understudy plot, excerpted to show four different understudy scenarios in the musical *She Loves Me*. Scenario One is a lead character out, covered by an understudy not part of the regular cast. Specific music and blocking moments requiring work with the orchestra and other principal actors are highlighted. Scenario Two addresses a night when one ensemble member is out, and her role is covered by a second ensemble member who still performs her primary role. In addition to two pieces of choreography to run, this situation requires a few prop adjustments to accommodate the double duty. Scenario Three is a double understudy, featuring an ensemble member stepping up to a principal role and a second ensemble member playing two roles. This brings with it a new fast costume change, which should be walked through. Our final scenario is a role that would be dropped. In this production, the director opted to double the violin part of a particular song by adding an actor to play violin on stage. Because this was an addition to the show, no outside understudy was cast. And because no other member of the company played the violin, the role would simply be eliminated should he fall ill.

By creating a chart to catalog all of these potential changes and rehearsal needs, the stage manager is prepared to effectively run the put-in rehearsal and to notify the cast, crew, and conductor about the specifics for any given night. The SM should begin this work during the rehearsal period, so that questions and uncovered roles can be addressed before the night of the performance.

FORMATTING THE PLOT

The understudy plot works best as a chart, set up in a spreadsheet or word-processing table. Individual columns exist for the understudy, prop and costume changes, specific rehearsal needs, and other important notes. Landscape layout provides sufficient room for all the columns,

She Loves Me
Understudy Plot

OUT:	Georg			
IN:	**Costume Changes**	**Prop Changes**	**To Rehearse**	**Notes**
Robert Schneider / Harry Kyle	None	None	"Perspective" & box stack Trip in "Tonight at Eight" "Tango Tragique" dialogue timing	

OUT:	Café/Shop Customer			
IN:	**Costume Changes**	**Prop Changes**	**To Rehearse**	**Notes**
Jane Smith / Susan Adams	None	Need handoff of bag in I-3 Move christmas present to SL table	Romantic Atmosphere Dance Tango Tragique Dance	Will Still Play Caroler in II-4 (just have one fewer customer in scene)

OUT:	Sipos			
IN:	**Costume Changes**	**Prop Changes**	**To Rehearse**	**Notes**
Jason Mendez				
Scott Johnson As: Sipos	None	ASM be ready to help him pick up the pile of boxes!	"Perspective" & Box Stack 12 Day Xmas fight with one fewer customer	
Chris Mitchell As: Keller	Chris will have new Quick Change to café customer	None	None	

OUT:	Violinist			
IN:	**Costume Changes**	**Prop Changes**	**To Rehearse**	**Notes**
Joe Hicks / None	None	None	None	No violinist in café scene at all (just orchestra part)

Figure 7.5 An adapted excerpt of an understudy plot for a production of *She Loves Me. (footer is cropped out)*

without using a small font or wrapping a large amount of text. Ample white space makes the document easy to read quickly. In order to further facilitate the notification process, the SM might opt to include telephone numbers right on the plot.

Because it is unlikely to be widely distributed, the stage manager opted to use color to highlight each scenario (which actor is out) and print the small number of copies required. Each member of the SM team will need a copy. Only a limited version of this information will be needed by other areas. Lighting and sound are unlikely to be affected at all and will need no information. Both front-of-house and the costume department would need to know who understudies whom—for signs and clothing, respectively. But neither area would be concerned with rehearsal needs or prop adjustments. Modifying your cast list to include a third column for understudies is often a satisfactory way to provide them the necessary details.

NOTIFICATION

Whenever an understudy is performing in an AEA production, the theatre is required to inform the audience by using two of three methods: a sign in the lobby such as the one in Figure 7.6, an insert in the program, or an announcement before the show begins. Non-AEA theatres will typically also provide this information to the audience, although their efforts might be limited to only one of these methods.

NOT JUST FOR ILLNESS

In professional theatre, an understudy may not simply perform in the event of a sudden illness in the cast. Depending on the length of your run, your actors could be eligible for vacation. And in the case of an extreme run (think of *Phantom of the Opera*), it is unlikely the cast

Figure 7.6 The understudy sign prepared for the audience at a production at the Shakespeare Theatre in Washington, DC. Photo by Christopher Anaya-Gorman.

will stay the same forever. In this instance, you might be preparing a replacement rather than an understudy. Regardless of the situation, the SM should approach working with new cast members the same way.

CHANGING CREW

In addition to replacement actors, the stage manager may have occasion to work with substitute crew members. The same vacation or illness situations can give rise to the need for alternate technicians. When working with IATSE crew, the union steward or head carpenter will make arrangements for a replacement; in an academic setting, this might be the job of the stage manager—or more likely the faculty production manager or technical director. The important considerations for replacement crew members will be to orient them to the backstage setup, explain the relevant paperwork and how to find their duties, and to practice tricky moves as best you can within the available time. Whenever a new technician is on the deck, the ASMs should pay extra attention to those backstage jobs, ready to provide assistance or additional in-the-moment direction to help the show proceed as though no one is new that night. Replacement crew members may have the chance to shadow their technician for one or more shows before taking over those duties. Availability, schedule, and finances will determine the feasibility of this—and will vary from theatre to theatre.

EMERGENCY PLANS AND PROBLEM-SOLVING

Understudy plots prepare the stage manager to handle emergency situations arising with the actors, but the list of situations that could occur is unfortunately much longer than the cast list. In order to be prepared, the stage manager will need to collect information about responding to a wide range of scenarios.

TECHNICAL PROBLEMS WITH THE SHOW

The first category of problems to solve is handling the breaking or malfunctioning of production elements. Think through potential issues in advance and inquire about solutions so that you can clearly and quickly communicate adjustments during a performance. Even a thorough preshow check cannot ensure nothing will go wrong. The key is to remain calm and to find a way to keep the play moving forward. Not every problem will be noticed by the audience. And those that are noticed will be quickly forgotten if you are prepared and able to respond quickly.

A single lighting instrument burning out is not necessarily impactful—unless it is the only light on during a speech or song. Jumping quickly to another cue or bringing up a follow spot or nearby light allows you to keep going. If the entire light board fails, can you turn on the work lights while the situation is investigated? A scene change unexpectedly in silence might be awkward; the lack of the doorbell cue to prompt the next line will be noticeable. Can you ask someone offstage to knock? Scenic malfunctions can be trickier. Make sure you and your crews understand the mechanics of individual pieces—which components have the potential to break or how to switch to manual operation. New stage managers will have less experience to draw upon in the moment, but taking the time to ask questions in advance can offset this limitation.

If the problem cannot be handled without stopping, the SM may need to halt the performance to allow a repair to happen. Make sure you have a working microphone to make announcements to the audience. Write out the speech in advance, so you won't have to think about what to say. Notify the house manager as soon as you stop. And when the problem is fixed, let everyone know you are ready to get under way again. (A sample set of announcements can be found in the appendix.)

FACILITY PROBLEMS AND OUTSIDE FORCES

Not all situations the stage manager encounters can be fixed with gaff tape, or even a five-minute hold. When working at a theatre for the first time, be sure to learn about the emergency procedures in place for problems beyond the scope of your show.

This can include such events as:

- Losing power
- Fire
- Tornadoes or hurricanes
- Rain (in an outdoor theatre)
- Earthquakes
- Gas leaks
- A broken elevator or other building problem
- Medical emergencies
- Building lockdowns

Many of these scenarios will require you to contact specific theatre personnel or local emergency services. If your theatre does not have a list of procedures and phone numbers, collect the most important details and write them down for yourself. Academic theatres are generally governed by a set of university policies that extend beyond just your department. A trip online may be all you need to find the specifics. By having the information up front, the SM can remain in problem-solving mode during an emergency rather than having to gather information before determining how to proceed.

Another important aspect of solving problems is understanding limitations. Recognize when everyone's best efforts cannot fix a malfunctioning scenic unit, and then move on to how to live without it for today. This might require an explanation to the audience, but could the show go on anyway? Even if that resolution is not your first choice, think about the long term. Don't sacrifice future performances with a quick fix that permanently alters something.

Perhaps the most useful strategy to avoiding problematic situations is to take steps to ensure they won't happen at all. I often believe there is some sort of cosmic "force field" that comes from having a backup—thinking through the possibilities in advance seems to keep them from happening at all. In addition, stay on top of what is in your control. The SM has no power over the weather, but can make sure that the preshow checks are taking place. You did not give that actor the flu, but did you verify the sign-in sheet right at call time to start the process of finding someone who hasn't arrived? Remaining proactive, even at the end of a long week of shows, always pays off.

The stage manager has the authority to halt a performance, but you are rarely in the position to cancel a show. This responsibility lies with someone above your pay grade—a fact I have never resented! Know who makes those decisions so you can reach that person in an emergency situation. Make the call early enough so that your superior can be aware of the problem-solving efforts under way, effectively and calmly communicating your actions. You may still be told to find a way to go on, but once again, creating a conversation rather than dropping a bomb will help you guide the situation to a successful resolution.

Whether the production lasts a week or a month, the stage manager should approach each set of performances equally prepared. You may not give many actor notes during a one-weekend run, but food poisoning, thunderstorms, and computer malfunctions are not discriminating events. A solid foundation in the artistic priorities, backed up with technical knowledge and clear communication with your team, will enable you to live up to your promise to bring the best possible show to each night's audience.

CHAPTER 8

Next Steps

As the final performance approaches, the stage manager will face one of two situations: closing the show or moving it to a new theatre. In both instances you will undertake some final organizational tasks and revisit your documentation of the production to ensure that it is thorough and complete.

MOVING THE PRODUCTION

If the end of the run does not mean the end of the show, the stage manager's final days will be spent preparing to move to a new location.

PREP FOR THE NEW VENUE

If you will be traveling with the show, find an opportunity to gather information about the new theatre space. The exact leadership role the SM will take for the move will be different at every theatre, but after clarifying your responsibility, ask your production team what is known so far. If the second run is a preplanned coproduction with a fellow theatre company, many of these details may have been discussed during the design process. If there are missing details (and there inevitably will be), find out if there is someone you can contact directly at the new venue, or if you should submit questions to be posed on your behalf. When given the chance to make contact yourself, the best sources of information, once again, will be speaking with the production manager or technical director and visiting the venue if possible.

Rather than simply looking for facts, this time you are conducting a comparative analysis between the original theatre and the new space. Some important concerns and questions to ask follow:

- Does the entire set fit? If not, what is changing?
- Amount of wing space.

- Location of dressing rooms and distance from the stage.

- Typical calling location for SM.

- Available technology and communication equipment, including headsets, cue lights, infrared, or other monitors.

- Access to theatre for setting up backstage, placing spike marks, and so on.

- Amount of time allocated for rehearsals and if any of it is actor-only time before tech.

- The location of these rehearsals: on stage, in a rehearsal room, or both.

- Specific theatre policies that will impact your work (These might be regulations about who can have keys, where available parking is located, work hours, and a variety of other things.)

Armed with these details, the SM can assist the production team with the transition by pointing out potential changes and helping to develop a schedule that will provide time for everything. Be sure that you understand the applicable rules before initiating work for the next run of the show. AEA stage managers are entitled to additional compensation for their work when a show is transferring to another venue.[1]

This discovery time is an opportunity to build relationships with the personnel at the next theatre. The stage manager should approach these conversations and emails with the same professionalism and clarity that have served you well thus far. Think back to your very first meeting with the director—allowing him or her to talk freely at the beginning gave you valuable insight into priorities, working style, and concerns. Once again, you want to listen and not just ask questions; you may be an expert on your show, but not on the new venue.

Equally important is to understand the limitations in your knowledge. Supervising the crew member running the automation computer does not mean that the SM knows how to program it. Defer questions to your production team when it is appropriate. You will not be judged harshly for recognizing someone else can answer a question more accurately, but you can create problems if you provide incorrect information.

The show may be the same, but the stage manager should be ready for changes at the next location nonetheless. It is highly unlikely the theatre setup will be identical. If there are no cue lights, think about another way to communicate to backstage in those moments. If the wing space is much more limited, consider if there are places on the back of your set walls where small shelves could be mounted to hold certain props. Start from the needs, and then find a way to meet them. Flexibility will be key to the transition, and your willingness to think creatively will help make the process more successful for everyone involved.

NEW AUDITIONS

Productions featuring children or local actors in ensemble roles may not bring the entire cast to the new venue, prompting supplemental auditions for replacement actors. The SM may be asked to assist with these auditions in the new city. If you participated in the original auditions, revisit the information you prepared at the time. If you were not part of the show at that point, you will need to locate or create paperwork to facilitate that process. You are likely to need the following:

- Audition forms that capture the same information as the originals.
- General information sheets with show details and character descriptions.
- A new show calendar with general dates and deadlines.
- Sides. Be sure to ask the director if the previous selections are still relevant. Depending on the roles to be recast, he or she may have different requests this time.

MAKING THE HANDOFF

The stage manager does not always stay with the show. You might participate in the transition for a few days and then depart, or you might hand off the show in your own theatre so the new stage manager is ready to take over when the production arrives in his or her facility.

If you are not traveling at all, the new SM will likely come to you. Expect to see your successor at some point during the final weeks of the run. He or she will want to watch the show, observe the call (possibly call the show, if permitted), walk through the backstage areas, and review your paperwork. The new stage manager is doing the same sort of comparative analysis—looking for differences between the two spaces to anticipate changes.

Even if you are disappointed that you will not move to the next location, that is no reason to make life difficult for your replacement. Take advantage of the transition time, not only to explain "what" but also "why." Is the current crew handing off the book to Actor X because he has to make a long cross behind the set and does not have time to get to the prop table? Because he worries about the big speech in the next scene and routinely forgets it? Or because your crew member had few tasks and you sought places to give him responsibilities to keep him invested in the show? Again, context is everything.

The same is true of cueing. If you have come to rely on a specific unconscious move an actor makes right before the visual trigger for a cue, share that insight. Is there a section of the show where the lines are never quite right? Be generous, and let the new SM know what typically happens, and how you call that page successfully. Theatre is a very small world, and building this relationship is just as important. You never know when you will cross paths with this colleague again, or when he or she will be asked for a referral when unable to take a job.

THE END OF THE LINE—OR IS IT?

If your production ends on closing night, the stage manager should make sure that all information in the prompt book is up to date and that the notes in your script are accurate. It may seem unlikely that you will revisit this show again, but opportunities may exist outside your immediate future.

On a professional production, it is not unheard of to remount a successful show in a subsequent season, or to tour the show to a location not foreseen during your original run. You may or may not be the stage manager of this next set of performances. Look at your cues. Did the growth of the show lead to a relatively permanent adjustment in cue placement that exists only in your head? If the call is different from the documentation in your script, you may not remember the changes later on. And if you do not stage manage the show next time, your notes are simply inaccurate.

AEA AND THE PROMPT BOOK

When working on an Equity production, remember that the prompt book remains the property of the theatre at the close of the show. The SM is unable to keep it for his or her own use. Additional rules apply to those final updates. The stage manager is required to keep the script accurate to the performance, but if the theatre requests other significant revisions or the preparation of a supplemental copy of the book, the stage manager is entitled to additional compensation for the work.[2]

The same is true for the run-of-show paperwork, including your preset list, shift plot, costume plot, and run sheet. By the fourth week of a run, the ASMs and crew may not refer to the paperwork as regularly as they did during previews. Similar small adjustments may have occurred, which should also be documented. The SM does not need to redistribute the paperwork, but should update the electronic version and print a single copy for the prompt book.

In academic theatre, the rationale behind final cleanup may be a bit different. A student stage manager may be asked to submit their prompt book as part of a grade for their work and want it to be an accurate reflection of the show. Or you may wish to retain specific script pages or pieces of paperwork as part of your portfolio. When talking about the show to a prospective employer, you would not want to answer questions about your methodology by replying, "Well, we didn't actually do it this way, but …"

Although it is rare for a university theatre production to be remounted, there are a few significant exceptions to that rule. If your department participates in the Kennedy Center American College Theater Festival (ACTF), the production could be entered into one of the regional festivals. A select number of shows are invited to perform at those festivals each year—often months after the original production. Accurate documentation will allow you to remember the show correctly, and to help identify any changes required by this move to a new facility. ACTF strives to present shows in venues similar to the original theatre, but even if you are still in a proscenium, you may have a different amount of backstage space, dressing room locations that prompt additional quick changes, or even different cueing based on the lighting setup.

The **Kennedy Center American College Theater Festival** is a national festival honoring and celebrating academic theatre work around the United States. Participating universities have the opportunity to enter work for adjudication—providing students valuable feedback, professional development, and recognition. "Through state, regional, and national festivals, participants celebrate the creative process, see one another's work, and share experiences and insights within the community of theatre artists. [The festival] honors excellence of overall production and offers student artists individual recognition through awards and scholarships in playwriting, acting, criticism, directing, and design."[3]

Certain productions find their way into college repertoires in the same way that they do in professional theatres. *A Christmas Carol* is a good example. My university presents it every four years—ensuring that every student can experience the show once during their college career. The set and costumes are kept in storage, and the director is always the same. The cast and stage manager will change, however. A good archival prompt script is a valuable resource to the next SM. It will help you to fill in gaps in the director's memory about how something was done the last time, and gives him or her a head start on the paperwork for this incarnation of the show.

PAPERWORK FOR OTHERS

In addition to production-specific details, the stage manager may be asked to provide other information at the close of a show. Professional theatres may request a final version of the contact sheet, which includes the actors' permanent information. This provides staff with a way to reach actors in the future, either to include in mailing lists about upcoming auditions or to mail relevant payroll forms at tax time. The final contact sheet is also a great networking resource for the stage manager. You now have an accurate set of addresses for sending holiday cards to new friends or updated résumés when in search of future employment.

Academic stage managers often participate in the evaluation process once a show has ended. Faculty members award grades, but may wish to incorporate specific feedback regarding the consistency of a crew member's work or the cumulative attendance record of an actor. Stage management is in the best position to provide an all-encompassing view of the work of many participants. If the SM is required to provide this type of information, department policy typically dictates the form it will take.

Such evaluations are your final avenue to demonstrate your ability to be tactful, timely, and specific—those communication hallmarks with you since pre-production. Now is not the time to share gossip or to play favorites. An objective, honest assessment of the work facilitates fair evaluation of your company members and helps to position you favorably for future assignments.

STRIKE

In academic and other non-Equity productions, the stage manager may also participate in strike: tearing down the set and returning props, costume pieces, and stock scenic units to their storage places. The SM may be asked to assist in communicating strike assignments and checking to see that all participants are present and working. At other times you will simply be one of many workers helping to complete tasks. If you are unfamiliar with your theatre's traditions, investigate what will be expected of you so that you can be active and helpful at the call.

Stage managers have their own strike tasks as well—these can include taking down information from posted callboards, helping to collect rental scripts for musicals, removing spike marks from the deck, cleaning out their work area in the booth, and completing paperwork on the final performance. The SM team should also be sure the rehearsal space is ready for the next production. If you have a quick transition from the rehearsal hall to the theatre, or if you will continue to use the hall during performances for any understudy or brush-up needs, you might not find the time to truly "move out" of your rehearsal room until the show ends. This means double-checking that spike tape has been pulled up from the floor, rehearsal props and costumes have been returned to their storage locations, show-specific signage has been taken down, and that the room is clean.

Once the last report has been filed and the ghost light turned on for a final time, cordially and professionally bring the project to a close. A successful stage manager will make a positive final impression. Then you can take a breath and get ready to dive into your next show.

Epilogue: Final Thoughts

As you make the transition to your next project, find time to reflect on the work you have just completed. Did you handle a specific challenge particularly well? Did you revise a piece of paperwork to be much more effective? Did you experience something totally new? Be proud of these successes, and file them away. But also look at places where you can continue to improve. Even a show that may have seemed unnecessarily complicated or even unpleasant offers the stage manager an opportunity to learn; knowing what not to do is sometimes more valuable than finding the perfect solution.

As a stage management educator, I often ask my students to engage in a more formal reflection in order to ensure it takes place. The following questions provide students with a structure in which to evaluate their work.

1. Were there any inherent challenges built into your show (size of cast, time of year, specific technical elements)?
2. How did you plan to address those challenges?
3. How would you rate your success, and why?
4. What challenges arose that you did not expect?
5. How (and how successfully) did you address those new challenges?
6. Did you try anything new on this show? What? Did it work?
7. Give one example of how something you did or experienced on a previous show helped you on this production.
8. In what aspect of stage management do you feel you were most successful?
9. What aspect of this production represents an area you still need to work on?
10. Looking back on the show, is there anything you would have done differently? Why?

One of the trademark possessions of a stage manager is our kit—that tackle box containing all those little odds and ends we rely on. Over the course of a career, a kit will grow, so that by the end it is nearly bursting with all of the unusual tools that have become useful over the years and it now seems difficult to do the job without. In many ways, growing as a stage manager is building a different, less-tangible kind of kit. Each production you work on gives you new skills and experiences, making you that much more prepared for your next project.

As your career progresses, remember that your primary goals on any production will be to build relationships, facilitate information sharing, and maintain your focus on the best interests of the show. Effective communication and professional interaction will position you for success every time! It is my hope that this book and the companion website found with the listing of this book at www.focalpress.com/9780415663199 provide you with some strategies and tools to help make that possible.

Let's face it: being a stage manager is not an easy job. It can feel at times that we live at the photocopier and are constantly caught up in the politics of a situation. Everyone else has the fun job, where they get to be creative. Despite the demands of this profession, I maintain that it requires both art and craft, and that achieving success as a stage manager is something to be truly proud of.

Several months ago, a colleague in an association of production managers to which I belong shared an inquiry he received about the true nature of stage management and its "qualification" as an artistic component of a theatrical production. With his permission, I share an excerpt of his response as the final thoughts in this book to remind us all that our efforts at communication are important, and all the work really is worth it in the end.

> *It's true that stage managers have to make use of certain technical skills to do their job. But that's no different than the technical skills required by a sound designer. Virtually all theatre artists need certain technical skills, and virtually all theatre artists are given specific direction. But to name the direction given to a designer as "collaboration" while naming the direction given to a stage manager as something else is just semantics. I disagree with anyone who doesn't recognize his or her stage manager as a fellow artistic collaborator.*
>
> *Stage managers use their knowledge and understanding of a director's vision to develop a strong sense of the show and how it flows from scene to scene. Directors and designers who collaborate with the stage manager to develop the best show possible are the ones who benefit the most. The stage manager must have, more than ANY other member of the team, a full understanding of the show: each actor, each set piece, each lighting and sound cue, and how each component individually and collectively moves through its individual moment. The stage manager's artistic ability and integrity is what, ultimately, transforms the show from its pieces into that magical whole.*[1]

Al Franklin
Production Manager, Steppenwolf Theatre Company

Appendix

Although we have reached the formal end of this book, we have seen numerous times within these pages that there is no such thing as too much information. This appendix has been created to provide you with an expanded look at several aspects of the SM world. These include a more detailed picture of Actors' Equity Association, a list of the items that can be found in a stage manager's kit, a set of emergency announcements to use in the event you need to stop a performance, even more paperwork, and collections of online resources and books to read.

ACTORS' EQUITY ASSOCIATION

Actors' Equity Association is the union of professional actors and stage managers in the United States. First formed in 1913, AEA represents these artists through a series of agreements with professional theatres around the country. The range of agreements is designed to address a variety of performance situations and levels of experience, providing workplace guarantees for as many individuals as possible.

JOINING EQUITY

Actors and stage managers may join the union either through the Equity Membership Candidacy program, where they earn points for weeks of work at participating theaters, or by being offered an Equity contract. In addition, members of other performers' unions such as the Screen Actors Guild/American Federation of Television and Radio Artists (SAG/AFTRA) for film, television, and radio performers or the American Guild of Musical Artists (AGMA) for opera and choral performers and stage managers have the opportunity to join Equity for a reduced membership fee.

CONTRACTS AND AGREEMENTS

AEA negotiates contracts with a variety of theatres around the United States. Some contracts represent a group of companies, while others are negotiated specifically with an individual venue. A series of smaller "codes" also exist for major cities such as New York and Los Angeles to provide structure for showcase performances. Each code or agreement outlines the relevant rules of employment—including salaries, work hours, safety considerations, audition requirements, and publicity regulations. A full list of Equity contracts can be found in the document library on the Actors' Equity Association website, but some highlights are listed here.

Sample Companies with Individual Agreements

Children's Theatre Company, Minneapolis, MN

Disney World, Orlando, FL

North Shore Music Theatre, Beverly, MA

Westport County Playhouse, Westport, CT

Sample Location-Specific Agreements

Bay Area Theatres   Companies producing a season of shows located in the Greater San Francisco area in theatres that have fewer than 400 seats

Chicago Area Theatres   A select group of nonprofit companies operating in the Greater Chicago area. As of 2012, the list of member theatres was as follows:

A Red Orchid

About Face Theatre

American Blues Theatre Itinerant

American Theatre Company

Artistic Home

Black Ensemble Theatre

Buffalo Theatre Ensemble

Chicago Dramatists

Chicago Shakespeare Theatre

Collaboraction

Congo Square Theatre

First Folio Theatre

Fox Valley Repertory

The Gift

Illinois Theatre Center

Lookingglass Theatre Company

Next Theatre Company

Oak Park Festival

Pine Box Theatre

Porchlight Music Theatre Chicago

Provision Theatre Company

Remy Bumppo Theatre Company

Rivendell

Route 66 Theatre Company

Seanachai Theatre Company

Silk Road Theatre Company

Steppenwolf Theatre

Teatro Vista

Theatre at the Center

Theatre Wit

Timeline Theatre Company

Victory Gardens Theatre

Writers' Theatre

Sample National Agreements

Theatre for Young Audiences (TYA)   Companies who produce plays or musicals written or adapted for youth up through and including high school–aged children

Casino Theatres   Casinos or hotels that operate theatres or other performance spaces on their property

Council of Regional Stock Theatres (CORST)   Companies operating exclusively in the summer that offer consecutive productions of a series of plays during their period of operation each year. As of 2012, the list of member theatres was as follows:

Barnstormers, Tamworth, NH

Flat Rock Playhouse, Flat Rock, NC

Maine State Music Theatre, Brunswick, ME

Mountain Playhouse, Jennerstown, PA

Peninsula Players, Fish Creek, WI

Peterborough Players, Peterborough, NH

St. Michael's Playhouse, Colchester, VT

Totem Pole Playhouse, Fayetteville, PA

Williamstown Theatre Festival, Williamstown, MA

League of Resident Theatres (LORT)   The largest subgroup of AEA theatres, composed of 74 major nonprofit theatres throughout the United States. LORT theatres are subdivided into five categories (A, B+, B, C, D) based on the number of seats and the average annual box office income for the past four years.

ACT Theatre, Seattle, WA

Actors Theatre of Louisville, Louisville, KY

Alabama Shakespeare Festival, Montgomery, AL

Alley Theatre, Houston, TX

Alliance Theatre, Atlanta, GA

American Conservatory Theatre, San Francisco, CA

American Repertory Theatre, Cambridge, MA

Arden Theatre Company, Philadelphia, PA

Arena Stage, Washington, D.C.

Arizona Theatre Company, Tucson and Phoenix, AZ

Arkansas Repertory Theatre, Little Rock, AK

Asolo Repertory Theatre, Sarasota, FL

Barter Theatre, Abingdon, VA

Berkeley Repertory Theatre, Berkeley, CA

Capital Repertory Theatre, Albany, NY

CENTERSTAGE, Baltimore, MD

Center Theatre Group, Los Angeles, CA

Cincinnati Playhouse in the Park, Cincinnati, OH

City Theatre Company, Pittsburg, PA

Clarence Brown Theatre Company, Knoxville, TN

The Cleveland Play House, Cleveland, OH

Court Theatre, Chicago, IL

Dallas Theatre Center, Dallas, TX

Delaware Theatre Company, Wilmington, DE

Denver Center Theatre Company, Denver, CO

Florida Studio Theatre, Sarasota, FL

Ford's Theatre, Washington, D.C.

Geffen Playhouse, Los Angeles, CA

Geva Theatre Center, Rochester, NY

George Street Playhouse, New Brunswick, NJ

Georgia Shakespeare, Atlanta, GA

Goodman Theatre, Chicago, IL

Goodspeed Musicals, East Haddam, CT

Great Lakes Theatre Festival, Cleveland, OH

Guthrie Theatre, Minneapolis, MN

Hartford Stage, Hartford, CT

Huntington Theatre Company, Boston, MA

Indiana Repertory Theatre, Indianapolis, IN

Kansas City Repertory Theatre, Kansas City, MO

Laguna Playhouse, Laguna Beach, CA

La Jolla Playhouse, La Jolla, CA

Lincoln Center Theatre, New York, NY

Long Wharf Theatre, New Haven, CT

Maltz Jupiter Theatre, Jupiter, FL

Manhattan Theatre Club, New York, NY

Marin Theatre Company, Mill Valley, CA

McCarter Theatre, Princeton, NJ

Merrimack Repertory Theatre, Lowell, MA

Milwaukee Repertory Theatre, Milwaukee, WI

Northlight Theatre, Skokie, IL

The Old Globe, San Diego, CA

Pasadena Playhouse, Pasadena, CA

People's Light and Theatre Company, Philadelphia, PA

Philadelphia Theatre Company, Philadelphia, PA

Pittsburgh Public Theatre, Pittsburgh, PA

PlayMakers Repertory Company, Chapel Hill, NC

Portland Center Stage, Portland, OR

Portland Stage Company, Portland, ME

Repertory Theatre of St. Louis, St. Louis, MO

Roundabout Theatre Company, New York NY

Round House Theatre, Bethesda, MD

San Jose Repertory Theatre, San Jose, CA

Seattle Repertory Theatre, Seattle, WA

Shakespeare Theatre Company, Washington, DC

Signature Theatre, Arlington, VA

South Coast Repertory, Costa Mesa, CA

Syracuse Stage, Syracuse, NY

Theatre for a New Audience, New York, NY

TheatreWorks, Palo Alto, CA

Trinity Repertory Company, Providence, RI

Two River Theatre Company, Red Bank, NJ

Virginia Stage Company, Norfolk, VA

The Wilma Theatre, Philadelphia, PA

Yale Repertory Theatre, New Haven, CT

Commercial Theatre

Production Contract   Broadway theatres and national tours controlled by producers who are members of The Broadway League

Special Arrangements

<u>Guest Artist Agreement</u>   Allowing educational and nonprofit community theatres to hire up to three AEA actors and one AEA stage manager

<u>Special Appearance Agreement</u>   Allowing small theatres outside of major cities (such as New York, Chicago, and Los Angeles) with fewer than 200 seats to hire up to three AEA actors

OTHER INFORMATION

Actors' Equity Association maintains a wealth of other information for its members, including a jobs board, forms, and information for a production's stage manager and deputy, and a listing of current productions not operating under union rules but potentially misleading members about this fact.

Please visit **www.actorsequity.org** for these and other details about the union.

THE STAGE MANAGER'S KIT

Most stage managers have a collection of essential supplies with them in rehearsals. Often kept in a tackle box or toolbox of some kind, the SM kit is a blend of office supplies, first-aid supplies, tools, and other handy items. When working in larger, more established theatres, you will find that some of these items are regularly provided. Newer stage managers, or those working in smaller venues, may wish to consider items from the following list in order to be "ready for anything." Do not, however, feel obligated to go out and buy it all!

Office Supplies

- Binder clips
- Click erasers
- Highlighters
- Hole protectors
- Hole punch
- Hot-glue gun
- Paper clips
- Pencils
- Pens
- Post-it notes
- Ruler
- Scale rule
- Scissors
- Scotch tape
- Sharpies
- Stapler
- Staple remover
- White-out pens

Equipment

- CD player, MP3 player, or iPod
- Laptop, netbook, or tablet computer
- Portable printer
- USB drive

First Aid/Actor Comfort

- Ace bandages
- Antibacterial hand cleanser
- Antiseptic ointment

Aspirin and/or other pain relievers

Antacid

Band-Aids

Bobby pins or hair bands

Cough drops

Dental floss

Emery boards

Eyedrops

Ice packs

Kleenex

Saline solution

Sterile gloves

Tampons

Tweezers

Backstage Tools or Equipment

Batteries

Clip light

Extension cord

Flashlight

Gaff tape

Leatherman or other all-purpose tool

Needle and thread

Power strip

Safety pins

Spike tape

Small screwdriver

Small wrench

Stopwatch

Tape measure

Your own comfortable headset

Props or Other Miscellaneous Items

Bell

Crayons or colored pencils

Deck of cards

Lighter or box of matches

Ribbon or string

Whistle

EMERGENCY ANNOUNCEMENTS

If your theatre does not have a set of standard announcements to use when stopping a performance during an emergency, use the following samples as a place to start.

TORNADO/ WEATHER SPEECH:

Ladies and gentleman, may I have your attention, please:

We have been alerted to a weather emergency and need to exit the theatre. Please remain calm and move with the rest of your row as directed toward the side doors and down into the basement.

Thank you.

FIRE SPEECH:

Ladies and gentlemen, may I have your attention, please:

We are experiencing technical difficulties. Our safety code requires that everyone leave the theatre through the nearest exit as quickly as possible. Please remain calm and move with the rest of your row as directed. Further information regarding the performance will be available outside shortly.

Thank you.

<u>POWER OUTAGE SPEECH (DELIVERED BY ASM FROM THE DECK):</u>

Ladies and gentlemen, may I have your attention, please:

We are currently experiencing a power outage. We will wait to see if the power can be restored in a timely manner and will update you as soon as we have more information.

Thank you.

<u>POWER OUTAGE (IF MORE THAN FIVE MINUTES)</u>

Ladies and gentlemen, may I have your attention, please:

We have determined that the blackout is affecting (only this building/the entire block). While we investigate how long the blackout will last, please feel free to stand up to stretch your legs. Ushers can also help you reach the lobby and restrooms. We will make another announcement once we know the extent of the power problem.

Thank you for your patience and understanding.

<u>MEDICAL EMERGENCY SPEECH:</u>

Ladies and gentleman, may I have your attention, please:

Due to a medical situation backstage, we need to pause the performance at this time. If there is a doctor in the audience who is willing to provide assistance, please go to the lobby and identify yourself to the house manager. We ask everyone else to remain in their seats, and we will resume the performance as soon as possible.

Thank You.

<u>MEDICAL EMERGENCY IN THE AUDIENCE SPEECH:</u>

Ladies and gentleman, may I have your attention, please:

Due to a medical situation, we need to pause the performance at this time. If there is a doctor in the audience who is willing to provide assistance, please go to the lobby and identify yourself to the house manager. We ask everyone else to remain in their seats, and we will resume the performance as soon as possible.

Thank You.

<u>TECHNICAL DIFFICULTIES SPEECH:</u>

Ladies and gentlemen, may I have your attention, please:

We are currently experiencing technical difficulties and need to pause the performance at this time. We ask you to please remain in your seats, and we will update you with further information as it becomes available.

Thank you.

<u>TECHNICAL PROBLEMS RESOLVED:</u>

Ladies and gentlemen:

Thank you again for your patience. We have resolved our technical difficulties and are now ready to resume tonight's (today's) performance.

Thank you for your patience and understanding.

<u>TECHNICAL DIFFICULTIES THAT AREN'T FIXED QUICKLY</u>

Ladies and gentlemen:

We are still working to resolve our technical difficulties. For your comfort, we will be bringing up the house lights. Please feel free to stand up to stretch your legs. We hope to resume the production in _____ minutes.

Thank you.

MORE PAPERWORK

As a bonus to the written communication tools already presented in this book, I offer you a few extra resources to facilitate your production process. These samples are also included on the book's website.

In addition, I have included a small collection of the paperwork I use as a stage management educator—including a contract to be signed at the outset of a production (a cross between a professional contract and a syllabus) and evaluation tools to be used after strike.

The paperwork provided is as follows:

- An emergency information form for actors and technicians
- A template for collecting biographical information for the program
- A sample of an information sheet passed out to actors in an academic cast on the first day of rehearsal
- A form for organizing and scheduling costume fittings
- Checklists for the SM team for load-in and strike
- Contracts for the stage manager and assistant stage manager, along with a list of prompt book contents
- An evaluation completed by the stage management supervisor
- An evaluation completed by the director of the production

Theatre or Department
Emergency Medical Information Sheet

This information will be kept confidential, and will be used only in the case of a medical emergency.

General Information:

Name: _____   Birthday: _____

Phone: _____   Alternate Phone: _____

Email: _____

Address: _____

_____

Emergency Contact Information:

Person to notify: _____   Relationship: _____

Phone(s): _____

Are you currently being treated for any medical condition? If yes, please specify.

_____

_____

Allergies (including foods): _____

_____

_____

Are you currently taking any prescription or nonprescription medications? If yes, please specify. _____

_____

_____

Have you recently received treatment for any major medical problem? If yes, please specify.

_____

_____

_____

_____   _____

Signature   Date

BIOGRAPHY

Please write in the third person and limit your biography to 50 words or less.
Change to your standards as appropriate!

NAME: _____

_____

_____

_____

_____

_____

_____

_____

BASIC INFORMATION & EXPECTATIONS

Rehearsal Location: Toland Theatre

Rehearsals: September 12 through October 7. Monday through Friday from 6:30-9:30 p.m.

Tech: October 10–12. Call will be at approximately 5:45 p.m.

Performances: October 14–15, 20–22 at 7:30 p.m., October 16 and 23 at 2:00 p.m.

Important Numbers:

Laurie Kincman (SM)	(XXX) XXX-XXXX office, (XXX) XXX-XXXX cell (the cell phone is ALWAYS the best way to get me!)
Costume Shop	(XXX) XXX-XXXX
Box Office	(XXX) XXX-XXXX

Expectations:

1. Except for previously submitted and approved conflicts, assume you will be called every night for rehearsal. A detailed breakdown will be posted on the callboards on Friday nights for the following week.

2. Arrive at least 10 minutes before the scheduled call.

3. Sign in upon arrival.

4. Call the stage manager if you are going to be late for any reason at all. That means even if you are walking in two minutes late.

5. If you have any new or potential conflicts that were not included on your audition form, please see Laurie ASAP.

6. If you need to do warm-ups, please be done before rehearsal starts.

7. There is no eating or drinking in the theatre. (Water is the only exception.)

8. It is your responsibility to attend all scheduled costume fitting appointments on time. If you are going to be late or must cancel the appointment, please call the costume shop (or Laurie, if you are unable to reach Joe).

9. You may not change your appearance—including getting a haircut—without consulting costume/makeup designer Joe Anderson first!

10. Please be quiet and respectful of others during rehearsal. If you are not in a scene but are at rehearsal, please keep the noise down. Bring homework or a book to read if you know you will be waiting around. We will try to only call you for the time we need you to rehearse, but we can not make any guarantees.

11. Check e-mail daily. (Talk to me if this is a problem for you.)

12. Check the call-board on a daily basis. There is a traditional call-board at the end of the theatre office hallway, and an electronic version found online at http://www.uwlax.edu/theatrecallboard.

13. Bring a pencil to rehearsal!

If you have any questions or concerns at all, I am always available! ☺

Laurie Kincman
Stage Manager
(XXX) XXX-XXXX cel
lkincman@uwlax.edu

NAME OF SHOW

FITTINGS

ACTOR
REQUESTED
& FITTING
LENGTH

*By listing out costume
shop requests here,
you can easily give this
sheet to an ASM to
schedule, and cross off
names once he or she
has been successful.*

Day: _____

1:00 pm_____

1:15 pm_____

1:30 pm_____

1:45 pm_____

2:00 pm_____

2:15 pm_____

2:30 pm_____

2:45pm_____

3:00pm_____

3:15 pm_____

3:30 pm_____

3:45 pm_____

*Note: adjust the times listed next to lines above for the
appropriate availability in your costume shop!*

Day: _____

1:00 pm_____

1:15 pm_____

1:30 pm_____

1:45 pm_____

2:00 pm_____

2:15 pm_____

2:30 pm_____

2:45pm_____

3:00pm_____

3:15 pm_____

3:30 pm_____

3:45 pm_____

Note: This form is based on one originally developed at the University of Arizona

STAGE MANAGEMENT LOAD-IN CHECKLIST

☐ Sweep and clean backstage areas as necessary

☐ Place prop tables

☐ Cover prop tables

☐ Label prop tables

☐ Assign and label spaces in prop cabinets

☐ Assign and label parking spaces on deck for scenery and furniture

☐ Tape out sight lines if needed

☐ Confirm spike colors on fly rail if needed

☐ Safety taping

☐ Glo taping

☐ Check for adequate run lights

☐ Check headset locations and amount of cable

☐ Check quick-change areas

☐ Backstage seating for actors/crew

☐ Check first-aid supplies

☐ SM: Check tech table for necessary equipment and its placement

☐ ASM: Set up your home base backstage (music stand, light, chair, etc.)

☐ Sign-in sheet for cast/crew/board operators

☐ Preset list completed and copied

☐ Shift plot completed and copied

☐ Costume paperwork done and copied

☐ Prop cabinet check-in sheets completed and posted

☐ Any green room props/food setup needed

STAGE MANAGEMENT STRIKE LIST

☐ Be sure headset is coiled up and out of the way

☐ Finish postshow props strike as normal (but faster)

☐ Be sure all costume pieces have been cleared to dressing rooms

☐ Make sure props are retrieved from green room and dressing rooms

☐ Remove and throw away paper on prop tables

☐ Return prop tables to storage location

☐ Pull up (or have crew pull up) safety and parking tape

☐ Strike any show-specific storage or prep items

☐ SM: Clear show and personal items out of booth

☐ Strike callboard

☐ SAVE crew sign-in sheets for use in crew evaluations

☐ ASM: Clear show and personal items from home base area

☐ BE SURE the spike tape in your rehearsal room is pulled up

☐ Take down running orders or any other show-specific signage (including in dressing rooms)

☐ Return any chairs pulled for cast and crew to their previous home

☐ Return water jugs, extra first-aid kit, or any other actor amenity supplies

☐ Double-check that actors' personal belongings have been struck from dressing rooms

☐ Clean up green room as needed

☐ Fill out (or schedule time to fill out) crew evaluations

STAGE MANAGER GUIDELINES
DEPARTMENT OF THEATRE ARTS

ASSIGNMENT

Name	
Production	Semester
Position	Theatre

IMPORTANT DATES

	Date		Date
Keys Checked Out		Tech Paperwork Due	
First Rehearsal		Run Sheet Due	
Crew Meeting		Prompt Book Due	
Strike		Other:	
Keys Due Back			

TECH PAPERWORK: This includes everything you will be giving to your crew: your preset list, shift plot, rail cue sheet, quick change plot, and whatever else is necessary for your show.

RUN SHEET: A detailed accounting of your activities from the moment you arrive at the theatre to the moment you go home, which would allow someone to fill in for you if you were unable to attend a performance.

GENERAL EXPECTATIONS

- Attend at all auditions, rehearsals, prep/SM load-in activities, meetings, and performances.

- Maintain good communication with all production areas throughout entire production process.

- Maintain clear and timely meeting minutes and rehearsal reports:
    o Meeting minutes to be sent out within 48 hours of a production meeting.
    o Rehearsal and performance reports to be sent out by 8 a.m. the following day (including weekends).

- Have a positive, proactive attitude.

- Maintain good team spirit, cooperation, and respect for the other members of the stage management team.

- Have respect for your director, production team, actors, understudies, and crew.

- Delegate responsibilities to your ASMs, and provide support and assistance when needed to complete those tasks.

- Ask questions if you aren't sure about something or need help.

- Despite the schedule or demands of your production, keep up with the work in your other classes. If you anticipate problems, please talk with Laurie BEFORE you are headed for trouble!

BEFORE REHEARSALS BEGIN

- Meet with your director to get information about the plan for rehearsals.

- Meet with the SM supervisor and confirm the names of your ASMs and their contact information, and confirm the important dates and special activities for your show.

- Create a version of the actor contact sheet and actor conflict calendar to be double-checked by the cast on the first day.

- Begin to assemble your prompt book.

- Make the character/scene breakdown—ideally to be included in the actor packet.

- Collect/create the items needed for the actor packet.

DURING REHEARSALS

- Arrive at rehearsals 30 to 45 minutes before they are scheduled to begin to ensure you are set up for the night.

- Take blocking in your script.

- Facilitate the scheduling of costume fittings, interviews, or other activities for the actors.

- Keep items like your prop list up to date, and share those updates with the appropriate departments.

- Make sure the SM team is ready to prompt and take line notes once the actors have reached their off-book deadline.

- Meet at least once a week outside of rehearsal time with your SM team to discuss upcoming events, changes, problems, paperwork, or whatever else may be next on your horizon (this may just be coming 15 minutes early or staying 15 minutes late once a week).

- Organize the crew meeting for your show, and create the paperwork with important dates.

- Check in with the production departments at least once a week—you will probably want to visit the shop/theater every day before 5:00 p.m. to know what is in store for you that night, though!

- Oversee the creation of the paperwork the crew will need to run the show: a preset list, a shift plot, and a quick change plot if necessary.

- TURN IN TO LAURIE a draft of all the paperwork for your crew no later than one week before tech rehearsals begin.

- RESERVE the Sunday before tech rehearsals as a time to finish preparing the theater and/or your paperwork in case you need it.

- Have all cues and standbys written in your script prior to the beginning of tech rehearsals.

- Update your script as needed based on notes/changes during tech and dress rehearsals.

DURING PERFORMANCES

- Attend all performances and call cues as set during tech rehearsals.

- By opening night, create your run sheet.

- By opening night, be familiar with any emergency procedures that could come up for your show.

AT THE END

- Attend strike.

- Complete crew evaluations as requested by production area supervisors.

- Turn your prompt book in to Laurie by the end of the day following your strike.

ASSISTANT STAGE MANAGER GUIDELINES
DEPARTMENT OF THEATRE ARTS

ASSIGNMENT

Name	
Production	Semester
Position	Theatre

IMPORTANT DATES

	Date		Date
Keys Checked Out		Tech Paperwork Due	
First Rehearsal		Run Sheet Due	
Crew Meeting		Prompt Book Due	
Strike		Other:	
Keys Due Back			

TECH PAPERWORK: This includes everything you will be giving to your crew: your preset list, shift plot, rail cue sheet, quick change plot, and whatever else is necessary for your show.

RUN SHEET: A detailed accounting of your activities from the moment you arrive at the theatre to the moment you go home, which would allow someone to fill in for you if you were unable to attend a performance.

GENERAL EXPECTATIONS

- Maintain a positive, proactive attitude.

- Ask questions if you aren't sure about something or need help.

- Maintain good team spirit, cooperation, and respect for the other members of the stage management team.

- Have respect for your director, production team, actors, understudies, and crew.

- Despite the schedule or demands of your production, keep up with the work in your other classes. If you anticipate problems, please talk with Laurie BEFORE you are headed for trouble!

BEFORE REHEARSALS BEGIN

- Help run auditions for your show (if you are assigned before they occur).

- Help the stage manager with scripts and other paperwork for the first day.

DURING REHEARSALS

- Arrive at rehearsals 30 to 45 minutes before they are scheduled to begin so that you can be set up for the night, as requested by the SM.

- Be attentive during all rehearsals (which means no homework, reading, or other nonshow-related work).

- Take good notes on your assigned area (props, costumes, etc.) in your script and check in with the stage manager and/or production area head if you have questions.

- Participate in prompting and taking line notes once the actors are off-book as coordinated by the SM.

- Help the SM and other ASMs put everything away at the end of the night, and don't leave until dismissed by the SM.

- Work with your SM and fellow ASMs to create the paperwork you will give to the crew to teach them how to set up and run the show.

- Be willing and flexible to help with nonassigned areas, special projects, emergency situations, or changes.

- Attend the crew meeting and be prepared to describe briefly to the crew what their jobs will be.

- Meet at least once a week outside of rehearsal time with your SM team to discuss upcoming events, changes, problems, paperwork, or whatever else may be next on your horizon (this may just be coming 15 minutes early or staying 15 minutes late once a week).

- TURN IN TO LAURIE a draft of all the paperwork for your crew no later than one week before tech rehearsals begin.

- RESERVE the Sunday before tech rehearsals as a time to finish preparing the theatre and/or your paperwork in case you need it.

- Update crew paperwork as needed during tech rehearsals.

DURING PERFORMANCES

- Attend all performances, and work to ensure that crew carries out all assignments as set during tech rehearsals.

- By opening night, create a run sheet.

- By opening night, be familiar with any emergency procedures that could come up for your show.

AT THE END

- Attend strike.

- Help to complete crew evaluations as requested by production area supervisors.

- Turn your prompt book in to Laurie by the end of the day following your strike.

GUIDELINES FOR PROMPT BOOKS

The following is a general list of the many things that can and possibly should end up in your completed prompt book at the end of a show. Some items (like contact sheets) will always be needed. Other items may be specific to your show or theater. It is also possible that your show will have a specialty consideration (like kids) that may warrant attention and paperwork, and would therefore be added to the list for this production.

Ultimately your book should reflect your work on the production, and contain all the information you need to do your job. It will be a combination of things you have received and things you have created.

ASMs do not need to have all of the cues and blocking in their scripts, but should instead have the notes they took during rehearsal.

- ✓ Cast list
- ✓ Character/scene breakdown
- ✓ Contact sheet(s)
- ✓ Distribution lists (who receives what documents: rehearsal reports, production meeting minutes, etc.)
- ✓ Schedules and calendars
- ✓ Script labeled with acts and scenes:
    - o With blocking and blocking key (from your ASM, if this was not your job)
    - o With line-notation key (from your ASM, if this was not your job)
- ✓ Copies of reports, minutes, and other communication
- ✓ Sections containing information collected from or generated for each department (scenery, props, costumes, lights, sound, etc.)
- ✓ Backstage plot (e.g., scene shift charts, rail cues, prop tracking, prop table lists, costume quick changes—any piece of paper you generated that had to do with the actual running of the show needs to be included)
- ✓ Groundplans
- ✓ Run sheet (SM should also have copies of ASM run sheets)
- ✓ Emergency information and plans
- ✓ Front-of-house information sheet (SM only)

The prompt book should be in a three-ring binder with LABELED DIVIDERS BETWEEN EACH SECTION. You can purchase label packets at the bookstore or any office supply store.

Thoroughness is key. Think of it as a record that could be used as a basic structure, should the show ever be remounted. All of the information to take over your job, should you become unavailable, should be readily accessible in the book.

Review this list periodically throughout your show. If you haven't begun working on an item on this list, one of two things will be true—it might not be needed for your show, or it might be something you should be doing! If you don't know which is true in your case, please just ask.

NEATNESS, CLARITY, AND THROROUGHNESS COUNT TOWARD YOUR GRADE!

Production Assignment/Prompt Book
Evaluation

NAME:

SHOW:

1. **Organization & Thoroughness**   1   2   3   4   5   6   7   8   9   10

    Comments: _____

    _____

2. **Attention to Detail**   1   2   3   4   5   6   7   8   9   10

    Comments: _____

    _____

3. **Accessibility of Information**   1   2   3   4   5   6   7   8   9   10

    Comments: _____

    _____

4. **Clarity of Script Notes**   1   2   3   4   5   6   7   8   9   10

    Comments: _____

    _____

5. **Tech Paperwork**   1   2   3   4   5   6   7   8   9   10

    Comments: _____

    _____

6. **Run sheet**   1   2   3   4   5   6   7   8   9   10

    Comments: _____

    _____

7. **Communication Skills**   1   2   3   4   5   6   7   8   9   10

    Comments: _____

    _____

8. **Work with your SM team**   1   2   3   4   5   6   7   8   9   10

    Comments: _____

    _____

9. **Work with Cast and Crew**   1   2   3   4   5   6   7   8   9   10

    Comments: _____

    _____

10. **Flexibility/Problem Solving**   1   2   3   4   5   6   7   8   9   10

    Comments: _____

    _____

11. **Effectiveness**   1   2   3   4   5   6   7   8   9   10

    Comments: _____

    _____

12. **Growth**   1   2   3   4   5   6   7   8   9   10

    Comments: _____

    _____

    General Comments:

STAGE MANAGEMENT FEEDBACK FORM

Dear Directors,

The following sheet is designed to allow you a chance to offer feedback on the stage management team assigned to your production. Comments, both positive and negative, will help me to continue their development and allow me to better assist you on future productions. I appreciate your taking the time to share your thoughts. Please return this sheet to me, and let me know if you have any questions.

Thanks,

Laurie Kincman
Production Manager

PRODUCTION: _____   DIRECTOR: _____

STAGE MANAGER/ASM: _____

Please evaluate the stage manager or assistant stage manager on the following skills (1-lowest, 5-highest)

ORGANIZATION & COMMUNICATION SKILLS

Punctuality	1	2	3	4	5
Proactiveness/Anticipation	1	2	3	4	5
Attention to Detail	1	2	3	4	5
Identifying Problems	1	2	3	4	5
Problem Solving	1	2	3	4	5
Follow-Through/Persistence	1	2	3	4	5
Verbal Communication	1	2	3	4	5
Written Communication	1	2	3	4	5

MANAGEMENT SKILLS

Leadership	1	2	3	4	5
Flexibility/Responsiveness to Changes	1	2	3	4	5
Ability to Manage ASMs	1	2	3	4	5
Ability to Meet Director's Needs	1	2	3	4	5
Ability to Function Effectively in Rehearsals	1	2	3	4	5
Interaction with Production Team	1	2	3	4	5
Maintenance of Production After Opening	1	2	3	4	5
Respect for Others	1	2	3	4	5
Respect from Others	1	2	3	4	5
Acceptance of Different Points of View	1	2	3	4	5
Attitude	1	2	3	4	5

Please see the back side!

Please comment on situations in which the stage manager or assistant stage manager did particularly good work.

Please comment on any areas in which the stage manager or assistant stage manager is in need of improvement.

Would you work with this stage manager or assistant stage manager again?

Please share any other thoughts not otherwise addressed on this form.

Thank you again for taking the time to share this feedback!

WEB RESOURCES

Actors' Equity Association—www.actorsequity.org

SMNetwork—www.smnetwork.org

An online community of stage managers for sharing experiences, answering questions, and exploring current trends

United States Institute for Theatre Technology—www.usitt.org

A nonprofit service organization that unites students, practitioners, and educators working in all aspects of theatrical design, management, and production through workshops, publications, annual conferences, and online resources

Stage Managers Association—www.stagemanagers.org

A national networking community created by and for stage managers

Stage Directors and Choreographers Society—www.sdcweb.org

The union for professional directors and choreographers working in theaters throughout the United States

American Guild of Musical Artists—www.musicalartists.org

The union for opera and choral performers and stage managers

IATSE—www.iatse-intl.org

The International Alliance of Theatrical Stage Employees, Moving Picture Technicians, Artists and Allied Crafts of the United States, Its Territories and Canada represent professional designers and technicians in the entertainment industries

Theatre Communications Group—www.tcg.org

A nonprofit service organization whose defined mission is "to strengthen, nurture and promote the professional not-for-profit American theatre." It does this through annual meetings and conferences, special research reports, and other online and in-person training opportunities. TCG manages ArtSearch, one of the most comprehensive collections of available jobs and internships in the arts.

ArtsJournal—www.artsjournal.com

A collected digest of the top issues, ideas, and stories in the visual and performing arts

SUGGESTED READING

THEATRE MANAGEMENT AND PRODUCTION

The Backstage Guide to Stage Management. Third Edition. Thomas A. Kelly. New York: Back Stage Books. 2009.

The Backstage Handbook. Third Edition. Paul Carter. New York: Broadway Press. 1994.

Backwards and Forwards: A Technical Manual for Reading Plays. David Ball. Illinois: Southern Illinois University Press. 1983.

Designing with Light. Fifth Edition. J. Michael Gillette. New York: McGraw-Hill. 2007.

On Directing. Harold Clurman. New York: Fireside. 1997.

Essentials of Stage Management. Peter Maccoy. New York: Routledge Press. 2004.

Illustrated Theatre Production Guide. John Holloway. Massachusetts: Focal Press. 2002.

Producing Theatre: A Comprehensive Legal and Business Guide. Third Edition. Donald C. Farber. New Jersey: Limelight Editions. 2006.

Sound and Music for the Theatre: The Art and Technique of Design. Third Edition. Deena Kaye and James Lebrecht. Massachusetts: Focal Press. 2009.

Stage Rigging Handbook. Third Edition. Jay O. Glerum. Illinois: Southern Illinois University Press. 2007.

Theatre Management: Producing and Managing the Performing Arts. David M. Conte & Stephen Langley. California: Quite Specific Media. 2007.

Theatrical Design and Production: An Introduction to Scene Design and Construction, Lighting, Sound, Costume, and Makeup. Seventh Edition. J. Michael Gillette. New York: McGraw-Hill. 2012.

Working Together In Theatre: Collaboration & Leadership. Robert Cohen. New York: Palgrave Macmillan. 2011.

DOCUMENT DESIGN

The Non-Designers Design Book. Third Edition. Robin Williams. Berkeley CA: Peachtree Press. 2008.

The Practical Guide to Information Design. Ronnie Lipton. New Jersey: John Wiley & Sons, Inc. 2007.

Thinking with Type, Second Edition. Ellen Lupton. New York: Princeton Architectural Press. 2010.

White Space Is Not Your Enemy. Kim Golombisky & Rebecca Hagen. Massachusetts: Focal Press. 2010.

COMMUNICATION & LEADERSHIP

Being Wrong: Adventures in the Margin of Error. Kathyrn Schulz. New York: Harper Collins Publishers. 2010.

Difficult Conversations: How to Discuss What Matters Most. Second Edition. Douglas Stone, Bruce Patton, and Sheila Heen. New York: Penguin Books. 2010.

It's the Way You Say It: Becoming Articulate, Well-Spoken and Clear. Carol A. Fleming. New York: iUniverse. 2010.

The Silent Language of Leaders: How Body Language Can Help or Hurt How You Lead. Carol Kinsey Goman. San Francisco, CA: Jossey-Bass Publishers. 2011.

Winnie the Pooh on Problem Solving. Roger E. Allen and Stephen D. Allen. New York: Dutton Press. 1995.

Notes

INTRODUCTION

1. The summary definition offered for a stage manager according to Actors' Equity Association is compiled from job description items found in the 2009–2012 League of Resident Theatres (LORT) Rulebook, the 2009–2012 Production Rulebook, and the 2008–2010 Council of Resident Stock Theatres (CORST) Rulebook. Due to the fact that AEA oversees 62 individual types of agreements relating to every possible category of professional live theatre, there is no single, all-inclusive definition. I have taken key elements from the working descriptions in these three agreements to create this summary.

2. Maccoy, Peter. 2005. *Essentials of Stage Management*. New York: Routledge Press. 39–40.

3. Fleming, Carol A. 2010. *It's the Way You Say It: Becoming Articulate, Well-spoken and Clear*. New York & Bloomington: iUniverse, Inc. 98.

CHAPTER ONE

1. "Examples of Body Language," Separated Parenting Access and Resource Center. Accessed on May 21, 2012, http://www.deltabravo.net/cms/plugins/content/content.php?content.367.

CHAPTER TWO

2. Williams, Robin. 2008. *The Non-Designer's Design Book*. Third Edition. Berkeley California: Peachpit Press. 153–160.

3. "Adobe Acrobat," Adobe Systems, Incorporated. Accessed May 4, 2012. http://www.adobe.com/products/acrobat/acrobatpdf.html.

CHAPTER FOUR

1. Actors' Equity Association, CORST Rulebook 2008–2010, rule 55 (E)(2).

CHAPTER FIVE

1. Stone, Douglas, Bruce Patton, Sheila Heen. 2000. Introduction to *Difficult Conversations: How to Discuss What Matters Most*. Second Edition. New York: Penguin Books. xxix–xxx.

2. Burnell, Holly. Interview with author. August 21, 2012.

3. Smith, Nicole. Interview with author. August 15, 2012.

4. Actors' Equity Association, LORT Rulebook 2009–2012, rule 13 (B)(2).

CHAPTER SIX

1. Harris, Kristen. Interview with author. August 17, 2012.

2. Threadgill, Susan. Comments shared with Production Managers Forum (excerpted with permission). June 1, 2012.

CHAPTER SEVEN

1. Actors' Equity Association, LORT Rulebook 2009–2012, rule 37 H (2)–(6). Similar rules exist in most other agreements, although the number of understudies/swings or the compensation to be received may differ.

CHAPTER EIGHT

1. Actors' Equity Association, LORT Rulebook 09–12, rule 63 J (1)–(3). Similar rules exist in most other agreements, although the amount of compensation may differ.

2. "Kennedy Center American College Theatre Festival." Accessed July 1, 2012. www.kcactf.org.

3. Actors' Equity Association, LORT Rulebook 09–12, Rule 63 (G). Similar rules exist in most other agreements, although the amount of compensation may differ.

EPILOGUE

1. Franklin, Al. Comments shared with Production Managers Forum (excerpted with permission). June 1, 2012.

PRODUCTION CREDITS

Throughout this book, examples have been drawn from several productions of the University of Wisconsin-La Crosse Department of Theatre Arts, chaired by Joe Anderson. Unless otherwise noted, all images and production paperwork were created or overseen by Laurie Kincman, stage manager.

Rent

Directed by Mary Leonard

Scenic & Lighting Design by Mandy Hart

Costume Design by Joe Anderson

Technical Direction by Ron Stoffregen

Assistant Stage Managers: Cara Cook, David Hartig

Twelfth Night

Directed by Walter Elder

Scenic Design by Mandy Hart

Costume Design by Michelle Collyar

Lighting Design by Nick Mompier

Technical Direction by Ron Stoffregen

Assistant Stage Managers: Cara Cook, Melissa Heller, Quinn Masterson

Urinetown

Directed by Mary Leonard

Scenic Design by Victoria Halverson

Costume Design by Joe Anderson

Lighting Design by Mandy Hart & Andrew Appold

Technical Direction by Ron Stoffregen

Assistant Stage Managers: Shelby Krarup, Erica Perrin

The Farnsworth Invention

Directed by Mary Leonard

Scenic Design by Mandy Hart

Costume Design by Joe Anderson

Lighting Design by Brent Bankes

Technical Direction by Ron Stoffregen

Assistant Stage Managers: Rachel Holtz, Scott Jenks

Author Biography

LAURIE KINCMAN is a faculty member in the Department of Theatre Arts at the University of Wisconsin—La Crosse, heading the undergraduate emphases in stage management and arts administration. She also serves as the department's production manager. Her professional credits as a stage manager and production manager include work with the Old Globe Theatre, Malashock Dance & Company, Shakespeare Festival/LA, Opera Pacific, the California Ballet Company, American Stage Festival, and for choreographers Jessica Iwanson and Donald McKayle.

Laurie holds a dual BA in drama and political science from Dartmouth College and an MFA in stage management from the University of California, Irvine. She is the winner of a Pacific Southwest Regional Emmy Award for Lighting Direction for the KPBS-TV production of "The Gypsy's Wife." Laurie is a member of the United States Institute for Theatre Technology, the Production Managers Forum, the Stage Managers Association, the Association for Arts Administration Educators, and Actors' Equity Association.

Index